D0267609

Interwar Britain
A Social and Economic History

Interwar Britain

A Social and Economic History

SEAN GLYNN
and
JOHN OXBORROW

London   George Allen & Unwin Ltd
Ruskin House   Museum Street

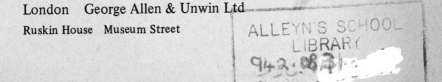

First published in 1976

Printed in Great Britain
in 10 point Press Roman
by Clarke, Doble & Brendon Limited
Plymouth, Devon

Acknowledgements

We would like to acknowledge the assistance of Dr J. A. Dowie and Dr J. Hatcher of this university and Professor J. W. McCarty, of Monash University, who have read and commented on individual chapters of this book. Professor S. B. Saul, of Edinburgh University, read the whole manuscript and made many valuable suggestions, which we have done our best to incorporate. Responsibility for the contents remains entirely our own.

Mr J. Pell, of the audio-visual aids unit of this university, drew the three charts in Chapter 1. We are grateful for his assistance.

SEAN GLYNN
JOHN OXBORROW

University of Kent at Canterbury

Contents

Tables

Charts

Chapter 1

Economic Growth
and Living Standards

I *Introduction*

The interwar years present a paradox in British history. The popular image is of a period of depression and distress at home, with a gathering storm of fascism abroad. On the other hand, to set against that image, is the record of economic growth. This record suggests that the interwar years were a period of economic progress, with rising material standards. This paradox is to a great extent real and is unlikely to be resolved by historical research. The interwar years in Britain do have this two-faced aspect. The popular image of a period of depression is soundly based on the very high level of unemployment which prevailed throughout. This brought distress and suffering to large areas and sections of the population. But equally for those who remained in employment, and even in the worst years of the period this was always the majority, economic growth was arguably yielding substantial benefits.

The two faces of the interwar years are therefore both real and both should have their place in any history of the period. Generally in writing about the period there has been a tendency for the two interpretations to remain separate; popular versions stress the more pessimistic view, while emphasis on the record of economic growth is largely confined to academic works or textbooks. In this book we attempt to give due weight to both aspects. We do not however attempt to arbitrate between them. No summary judgement of the period is possible. The interwar years were a period which combined abnormally high unemployment with fairly rapid economic growth. They were a period in which there was significant progress in the development of social policy and particularly in housing standards. But it will also be argued that these years offered opportunities in the social sphere which were by no means fully grasped.

In the remaining sections of this chapter, we present the record of economic growth and try to assess its effects on the population. Chapters 2 and 3 deal with the general economic environment in the international economy and at home respectively. In Chapter 4 on economic policy we consider government reactions to the problems of the period. In the remaining chapters we return to more specifically social issues. Chapter 5 deals with the question of unemployment, which is of central importance in any assessment of the period. Following on from this, Chapter 6 discusses the position of the labour movement more generally. Chapters 7, 8 and 9 discuss population, housing and social policy. In each of these areas there were developments which had effects on the welfare of the population.

II *Economic Growth*

Interest in the size of output of the economy and changes in this output is very old; it can be traced back at least to the seventeenth-century statisticians like William Petty and Gregory King. Measurement of the output of an economy is difficult since that output contains so many different products. Money is used as the measuring rod which enables these different products to be combined into a single total, but where comparisons have to be made between two different economies, or, what is conceptually the same problem, between the same economy at two different points in time, the use of money values has many problems. Complications arise with the introduction of new products (or the improvement of old ones which makes them in effect different products), the change in the level of prices, and the varying classes of product included in the total. In the course of the development of techniques of measurement, certain definitions have come to be accepted about what is included and what excluded, how price changes are to be dealt with and so on. These accepted definitions are not the only possible ones and there is much room for debate about the relevance of the results to welfare. Nevertheless, until very recently, the conventional measures of national income have been accepted as being significant, it usually being presumed that growth benefited the populations concerned and hence could be seen as a good thing. In the period after the second world war, economic growth came to be a policy objective for governments, both in industrial and in developing countries. This increased interest in growth — 'growthmanship' as Professor Postan has called it[1] — has been reflected in increased academic interest in the rate of economic growth in the past. Economists have attempted to reconstruct national income accounts for the United Kingdom as far back as the data permit. This work has been centred at the Department of Applied Economics at Cambridge

University. In 1972 C. H. Feinstein published his *National Income, Expenditure and Output of the United Kingdom, 1855-1965.* This massive work is the outcome of more than a decade's study, and it seems unlikely that any future research will substantially modify the figures he presents. Feinstein's conclusion is that the annual growth rates of the UK economy can be calculated back to 1855 and up to 1929 with a margin of error of about 0·5 percentage points.[2] After 1929, the margin of error is much less, and after 1945 the official national income statistics can be regarded as exact for most purposes. Determined attempts have been made to carry the figures back before the mid-nineteenth century.[3] The margin of error is inevitably wider and here we shall use Feinstein's figures from 1855 to place the interwar economy in perspective.

Embarking on a discussion of these figures implies that they are at least to some extent significant, despite the problems about compiling them which have already been mentioned. Recently, in the late 1960s and early 1970s, an 'anti-growth' or 'environmental' literature has appeared, which has in many cases gone further than casting doubt on the connection between conventionally measured growth and welfare and has suggested that growth actually reduces welfare. This literature has led to an extensive controversy[4] and in general governments have not abandoned their concern with growth. In the period with which we are concerned, as in all periods, it is clear that many factors will affect the welfare and happiness of the population other than the level of output in the economy. Some of these things are discussed in later chapters. In the later part of this chapter some attempt is made to show the ways in which growth was bringing benefits to some sections of the population in the form of higher consumption and the availability of new products. This reflects the outcome of the research into national income in the period, which has shown that rates of growth in the interwar years were quite high compared both with other countries and with previous periods in this country. The interwar years have traditionally been seen as years when the overriding social and economic problem was unemployment. No attempt is made here to minimise the social evils of unemployment. Ultimately, it is not possible to strike a definitive balance of welfare between the improvement of material conditions for certain groups of people and the psychological and material losses of those who were unemployed. But it is argued that the growth which occurred benefited a large proportion of the population, and perhaps nearly everybody would have been worse off without it. But this is certainly not a proposition that could ever be disproved in a rigorous way, and it is argued only by description and example.

Table 1.1 *Gross Domestic Product per Head: United Kingdom, 1855-1965* (£s at constant 1913 prices)

Years	Value for the year or average for years shown
1855	26
1857-1866	28½
1866-1873	31½
1873-1882	34
1882-1890	37
1890-1900	41½
1900-1913	45½
1900	45
1920	45 (including all Ireland)
1920	47 (excluding the Republic)
1924-1937	52
1937	60
1951-1965	82
1965	98

Source Feinstein, table 17, p. T42.

The course of gross domestic product per head in the United Kingdom between 1855 and 1965 is given in Table 1.1. The figures are taken from the work by C. H. Feinstein already referred to and are in £s per head at 1913 prices.[5] The sizeable technical difficulties of producing such figures for such a long period have already been hinted at. Not the least is the ceaseless change in the prices of different parts of the output of the economy. A further problem is the way in which, in the course of economic change, new products and new services appear in the output of the economy, whilst others disappear. It is the task of the applied economist to deal with such problems, but they are not in principle capable of any determinate solution. While there are generally accepted procedures for dealing with price changes and the incorporation of new products, the agreement is in the nature of a compromise rather than a solution. However, it will clearly not do to consider the growth of the value of the output of the economy in current prices; a doubling of the price level would double the total value of the gross domestic product, but it would double nothing else. Hence the measure in which we are interested must be a constant price measure, and the difficulties and uncertainties of correcting for changes in prices must be faced.

The methodological difficulties inherent in any statement about economic growth have been stressed, because otherwise the conclusions to be presented about economic growth in the interwar years might appear to be much more definite and straightforward than they really are. But once the foregoing qualifications and difficulties have been passed, though it is hoped not forgotten, the quantitative conclusions can be stated fairly shortly. Between 1857 and 1965 the gross domestic product per head of the United Kingdom grew at 1·2% per annum.[6] What is required is to set the interwar years into perspective in this long period. The most appropriate choice of sub-periods for analysis is always a matter for discussion and many different schemes have been presented by different writers. The two features which present themselves most readily as landmarks within the long period are the peaks of the trade cycle and the world wars. The peaks of the trade cycle are important, since any subdivision of the period which ignored them would be liable to confuse increases in GDP per head caused by reducing unemployment with increases due to the actual growth of the productive capacity of the economy. Obviously if unemployment in one year is, say, 10% and in another only 5%, output is likely to be higher in the latter year. But this will not tell us by how much the productive capacity of the economy has grown between the two years, unless we discount that part of the increase due to the fall in unemployment. The simplest way of doing this is to choose sub-periods so that the dividing years have about the same level of unemployment. Where the sub-periods are long, or the levels of unemployment involved are low, so the choice of end years becomes less important. This problem however is quite prominent in relation to the interwar years where levels of unemployment are very high. Cutting across the trade cycle are the two world wars. These events loom so large in history and had such major effects on the economy, that historians have inevitably been led to divide up history into periods which take account of them. Hence this book deals with the 'interwar period'. It is necessary therefore to offer a scheme of sub-periods which takes both the trade cycle and the wars into account.

Between 1855 and 1900, there were no major interruptions of the size of the two world wars in the course of economic growth, and during this time the trade cycle proceeded fairly regularly with a period of between seven and ten years. In this time, there were six trade cycle peaks — 1857, 1866, 1873, 1882, 1890 and 1900. The average per capita rate of growth over the whole period was 1·1% and the rates of growth in the periods between the trade cycle peaks were as follows:

1857-66	1·1%
1866-73	1·5%
1873-82	0·9%
1882-90	1·2%
1890-1900	1·1%

In so far as there is a 'normal' rate of growth in the second half of the nineteenth century this period provides it. All the sub-periods are fairly close to the average for the whole. The average itself, of 1·1%, may sound a rather unspectacular figure, but it should be remembered that 1·1% per annum compound is a rate that doubles GDP per head in sixty-four years. Apparently unspectacular rates of growth such as this are in fact very much higher than anything that happened before the industrial revolution. Maintained over the two hundred or so years since the start of the British industrial revolution they have transformed the economy of this country and indeed of the world.

The years 1900 to the outbreak of war in 1914 are here treated as a special sub-period, not directly related to the trade cycle, though the cycle peaking in 1900 is its starting point. There is in fact another peak in 1907. The justification for treating 1900-14 separately is that it is a period of unusually slow growth in historical perspective. The actual period taken for calculation is the thirteen years 1900-13, since 1914 is already showing the effects of the war. In those thirteen years the average rate of growth of GDP per head was 0·7% per annum. If the figures are correct, this marks out this period as a highly exceptional one in modern British economic history.

Coming to the interwar years themselves, the problem of deciding which years to use for comparison is difficult. Unemployment is higher in nearly all years of the period than it was before or after, and there is a major reduction of working hours immediately after the war. However, within the interwar years themselves these things can be held roughly constant by choosing years of equal unemployment for comparison, and by choosing a starting year after the reduction in working hours had been accomplished. Either 1923-37 or 1924-37 meets these requirements reasonably well; the rate of unemployment for the whole labour force is about equal in the first pair of years, while the unemployment among the insured labour force is about equal in the second pair. And 1924 is well after the completion of the postwar reduction in working hours. Actually it makes very little difference which pair is chosen, and 1924-37 is the most commonly used. The rate of growth of GDP per head in this period is 1·8% per annum. Any attempt to link 1900 with an interwar year cannot escape these problems so easily. GDP per head in 1918 was 20% higher than it had been in 1900, and most of this increase had occurred in the war itself. But the figures for the war years are less reliable than for peacetime years, and less meaningful, since much of the output was devoted to war materials. Immediately after the war, by 1920, hours had been reduced throughout much of industry to about 48 per week instead of the 54 per week typical of the prewar period. Southern Ireland was detached from the United Kingdom in 1920 and unemployment in 1921 leapt up to 9·6% of the labour force. Hence the figures for 1920 and 1921 show a gross domestic product per head about the same as in 1900, giving a twenty-year period with roughly zero growth, but this is subject to the qualifications discussed above. Finally, there is the period after the second world war. Here unemployment rates are much lower and fluctuate over a very small range. For our purposes of broad comparison then, the choice of years in this period is not too critical and 1951-65 is chosen to give a reasonably long run. The per capita growth rate over these years was 2·3% per annum. Linking the interwar years with the postwar period involves complications similar to those already discussed over the first war and will not be pursued further here.

The scheme which we have discussed then looks like this:

(a)   'Nineteenth century growth rate' — taken between trade cycle peaks from 1857-1900; all periods between 0·9 and 1·5% per annum and average 1·1%.

(b)   The period between 1900 and 1920-1. This is an exceptional period in many respects. The growth rate in the early part up to 1914 is unusually slow by nineteenth century standards. The war is a major disruption and after the war various other factors complicate the issue. It is however clearly a period of slow growth.

(c)   The interwar years. Using the period 1924-37 for the reasons discussed, the rate of 1·8% marks an acceleration in the rate of growth over previous experience.

(d)   The postwar period. The rate of 2·3% is a further acceleration in the rate of growth.

In interpreting this pattern, it is necessary to remember the margin of error in the figures. It is possible that the rate of growth in the period 1924-37 was not in fact higher than between 1857 and 1900. If the error in the latter period was downwards and in the former upwards, both by 0·5%, then the periods almost exactly change places in their relative growth rates, 1855-1900 coming out as 1·6% and 1924-37 as 1·3%. All that one can say with any conviction is that growth in the interwar years was probably about the same as in the second half of the nineteenth century. Most observers are less cautious than this over the figures and assume that they do support the assumption that the interwar years saw an acceleration of growth; an acceleration which proceeded further in the post-1950 period. The evidence does seem to support a view that growth in the interwar years was at least what might be described as 'normal'. The word 'normal' here is meant to contrast the growth performance of this period with the 'abnormal' period which immediately preceded it. Part of the 'abnormality' of this preceding period is due to the war, but 1900-14 is also a period of very slow growth for which there is no such obvious explanation. It does therefore seem reasonable to see the whole period 1900-20 as a major hiatus in the history of British economic growth, and also to see the interwar years as a period when growth was resumed to at least the pre-1900 or 'normal' rates, and probably at a higher rate. If the interwar rate really was higher, which the figures suggest although they do not finally prove it, then this higher rate can also be seen as part of a long-term acceleration in the rate of growth which was resumed after the further interruption of the second world war.

This then is the historical pattern of growth of GDP per head. The other obvious way of looking at growth is to make comparisons with other countries rather than between different periods for the same country. Unfortunately this takes us into statistics which are probably rather less reliable than the British figures, or subject to more qualifications. American GDP figures are about as accurate as the British, but the rapid growth of American population, the rapid expansion of the American 'frontier' in the nineteenth century, and the abundant supply of indigenous raw materials make direct comparisons with the USA of limited significance. In the interwar years, comparison is difficult because of the far greater severity of the post-1929 depression in the USA, which means that there is no even approximately 'normal' year in the 1930s with which to make comparison. However, for what it is worth, output per capita in the USA between 1870 and 1960 grew at 1·9% per annum, compared with 1·2% for the UK and 1·8% for Germany.[7] Remembering the likely margins of error, this suggests that over this period the UK had had a somewhat slower growth rate than these two major industrial countries. For the period over which there are comparable figures in the nineteenth century — that is from 1871 onwards — both Germany and the USA appear to have grown faster than Britain, the USA at 2·5% and Germany at 1·9%, between 1871 and 1901. Between about 1900 and 1913, the growth rates of all three countries are reduced; the British rate to 0·7% compared to 1·5% and 1·3% for the USA and Germany respectively.

For the interwar period comparisons are made difficult by the disruption of the war and the depression. It is possible to find years of approximately equal unemployment in both countries. In the USA in 1921 and 1937 unemployment was 11·4% and 14·2% of the labour force respectively, and the per capita growth rate between these years was 1·7% per annum.[8] In Germany, the volume of total output did not recover its prewar value until 1927, due to hyper-inflation, the French occupation of the Ruhr and other disturbances consequent upon the war. In 1928 German unemployment was 3·8% of the labour force and in 1937 it was 2·7%. The German growth rate between these years was 2·2% per annum, although this is not a very meaningful figure, since almost the whole of this growth occurred after 1934. Between 1931 and 1933 German output had again fallen below the 1913 level. However, uncertain though the basis of such figures is, they are sufficient to show up the interwar years as a period when Britain's growth rate, relative to Germany and the USA, was higher than it had been in the nineteenth century. Between 1870 and 1913 the growth of these countries had probably been faster than Britain's; in the interwar years the difference disappears. Britain is no longer a relatively slow growing country. If France is brought into the comparison, the contrast is reinforced. Between 1870 and 1913 French growth had been 1·4% per capita; again faster than Britain's.[9] But by the end of the interwar period France's population was the same as in 1913 and her total output only 9½% higher. In the 1920s, France had grown faster than Britain, but French economic performance in the 1930s was worse than that of any other major industrial country, and reduced her growth rate for the interwar years as a whole to a very low level; if 1924 is compared with 1937 the growth of GDP per capita is minus 0·3% per annum. Thus it becomes clear that both historically and compared with other countries the British growth performance in the interwar years was relatively good. This conclusion is further reinforced if, to complete our comparisons, the period after the second world war is brought into consideration. In this period much more accurate statistics are available and the conclusion they offer is that, beyond doubt, Britain's growth was slow compared with nearly all other western European countries, and much slower than France or Germany. In the years after 1945, the slow rate of growth of the UK economy has become a major topic of discussion, research and policy. It is often suggested that Britain's growth has always been slow compared with other major industrial countries, but this does not seem to be true of the interwar years. Despite the common view of the interwar years as a time of 'depression' they appear from the statistics as years of fairly good growth performance and as the one period when Britain did at least as well, and perhaps rather better, than most other industrial countries.

III *The Causes of Growth*

The actual course of GDP per head from year to year in our period is given in the diagram (Chart 1). The main sub-divisions of the period stand out clearly. There is a postwar boom, followed by a sharp decline and then fairly steady growth in the 1920s, interrupted only by the General Strike of 1926 and the very prolonged coal strike of the same year. Then there is the check of the depression of 1929-33, followed by a recovery which gives the most rapid spurt of short-run growth recorded in the period, though this rapid growth was showing some tendency to level off in 1938. A line representing a steady rate of growth of 1·8% per annum per head has been added to the diagram, arranged so that it passes through the actual figures for the years 1924 and 1937. On ordinary graph paper such a line is not straight but curved, though on the scales chosen in this case the curve is so slight that it might not be noticed at first glance. This 1·8% line shows how the economy was faring each year in relation to a 'target' rate of growth of 1·8% per annum compound for GDP per capita.

What factors determine the rate of growth? Short-run fluctuations in output are explained largely by variations in demand, acting through changes in the level of employment, as in the case of the decline in output per head in the 1929-33 depression, the sharp recovery from 1933-8 and the decline in output in 1921. These short-run fluctuations will often appear to be of more significance to contemporaries than any other factor, but they do not play an important part in determining the long-run rate of growth of output per head. The longer run trend, which we have in the previous section tried to isolate from short-run variations as far as this was possible, may be thought of as being determined by three main factors: the growth of the capital stock per worker, improvements in technology and organisation, and the proportion of the population who are able and willing to work (but abstracting from involuntary unemployment). Between 1924 and 1937 the capital stock grew at 1·2% per annum.[10] It so happens that between those years the number of persons in employment also grew at 1·2% per annum, so that the capital per worker over this period remained approximately constant. Gross domestic product grew at 2·2% per annum. Total population grew at 0·4% per annum, thus giving the increase in GDP per capita already discussed of 1·8% per annum (2·2%-0·4%). GDP per member of

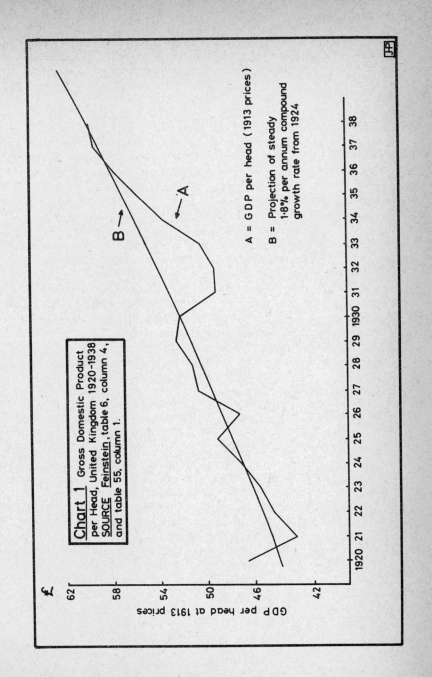

Chart 1 Gross Domestic Product per Head, United Kingdom 1920-1938
SOURCE Feinstein, table 6, column 4, and table 55, column 1.

£

GDP per head at 1913 prices

62
58
54
50
46
42

1920 21 22 23 24 25 26 27 28 29 1930 31 32 33 34 35 36 37 38

A

B

A = GDP per head (1913 prices)

B = Projection of steady
1·8% per annum compound
growth rate from 1924

the working population grew at 1% per annum; that is the 2·2% growth of total GDP minus the 1·2% per annum growth of the working population. We have already seen that since there was apparently no increase in the amount of capital with which each worker was equipped, the whole of this increase must have been due to improvements in technology and organisation.

The growth of the working population in this period is at first sight surprisingly fast, given the slowing down in the rate of population growth and the discouragements to participation in the labour force which prolonged high unemployment must have offered. The relevant statistics can be summarised as follows for the years 1924-37: [11]

Population growth	0·4% per annum compound
Growth of 15-64 age group	0·7% per annum compound
Growth of working population	1·2% per annum compound

It will be seen that the growth of the 15-64 age group, who form the great majority of the potential working population, was nearly twice as fast as the growth of population as a whole. This is likely to be a feature of any period in which the growth of population is slowing down due to a fall in the birth rate. The first effects of such a fall are to reduce the proportion of young dependants in the population. After a few decades, this will be offset by an increase in the proportion of old dependants, dependants here meaning simply people who are not potentially members of the working population. When the fall in the rate of growth of population is completed, the proportion of dependants in total is likely to be much the same as it was during the earlier period of fast growth. For instance, in 1871 the 15-64 age group was 59% of the total population, with 36% of the population being aged 14 or less, and only 5% being 65 or over. By 1961 the proportion of those aged 65 or over had already risen to 12%, but the 'young dependants' group had fallen to 23% leaving a 15-64 age group of 65%. However, in the interwar years the demographic situation was unusually favourable to economic growth. The fall in the proportion of young dependants resulting from the fall in the birth rate was already almost fully reflected in the figures. Thus by 1931 the under 15s were already only 24·3% of the population, almost a 'modern' proportion; in contrast the 65+ group were still only 7·5% of the total, thus leaving 68·3% of the population as potential workers aged 15-64. In 1937 the proportion had risen slightly further, to 69·3%, whereas in 1924 it had been only 66·7%. The demographic situation thus presented a special opportunity for growth in output per head of the total population in the interwar years. However, although the growth of the 15-64 age group was faster than the growth of the total population, it was slower than the growth of the working population, meaning those actually working or seeking work even though unable actually to find it. The concept 'seeking work' is not capable of any very precise definition, since it is impossible to be sure what proportion of the population might have opted to work if the employment position had been easier; almost certainly a larger proportion than actually did. Our actual definition of the 'working population' is those in employment plus the unemployed, the number of the latter being an estimate arrived at by correcting the numbers actually registered as unemployed under the insurance scheme to allow for the incomplete coverage of that scheme. Even with regard to the limitations of this definition, the increase in the 'working population' as a proportion of the 15-64 age group between 1924 and 1937 is quite striking. At the earlier date the working population was 66·1% of the age group; at the later date 70·6%. In the long historical perspective, both 'activity rates' are rather low; both in the nineteenth century and after the second world war typical rates were between 70 and 75% (e.g. 1964, 74%; 1861, 75%; 1891, 73%; 1911, 71%). But the 1937 figure does represent a return from the low figure for 1924 to something nearer the historical norm. The low figure for the 1920s reflects the discouragement to participation of the very high unemployment; the recovery in the 1930s can be seen as an adaptation to the continued high levels of industrial unemployment, which took the form of a rapid increase in employment in the service sector of the economy, particularly in retailing. Of the whole increase of the working population between 1924 and 1937 of 3·36 million persons, 875,000 went into the distributive trades, compared with only 550,000 into the whole manufacturing sector. A further 400,000 were absorbed by the building trades.[12]

Thus we have seen that of the growth of GDP per capita over these years, a substantial part can be accounted for by the excess of the growth of the working population over the growth of total population. However, GDP per member of the working population grew, as we have seen, at 1% per annum, and this seems to have been entirely due to improvements in technology or organisation. This rate of improvement was very much in line with previous peacetime experience, with the exception of the period from 1900 to 1913. This period of exceptionally slow growth seems to have gained almost nothing from technology.

The reasons for this are not clear. As R. C. O. Matthews puts it: 'There is scope for further study and more sophisticated hypotheses relating to this peculiar period.'[13] As far as the interwar period goes, technological improvements seem to have resumed their normal role in promoting the growth of output per head. This is not surprising when one considers the number of important innovations which were in progress during the period. Above all perhaps, electricity and the small electric motor offered the possibility of far more flexible layouts for factories and for the application of power to a wider range of processes, as for instance in small electric tools such as drills, saws and grinders. As far as industrial power went, the development of electricity was the most important advance since the invention of the steam engine. The internal combustion engine was another important development, and was closely associated with progress in the working of metals, and in the manufacture of new alloy steels, such as manganese steel. 'Artificial silk' or rayon had been developed in Britain in the early 1900s and its production increased rapidly after 1920. The first plastics, celluloid, casein and bakelite, had all been discovered by 1909, and the interwar years saw the beginnings of large-scale production. Radio had been pioneered just before the war and by 1935 'almost every English home was equipped to hear King George V broadcast on his Silver Jubilee day'.[14] Paper making had undergone a technical revolution with the innovation of the use of wood pulp as a raw material. Organic chemistry made rapid strides and its products found application in a wide range of industries, from cosmetics to explosives. The list of innovations spreading in the economy could be extended but these examples will serve to illustrate the process of technical change which lies at the heart of economic growth.

The pattern of changes in industrial working hours is at first sight a rather unexpected one. Reductions occur only at infrequent intervals and when they occur they are large. In between these major changes, working hours are extremely stable and resistant to change.[15] The reasons for this pattern are complex, but in summary one can say that normally the employees' demand for shorter hours and the employers' resistance to them are sufficiently evenly balanced to inhibit change. At certain times however, a combination of circumstances has broken through this barrier. The main driving force behind demands for reductions in hours has been the unions' fear of unemployment and desire for greater job security. When this fear was high, and when at the same time a rapid rise in wages coincided with a check in the rate of rise in prices or the existence of substantial accumulated savings, then the unions turned to the hours question. The four moments in recent history when this happened were the early 1870s, 1919, the late 1940s, and 1961-4.[16] Of all these, the most abrupt change occurred in 1919, when, in a single year, the 8-hour day became normal, as compared with the 9-hour day which had been the standard since the early 1870s. The particular combination of circumstances which prevailed in 1919 included the following elements: money wages and prices had been rising rapidly in the war, and small savings had been accumulated because of the shortage of goods; unemployment was low, and the union movement was strong, having greatly increased its membership and status in the war. On the other hand the fear of unemployment was high and the unions were anxious to avoid its recurrence. The fear was generated by technological changes, which had been accelerated in the war, and the possible increase in the labour force which would result if many of the people drawn into work in the war, especially women, decided to try and stay in competition for jobs. In these conditions, which have much in common with the other three periods of hours reduction, unions turned with success to the hours question. The change was led by the engineering and shipbuilding workers, and was swiftly followed by the majority of the industrial labour force. Hours of work in distribution and transport, and in agriculture, were much less standardised and in general longer. Nevertheless the arrival of the 8-hour day in industry, giving a working week generally of 48 hours, marks a major change in the working conditions of a majority of the British working population. The general statistic is confirmed by local observations, as for instance that made in the London School of Economics' *New Survey of London Life and Labour*.[17] 'Roughly speaking, the average London worker now [1928] has an extra hour a day to himself compared with then [1889]. The bulk of the total reduction took place in the years immediately following the war; since then the movement has practically ceased.'[18] There can be no doubt that this change was beneficial. The hours worked typically before the war meant that the opportunities for leisure or relaxation were minimal. It is a significant failing of national product statistics that they can attribute no value to leisure gained at the price of output foregone, and this is one of the many ways in which such statistics are inadequate indicators of welfare. The change in hours worked can have had no effect on the recorded interwar growth rates as it all occurred in the year or two following the war and there was virtually no further change in the rest of the period, and no change between the years we have used for the calculation of growth rates. But when thinking of living standards in the interwar years as compared with preceding periods, one needs to add in something for the 11% reduction in average working hours.

IV *Trend and Cycle in the Interwar Period*

So far we have been concerned mainly with trends in the rate of growth which deliberately abstract from year-to-year fluctuations in the economy. The choice of years which define the trends discussed is debatable. One could for instance attempt to compare the growth rate of the 1920s with that of the 1930s. It is argued here that such a comparison would not be very meaningful, since the ten years 1930-9 contain years of severe cyclical depression, but this is not true of 1920-9. Year-to-year growth rates in the early 1930s are therefore faster than anything which occurred in the 1920s, but much of this apparently rapid 'growth' is due not to the underlying trend of growth in the economy but to recovery from the depression. It must be stressed, though, that the separation of trend and cycle is always an arguable operation; a matter of interpretation and not of fact. The facts available are simply the points on the graph representing each year's output.

The main alternative interpretation which has been suggested for the growth trends of the interwar years is one which sees the 1920s as belonging to a period of slow growth running from 1900 until the early 1930s. This was suggested by R. C. O. Matthews.[19] D. H. Aldcroft, in a later article,[20] placed more stress on what he saw as the contrast between the interwar period as a whole, and the pre-1914 period as a whole. J. A. Dowie,[21] criticising Aldcroft, suggested the scheme, which has been in principle followed here, of using the years of approximately equal unemployment, 1924 and 1937, to define the trend of growth in the interwar years. In any case, as we are here concerned with the interwar years, we need some scheme which will enable us to talk about 'the rate of growth' in this period. This seems to be most usefully defined as the rate of growth between years of equal unemployment.

The phenomena of the 'trade cycle' is one which has received much attention. The trade cycle appeared to be a regular wave-like fluctuation in the levels of output and employment. Its regularity suggested that it might be a natural phenomena, and in the nineteenth century Jevons attempted to connect it to the sunspot cycle. Modern interpretations of the instability of economic activity see it as arising from man-made rather than natural phenomena.[22] Some of the regularity of the cycle was in any case more in the mind of observers than in reality. Different indicators of economic activity, such as employment, total output or investment, showed peaks and troughs at different times. Cycles varied in length and did not by any means always synchronise in different countries. The view of the cycle as a surprising and problematic phenomena assumes a view of normality as being stable. The modern view is basically that there is no particular reason why economic output should pursue a stable path; economic life is immensely complex and subject to large numbers of influences both from domestic and external sources. Modern theory shows how the economic system is liable to relatively large fluctuations when subject to such random disturbances. Modern economic policy has tried to devise means of providing stabilising mechanisms which will offset these tendencies.

The record of economic output in nineteenth-century Britain did however show what appeared to be a reasonably regular cyclic pattern. Most indicators of economic activity moved fairly closely together. In Section II, we have already made use of the trade cycle in the nineteenth century to define the periods to be compared with respect to rates of growth. In the interwar years however such regularity has largely disappeared. It is possible to see 1929 as the peak of one cycle and 1937 as the peak of the next. But it does not seem that much interpretative light is thrown on the situation by this approach. By far the most important cyclical phenomenon of the period is the downswing of the early 1930s, which started in 1929. This depression was worldwide. It was far deeper than any cyclical downswing of the nineteenth century. Many thought of it, with reason, as the 'crisis of capitalism'. That it was a very serious phenomenon can hardly be doubted. It does not seem very helpful to describe it simply as another cyclical downswing. Its magnitude demands special analysis. This we attempt to provide in Chapter 2, since the origins of the depression were essentially worldwide in scope.

The impact of the world depression on the British economy can be clearly seen in the graph of GDP per head (Chart 1). Output is rising in the 1920s, although throughout unemployment remains at historically high levels. But between 1929 and 1932 output falls and most indicators of economic activity turn downwards. Table 1.2 gives the details. From 1933 to 1937 there is a period of recovery and again the movement of five indicators is shown in Table 1.2. As far as Britain is concerned, the outstanding feature of her experience is the way consumers' expenditure was shielded from the depression. This was mainly because Britain was a large importer of foodstuffs and had herself a very small primary producing sector. The enormous fall in the price of primary produce was thus in some ways a benefit to her, though, as is discussed in Chapter 2, not an unmixed benefit.

If consumers' expenditure showed great stability, investment and exports showed the greatest fluctuations. Investment goods are typically the most unstable item in the output of industrial economies. Investment is by definition the installation of equipment that will generate extra output in the future. If for any reason people cease to think there will be a demand for that extra output, net investment (additions to the capital stock as opposed to replacements) is likely to fall to zero. If the depression becomes very severe, firms may cease to maintain their existing capital equipment, so that investment falls even further. The instability of exports is discussed in Chapter 2. In the 1930s the quantitative importance of exports in British output was much reduced. Throughout the interwar years the difficulties of certain large exporting industries in their overseas markets was at the centre of the unemployment problem. Further discussion of the problems of these industries will be found in Chapter 3.

Table 1.2 *Depression and Recovery, 1929-37*

Columns 1 and 2 show the percentage change, between the years shown, in the items in each row. Column 3 shows the proportion of the change in total final expenditure between 1932 and 1937 which is accounted for by each item, using its 1929 proportions in total final expenditure as a weight. Thus, for example, the item, 'consumers' expenditure' increased by 2·0% and 13·5% between 1929 and 1932 and 1932 and 1937 respectively. Its increase between 1932 and 1937 accounted for 46·7% of the whole increase in total final expenditure between those years. (Total final expenditure is a measure of output defined so that GDP is equal to total final expenditure less imports of goods and services. Its increase between 1932 and 1937, at 19·8%, was very similar to that in GDP.)

	1 1929-32	2 1932-7	3
Consumers' expenditure	+2·0	+13·5	46·7
Public authorities' current expenditure on goods and services	+5·0	+34·5	14·1
Gross domestic investment	−14·1	+47·5	20·1
Exports of goods and services	−32·2	+21·1	19·1
			100·0
Gross domestic product	− 4·9	+20·4	−

Source Calculated from Feinstein, table 5. Original figures at 1938 constant prices.

Some commentators have sought explanations of the timing of Britain's recovery in the 1930s. H. W. Richardson, in the standard work on the subject, has concluded that the building boom and investment in the new, mainly consumer durable, industries were the most important elements.[23] Richardson also stressed the importance of the stability of consumers' expenditure in moderating the depth of the downswing. The development of the 'new' industries, which sold most of their output in the home market, has been widely accepted as an important factor. Explanations which rely on the part played by particular industries, such as the 'new' industries or building, or particular components of output and expenditure, such as consumption or investment, do raise the difficult problem of exactly what is to count as an 'explanation'. If recovery is defined as a resumption of increases in GDP, and if GDP is in turn defined as having certain components, such as consumption and investment, then clearly increases in GDP must reflect an increase in at least one of its components. A measure of the relative importance of the various components of GDP in the recovery between 1932 and 1937 is given in Column 3 of Table 1.2. This shows the proportion of the total increase which was accounted for by the four components shown, using their relative shares in 1929 as weights. Thus although consumers' expenditure increased by only 13·5%, this increase made up 46·7% of the total, since consumers' expenditure has a large share of the total. Increases in government expenditure, investment and exports accounted for 14%, 20% and 19% respectively of the increase, However, to state these proportions is not of course to offer any explanation of the recovery, but merely to describe the form which recovery took.

Similar difficulties apply to any statement that any part of the increase in consumers' expenditure and/or investment was due to the expansion of the 'new' industries. The problem again is to define 'new' in such a way that it has any explanatory, as opposed to descriptive, force. If, as J. A. Dowie has emphasised in an article already referred to above, 'new' simply means expanding, then fairly obviously expansion cannot be explained by saying that it was due to the 'new' (that is expanding) industries. Further, as Dowie goes on to emphasise, even if 'new' can be defined in a way that is independent of 'expanding', there is a further requirement. If the 'new industry' argument is to reach the status of an explanation rather than a description, then all new industries must have been expanding, or in other words the 'newness' of an industry must have been sufficient cause for its being an expanding one. This condition would not be met if only some new industries were expanding and others were not, even if the ones that were expanding were the only industries, of any sort, that did so. The 'newness' of an industry would then be a necessary but not a sufficient cause of expansion, and we should still be left wondering what other features the expanding industries had in common which actually caused them to expand.

All this amounts to saying that to elevate a description to the status of an explanation, in anything approaching a rigorous sense, is very difficult. No description of the recovery of the British economy comes anywhere near meeting these requirements. Indeed it is very doubtful whether historians have ever, at any time, or in relation to any period or problem, produced explanations of the historical record in this rigorous sense. Rather they suggest features of the record which, at least in most people's minds, help to make it seem less obscure or surprising. Features of the recovery of the 1930s which have been suggested in this way include, apart from the growth of 'new' industries already discussed, the building boom and, with less emphasis, government policy on interest rates, tariffs and regional employment. These matters will all be referred to in more detail in later chapters.

Finally, it needs to be emphasised that, although in the discussion of the trends of growth rates, we abstract from cyclical variations, these variations from the trend were of the greatest significance to contemporaries. Throughout the interwar years, although the economy was growing at an historically respectable rate, it was all the time producing much less output than it could have done if there had been less unemployment. Even in the least depressed years of the period, roughly 10% could have been added to the output of the economy, by eliminating the majority of the unemployment, more or less 'at a stroke'. Goods and services produced during the period, at constant 1938 prices, totalled £97,536 million. If we arbitrarily assume that a 10% increase was possible in each year, by reducing the level of unemployment to more reasonable proportions, then the total output lost in the period comes to £9,754 million, or two years' output at the level of output actually prevailing in 1929. This loss of output through under-employment of the productive capacity of the economy is a quite separate phenomenon to the increase in the actual productive capacity itself. Not surprisingly, in the interwar years, the losses due to under-employment of capacity were seen as a far more urgent problem by contemporaries than the other question of the rate of growth of capacity. The failure to solve this problem of unemployment is central to the more popular view of the period as one of depression in general. It was not until the question of under-utilisation of capacity had been largely solved, at least for the time being, in the 1950s, that popular attention turned to the problem of the rate of growth. Ironically enough, the gloomy view of the interwar years, which arose mainly from the problem of under-employment of capacity, was, in Britain's case, to be immediately replaced by a gloomy view of the postwar years, which arose mainly from the newly discerned problem of Britain's slow growth of capacity.

v *Living Standards*

It is now time to investigate the relationships between the abstractions discussed so far and the concrete realities of life in interwar Britain. The aggregate statistics outlined above should give a general indication of standards of living. We would expect, other things remaining equal, to find that economic growth resulted in higher levels of consumption. The principal 'other things' were the distribution of income and the terms of trade. The former changed little after 1921, but the latter was an important influence in the direction of higher consumption.

The main direct evidence for what actually happened to living standards is the long series of social surveys, modelled on and inspired by the pioneers of all such work: Booth's survey of living standards in London in 1889 and Rowntree's *Poverty*, a survey of living standards in York in 1899. In the interwar years further surveys were taken in York, London, Merseyside, the 'five towns' (Reading, Northampton, Warrington, Stanley and Bolton), Southampton and Bristol. In addition national surveys of food consumption and total expenditure were carried out by the Rowett Institute and the Ministry of Labour respectively, in 1935 and 1938.

From this large mass of material certain general impressions emerge. In all the survey work, with the exception of the Rowett survey of food consumption, attention was focussed exclusively on the 'working class' and it was assumed that the working class was an easily identifiable group in society. The middle class was taken to be well off and to be in no need of social services or government assistance. Rather surprisingly, very little space is devoted in any of the surveys to the problem of precise definition of the working class. 'This report', says the Bristol survey, 'is concerned only with incomes which fall below middle-class levels and consequently it covers four fifths of all Bristol families.'[24] Rowntree's second survey of York,[25] after accounting for the working class, has a residual not surveyed of 35% of the population, and the new London survey had a residual of 28%. Possibly 25-35% of the population may have thought of themselves as middle class. But if one defined the middle class as persons living in households where the main earner was a non-manual worker with an income (earned or unearned) of more than £250 a year, then a figure of between 15% and 20% would seem more likely. Some of the difference between these 'subjective' and 'objective' proportions is accounted for by white-collar workers earning less than £250 a year. There would also be some young professional or managerial workers earning less than £5 a week at the start of careers which would soon take them well over this level. And again there were no doubt some elderly persons living on unearned incomes below the arbitrary £250 line, but still thinking of themselves, and being accepted as, on the middle-class side of the fence. Nevertheless the Rowntree residual of 35% does seem rather high, and possibly too little attention was devoted to the accurate drawing of this important social dividing line in the interwar surveys of living standards.

A second common feature of these surveys is their overriding concern with physical needs which they assume can be objectively calculated. The leading component of these physical needs calculations is the number of calories assumed necessary for 'physical efficiency', figures for which had by the beginning of the period become available as a result of progress in the study of nutrition. Starting from the number of calories and principal components of the minimum diet, it was possible to calculate a minimum cash cost, taking into account the accepted social norms of the working-class life style. To this could be added allowances for clothes, fuel and light, minimum insurance and transport commitments, 'sundries' and the rent actually paid by typical working-class families. The classic example of this type of calculation is Rowntree's in *The Human Needs of Labour*, the first edition of which was published in 1918, revised in the light of the new knowledge of nutrition in the 1930s, and used as the standard in his second survey of York in 1936. Rowntree elected to place most emphasis on a family of five: man, wife and three children, and it is this type of family that he uses for purposes of comparison throughout. In fact, families of this composition were highly untypical; the London survey commented in 1929 that 'the traditional statistical family of man earning, wife and three children dependent [is less] than 40 per thousand in the western area [of London] and 50 per thousand in the east'.[26] In nearly all the surveys, two and three person households are the most commonly occurring type, and the average number of persons in a household is usually a little under 3·5; 3·37 in York for instance,[27] 3·48 in London[28] and 3·35 in Bristol.[29] Rowntree's 'Human Needs' standard (as it came to be known after the title of the book) was as follows:

Man living alone	£1·29 per week
Man and wife living together	£1·60 per week
Man, wife and 1 child	£1·90 per week
Man, wife and 2 children	£2·06 per week
Man, wife and 3 children	£2·18 per week

These figures assume the head of the household is employed and exclude rent. Rent typically would be in the region of 35-50p per week and the rent allowed by Rowntree for a family of five was 47½p. Rowntree's survey of York in 1936 found that 31·1% of working-class families, or 17·7% of the whole population, failed to meet his standard.

The survey of Bristol, conducted in a prosperous city at the peak of the recovery of the late 1930s (in the summer of 1937), found that 30% of working-class families were either with 'insufficient income' (19·3%) or in poverty (10·3%). Rather more than a quarter of the Bristol working-class families in poverty were in 'utter destitution'. On Merseyside 30% of working-class families in 1929 fell below a 'human' needs' standard similar in essentials to that of Rowntree's.[30]

Precise comparability between these figures cannot be expected. In particular, the Bristol survey standard for 'insufficient income' is higher than the 'minimum human needs' standard though its poverty standard was lower, making no allowance for personal sundries of any sort other than basic household necessities.[31] Without claiming great precision, it might be suggested that half the families in the Bristol survey's 'insufficient income' class fell below Rowntree's 'human needs' level, giving a figure of 20% of families below this level, compared with the common result of 30% in other surveys. But one main inference from these figures is clear; that for the lowest third of working-class families in the income distribution, or about the lowest quarter in the population, life throughout the interwar period was hard. 'The wide gap that separates working-class standards from middle-class standards', wrote Herbert Tout in the Bristol survey, 'will strike all readers who have imagined for themselves what the standard means';[32] and indeed for all the vast weight of words in the earlier surveys, the concise sixty-four pages of the Bristol survey bring home as clearly as any the problems of life at the bottom of the income distribution. Of course one can comfort oneself with the thought that all things are relative; 'the minimum sum required to feed an Indian peasant is considerably less than that required to feed an English agricultural labourer', notes the Merseyside survey consolingly,[33] but Tout's unembroidered description of the poverty level suggests a life without interest or variety, existence rather than living. Lighting allowed was one 60 watt bulb for twenty hours a week. Two pairs of boots had to last three years, repairs to be done by the owner. Three pairs of trousers were to last two years; 'very often', it is noted, 'clothes can be purchased quite cheaply at jumble sales'. 'The minimum standard makes no allowance whatever for sickness, savings, for old age or burial expenses, holidays, recreation, furniture, household equipment, tobacco, drink, newspapers or postage.'[34] Yet in a prosperous city in a boom year, after seventeen years of fairly sustained economic growth, 10% of working-class families were below this spartan level, and another 19%, those defined as on an 'insufficient income', cleared it by a margin of less than 50%. In other towns, especially in South Wales, where no survey was done, and the north and west, and especially again in

Scotland and Northern Ireland, there can be no doubt that larger percentages, probably in the region of 30%, were fairly regularly at or below this dreary standard, and even where respectability was maintained as it so often was, 'the lace curtains often hid empty cupboards'.[35]

But below the level of the dreary and the uninteresting, and mixed inextricably with it, was the malnutrition. The most extensive survey conducted into nutrition was that of the Rowett Institute in 1935.[36] It divided the population into six groups by income per head, and estimated their income and food expenditure, by a process that includes many uncertainties due to lack of data.

Table 1·3 *Income and Food Expenditure*

Group 1	Income per head per week	Food expenditure per head per week	Numbers of persons in group (millions)	Percentage
I	Up to 50p	20p	4.5	10
II	50p-75p	30p	9	20
III	75p-£1	40p	9	20
IV	£1.-£1.50	50p	9	20
V	£1.50-£2.25	60p	9	20
VI	Over £2.25	70p	4.5	10
Average	£1.50	45p	45	100

Source J. B. Orr, *Food, Health and Income, appendix V, table II.*

Orr's conclusions were that the diet of the poorest group, Group I, was deficient in every nutritional constituent considered, and that Group II was deficient in all vitamins and minerals, though satisfactory in respect to protein, fat and carbohydrate. The third group was deficient in several important vitamins and minerals, and complete adequacy was reached only with Group IV.[37] This suggests that 30% of the population was suffering from a substantial degree of malnutrition. These conclusions have been criticised by A. L. Bowley on the grounds that inadequate account was taken of the differing needs of children and females, and a recalculation, which has not been published in detail, concluded that substantially lower percentages were undernourished.[38]

None the less, it seems likely that malnutrition, particularly of growing children, was quite widespread in interwar England. R. M. Titmuss and Le Gros Clark in 1939 concluded that 'over large regions of Great Britain, in Wales, Scotland and the greater part of the north, there is a strikingly high incidence of devitalising disease'.[39] The infant mortality rate for Scotland, which had been lower than the rate for England and Wales in the nineteenth century, was 35% above it by the mid-1930s. In Glasgow it was 109 per thousand, which contrasted with a rate of 38 per thousand in Hertfordshire. The Glasgow rate was only a marginal improvement on the average for the whole of Scotland in 1855.[40] Tuberculosis death rates had on average declined since before the war, but regional differentials had widened, Wales for instance rising from 130% above the national average to 171% above it.[41] These differentials and death rates were of course influenced by factors other than malnutrition, particularly housing.

Other evidence suggests that malnutrition particularly affected growing children, and among them, particularly teenagers. The apparent liveliness, or uncontrollability if one looks at it that way, of the modern teenager may be due in no small measure to the fact that he is now properly fed. Figures for the height and weight of teenagers, covering some 68,000 observations in five separate surveys, are given in *Food, Health and Income.* [42] They cover the years 1927 to 1935, and can be compared with similar measurements taken before the war. In all cases, public school boys, or Christ's Hospital school boys, used as 'fully nourished' controls, show large gains over their working-class contemporaries. Further, 'it appears that, in the last fifty years [1886-1936] though the average height for all classes has risen, there has been no marked change in the order of difference between classes'. [43] The number of rejected volunteers for the army had not changed substantially over the same fifty years,[44] remaining in the region of 30% (excluding those rejected for poor sight), though as far as can be told, there was little change in the physical standards adopted. Poor feeding, R. M. Titmuss suggested, was responsible for the stunted growth and slight build of many working-class adolescents. 'The majority of boys of 10 to 14 seem of average size but the youth of 14 to 18 is weedy in a disproportionate number of cases.'[45] The excessive weight of poverty that was borne by children is discussed further below.

So far we have kept our discussion focussed on the lower end of the distribution. In that lower 30% drabness was universal, malnourishment common, and severe hardship and poverty the lot of a substantial proportion, probably more than 10%, throughout the interwar period. When unemployment was at its peaks, and in the depressed regions, these figures may well be underestimates by a large margin. But if our first point is that 'optimistic' views of the interwar period can all too easily forget these realities, our second must be that whatever the state of affairs in the interwar period in general, it was a substantial and striking improvement on the period just before the war. Three surveys permit more or less direct comparisons: Bowley's *Five Towns* survey (1913-14 and 1924), Rowntree's two surveys of York (1899 and 1936) and Booth's survey of London (1889) which was followed up by the *New Survey* directed by Bowley from the London School of Economics in 1929. All are clear in their answer to Bowley's question, the title of his 1924 book, *Has Poverty Diminished?* The answer was yes.

'The improvement since 1913 is very striking. The proportion [of families] in poverty in 1924 was little more than half that in 1913. If there had been no unemployment, the proportion of families in poverty in the towns taken together would have fallen to one third, and of persons to a little over a quarter, of the proportion in 1913. All the towns except Stanley show an improvement in nearly the same ration: and it is found for both sexes and all ages.'[46]

The extent of family poverty in York in 1936 among the working class was only 44% of its 1899 level.[47] These poverty calculations of before the war of course set much harsher standards than the 'human needs' type standards to which we have been referring so far, but they are the only basis on which prewar comparisons can be made. But improvement there undoubtedly had been, and it seems that quite a lot of this improvement had occurred by 1924 if the *Five Towns* survey is any guide. Since by 1924 the national income per head was roughly the same as in 1914, the question arises as to how this component of the improvement, that which occurred across the years 1914-24, had come about.

This opens the wider question of the sources of rising living standards in the interwar years, and it can profitably be split into two: firstly the causes of the improvement between about 1914 and 1924 already referred to, and secondly the subsequent improvement to 1939. Basically the answer would seem to be that the first period saw a marked shift in distribution in favour of wage earners and the working classes; and that the second period saw little further change in distribution but a steady growth of national product reflected in rising standards at all points on the spectrum of distribution. Explanations relying on changes in income distribution for a period in which virtually no reliable figures for such distributions are available are bound to be speculative. Nevertheless, the work of E. H. Phelps-Brown and M. H. Browne[48] has shown that profits as a share of income generated within the industrial sector of the economy showed a marked fall in the great deflation of 1921-2. 'Profit margins were squeezed in the great postwar deflation, as they were in slumps generally, but this time the pressure was extraordinarily powerful and the market environment remained hard, so that when recovery came and the margins were restored, it was to considerably less than their prewar level.'[49] Hence income from employment was taking a larger share of total income, and although a larger proportion of this certainly went to salaries, this larger proportion was spread over a larger number of salary earners, and it seems at least reasonable to look here for some of the resources needed to account for a rise in the level of real wages since 1914.

The second form which redistribution took was through taxation and social expenditure. The war created a 'displacement effect'[50] by which conventional ideas about acceptable rates of taxation were displaced upwards under stress of war, and did not subsequently move down again. In addition, the stresses and expectations of the postwar situation led to large-scale extension of unemployment insurance in 1920. The extent of the redistribution was not very great, but was none the less significant. In 1937, to which the first detailed estimate available refers,[51] the income of the working classes was increased through redistribution by between 8% and 14% depending on assumptions made about the allocation of 'indivisible' items like defence. In 1924, before the major conversions of national debt to lower rates of interest in 1932, it is safe to say that the proportion redistributed was no higher, and probably lower than in 1937, but also that it was substantially greater than in 1914. Higher real wages, then, and a more extensive provision of social services, particularly unemployment insurance and assistance, stand out as two major reasons for the improvement between 1914 and 1924. The third major reason is the decline in family size. The fall in family size between Rowntree's two surveys of York, thirty-seven years apart, was from 4·04 persons to 3·37 persons. More general figures for the whole country are, surprisingly, not available. 'It is an extraordinary fact', comment A. M. Carr-Saunders and D. Caradog Jones, writing in 1937, 'that we do not know how many families there are with one, two, three or more children. This is a very serious gap in our knowledge of the social structure of the country.'[52] It is clear however that family size was falling. The average number of live births to couples married in the period 1920-4 was 2·38, and in 1925-9 2·19, compared with 3·37 and 2·90 to couples married between 1900 and 1909, and 1910 and 1914 respectively.[53] These figures do not tell us anything precise about surviving families at any instant in time, and the fall in the number of live births was offset to some extent, but not completely, by the fall in the number of children who died young. However, as we shall see below, the connection between poverty and number of dependent children in a family remained extremely strong throughout the interwar period.

If there was a substantial improvement in working-class living standards between 1914 and 1924, it is also true that there was a further rise between 1924 and the end of our period. This was due to economic growth, with relatively stable distribution, together with some further fall in family size and a further extension of social services. In addition, as primary product prices in world trade declined in the depression, food prices fell to the benefit of those, the lower end of the distribution, for whom they formed a larger than average proportion of expenditure. Consumers' expenditure per head grew throughout this period, falling only in two years: 1926 (because of the strike) and 1932 (because of the depression). In both years the recorded falls were so small as to be well within the margin of error of the figures, and it would be possible to suggest that consumers' expenditure shows a virtually uninterrupted rise throughout the interwar period from 1921 to 1938. Almost uniquely among industrial countries, consumption in Britain was little affected by the depression of 1929-33. And to come back to the Bristol survey, at the end of this development, the average income of Bristol working-class families was found to be, in 1937, double the minimum standard adopted as the poverty level. In the winter of 1937-8, following through into the summer of the 1938, the Ministry of Labour conducted an extensive survey into weekly expenditure of working-class households, where the head of the household was in employment.[54] The average weekly expenditure emerging from this investigation was £4·25,[55] with an average household size of 3·75, giving an average expenditure per head of £1·14. The average expenditure on food was £1·70 a week, or about 45p a head. With the most commonly occurring family sizes being those of two and three persons, it is clear that average expenditure at this level means that many working-class households were achieving a standard which really was beginning to be a standard of living, rather than a standard of existence. And all the available evidence confirms this impression. The average expenditure in the Ministry of Labour survey on 'other items', at £1·28 a week, suggests that many families were beginning to be able to diversify their expenditure in ways not dreamed of in 'human needs' calculations. For families in the upper half of the working-class income distribution, standards of housing, heating, lighting and feeding were better than ever before. There was greatly increased access to transport, in the form of buses, cycles, and, for a few, motor-cycles and occasionally cars; and to entertainment — cinemas, radio, newspapers. It seems reasonable to suggest that for the better-off half of the working class the rise in the level and the diversification of expenditure that took place in total between 1914 and 1939 was a crucial step out of the drab uniformity and low level of life that must have characterised the greater part of working-class existence before the war.

How can we reconcile the two pictures that have been drawn, of poverty on the one hand, and of progress on the other? There is in fact no conflict. We are dealing with a society with an uneven income distribution; a distribution that shades steeply from physical hardship to relative affluence. Although all classes gained, the gain was not enough to eliminate extensive malnutrition and physical stress, though it certainly reduced its incidence. There is not enough data to give a clear picture of family income distribution in relation to needs. The attempt by Sir John Orr referred to on page 38 is the nearest approach made to such a distribution for the whole population between the wars. The Bristol survey data enable a diagram to be given of the sample of Bristol working-class family incomes in relation to their 'standard needs' and a diagram of this sort is given in Chart 2. The height of each bar gives the percentage of families within the income range shown; for example, 3·2% of all families in the sample had family incomes within the range of 100-110% of their standard needs.

VI *The Sources of Poverty*
Why did poverty persist? The basic answer must be that a market economy distributes income in accordance with earning power, and not in accordance with needs. The basic economic unit is the household, that is a group of people (usually a family) sharing approximately the same living standards. The needs of the household depend on the number and age of its members. Its income will depend on the number and earning power of those members who can find work, or any social security payments to which its members are entitled. Throughout the interwar period, and indeed beyond, the ghost of the 'less eligibility' principle hovered over all social security payments. 'Thus where there are large families or special troubles, a conflict frequently arose between the conception of satisfying minimum needs, the *raison d'etre* of a *needs* service, and the necessity to maintain normal work incentives in the community.'[56]

Thus the scale of unemployment benefit and assistance, and public assistance rates, though well above Rowntree's 1899 poverty level, were generally below 'minimum human needs' standards as commonly

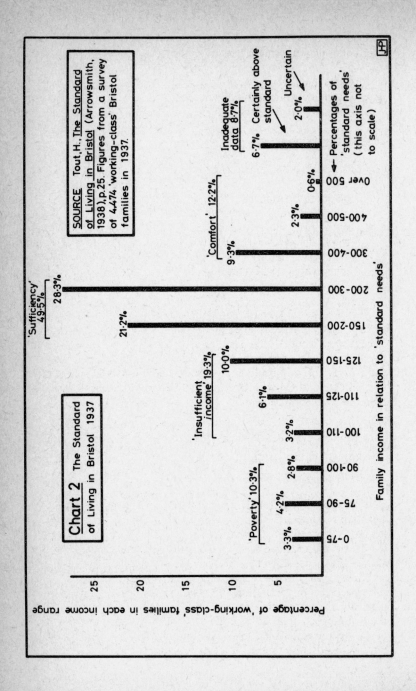

Chart 2 The Standard of Living in Bristol 1937

SOURCE Tout,H.,The Standard of Living in Bristol (Arrowsmith, 1938),p.25. Figures from a survey of 4,474 'working-class' Bristol families in 1937.

Percentage of 'working-class' families in each income range

Family income in relation to 'standard needs'

'Poverty' 10·3%
'Insufficient income' 19·3%
'Sufficiency' 49·5%
'Comfort' 12·2%
Inadequate data 8·7%

0-75 3·3%
75-90 4·2%
90-100 2·8%
100-110 3·2%
110-125 6·1%
125-150 10·0%
150-200 21·2%
200-300 28·3%
300-400 9·3%
400-500 2·3%
Over 500 0·6%

Certainly above standard 6·7%
Uncertain 2·0%

Percentages of 'standard needs' (this axis not to scale)

JP

defined in this period. A South Wales miner with three children paying a rent of 50p a week might receive: [57]

Wages in an average working week	£2·25
Unemployment insurance benefit	£1·75
Unemployment assistance	£1·80[58]

and (for comparison):

Rowntree 1936 human needs	£2·68 (employed)
	£2·52 (unemployed)
Rowntree 1899 poverty level (at 1936 prices)	£1·53
Bristol survey poverty level (1937)	£2·38
Average manual wage (1936)	£3·00 (approximately)
Average expenditure of working-class households (1938) (excluding the unemployed)	£4·25

Thus for the three-child family unemployment insurance was about 69% of minimum needs, the typical miner's wage about 84% and the average wage about 112%. As long as it had only one earner and four dependants such a family had little chance of a life appreciably above the poverty line and could easily, if unemployment or ill health struck, go well below it. On the other hand, if the family had only one child, then the calculation becomes:

Rowntree 1936 human needs	£2·15 (employed)
	£2·00 (unemployed)
Bristol 1937 poverty level	£1·78 (employed)
Unemployment insurance	£1·45

Here we can see that for the smaller family, even a miner's wage would clear the minimum level fairly easily, and unemployment insurance at least brings the family a little closer to it. Large family size in other words was not provided for by the wage system and because of this was also inevitably penalised by the social security system.

These figures however conceal another way in which large families suffered. Modern calculations of relationships between the minimum diets of children of different ages and of adults show that teenagers need more food than an adult. Further, in any reasonable calculation of 'human needs' which takes account of social pressures as well as physical needs, the total costs of maintaining a child rise steeply after the age of 10 to reach a peak in the late teens equal to about 125% of maintenance costs of an adult.[60] The Bristol survey attempted in 1937 to distinguish between the costs of children of different ages, but allowed no rates above those of an adult, and allowed 85% of an adult's food costs for a child between 10 and 14. Modern figures would suggest 95% or possibly even 100% as being a more appropriate average relativity for those years. Apart from the Bristol survey, it was normal to treat children as Rowntree did, as equivalent to 65% of an adult, a relativity that underestimates the average cost of a child as he grows up over the years from birth to school leaving at 14. It is true of course that before he leaves school he may start to contribute to the family income, though the total contribution before the age of 14 was unlikely to be large, and would be to some extent offset by the extra wear and tear on clothes, and demands for pocket money for small luxuries. In the outcome there can be little doubt that the small proportion of families, who in the interwar years raised the majority of the country's children, suffered a quite disproportionate burden of poverty. Only 9% of families in the Bristol survey had three or more children, but these families contained 41% of all the children. The child poverty rate in Bristol was double the average rate. In York Rowntree found a similar situation, with 52·5% of the working-class children under one year of age, and 39% of those between 5 and 15, living below his minimum standards.[61] 'The seriousness of this from the standpoint of the national physique can hardly be overstated', commented Rowntree.[62] The national physique aside, society's treatment of dependent children in this period must be considered a moral failure. Industrial society has placed steadily increasing pressure on that minority of families which rear the majority of the succeeding generation. By any standards this is one of the most important investment projects going on in the economy at any moment of time, and as society becomes more complex its importance increases. Inadequate resources were devoted to it during the interwar years.

If the fact of being young or having young children dependent was an important source of poverty in two stages of the family life cycle, the stages of childhood and child rearing, the next most likely time for poverty to arise was in old age. 'The poverty of old age is more acute than that due to any other single cause', noted Rowntree.[63] Both the non-contributory old age pension scheme of 1908 and the contributory pension scheme of 1925 provided pensions at the rate of 50p a week, the former Act at age 70 and the latter at age 65. Thus for all the interwar period a married couple living together aged over 70 would have an income of £1 a week. If this was their only resource, they were bound to be in poverty by any standards; the Rowntree

1899 poverty line, at 1936 prices, including 43p a week rent, being £1·17 for a man and a woman living together. For a person forced to live alone the position was even worse. Of course neither pension scheme was ever intended to be more than a supplement to savings or other income. Thus it was that whereas, for instance, in 1936 about, 2¼% of the population between 15 and 65 were driven to seek public assistance, the proportion for those over 65 was 8·7% and, re-emphasising an earlier point about child poverty, for those aged below 15 years, it was 4·5%.[64]

In between the three phases of family life where poverty was commonest came two phases of relative affluence: between the end of childhood and the start of child rearing and between the end of child rearing and the onset of old age. This pattern, emphasised by Rowntree in his earlier work, still shows clearly in the diagram which serves as a cover illustration in the Bristol survey, and is given here in Chart 3.

As the children grew up the family typically entered a phase where there was more than one wage earner. The average number of wage earners per family in the Ministry of Labour survey (1938) was 1·75; in London it was 1·72 (1929), in Bristol 1·46 (1937), while in York the average was 1·8. The presence of an additional wage earner, whether it was an adolescent, or a wife, or some other relation, was the surest route out of poverty. Only a very small proportion of working-class families with family incomes of £4 or over (perhaps about half of all working-class families in 1938) can have achieved this level of income through the unaided efforts of the wage earner; only about the top 10% of working-class weekly wages exceeded £4.

Whatever the number of wage earners, or their income, the disasters of illness, disablement or death were liable for any family to be superimposed on the life cycle of earnings in relation to need described above. Health insurance throughout the period was on a purely individual basis, taking no account of family responsibilities, so that illness of the head of the family could be a disaster indeed. About a half of the applicants for public assistance between the ages of 15 and 65 were sick or disabled, and in the Bristol survey these causes accounted for 9% of total poverty, with the absence of an adult male earner accounting for another 13%.[65]

VII *The Middle Classes*

The number of salary earners in Great Britain increased from 8·3% of the occupied population in 1911 to 13·8% in 1931 and 14·3% in 1938.[66] A further 6% were self-employed in 1931, a proportion that had steadily declined since the nineteenth century.[67] Data concerning the

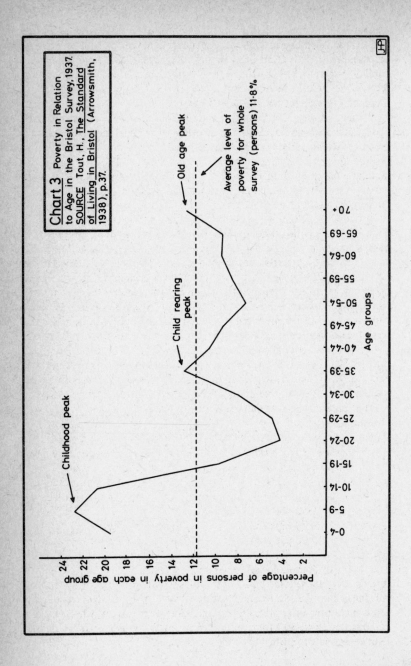

Chart 3 Poverty in Relation to Age in the Bristol Survey, 1937. SOURCE Tout, H., The Standard of Living in Bristol (Arrowsmith, 1938), p.37.

Old age peak

Average level of poverty for whole survey (persons) 11·8%

Child rearing peak

Childhood peak

Age groups

70+ 65-69 60-64 55-59 50-54 45-49 40-44 35-39 30-34 25-29 20-24 15-19 10-14 5-9 0-4

Percentage of persons in poverty in each age group

24 22 20 18 16 14 12 10 8 6 4 2

distribution of personal incomes in this period is scarce and insecure, but it seems that throughout the period about 12½% of pre-tax incomes exceeded £250 per annum. According to the estimate by Dudley Seers for 1938, the figure for incomes above this level was 12·8% and these incomes took 44·5% of all personal distributed income before direct tax and 40·4% after tax.[68]

Perhaps these 12% of top income receivers were most securely classifiable as middle class; the overlap of manual and non-manual incomes which arises after the second world war was only just beginning to be apparent in this period and in 1937 only 60,000 manual workers insured for unemployment earned over £250 a year.[69] No doubt many non-manual workers with salaries of less than £250 per annum thought of themselves as middle class, particularly teachers, shop assistants, and civil servants. The size of the 'subjective' middle class — those who thought of themselves as such — can only be guesswork, but considering the figures given above it seems unlikely that, on any objective definition, it was more than 20% of the population, and probably less. Unlike the working class, few people bothered to survey them or their households. They were not on the whole the concern of policy makers, who invariably excluded them from social security measures by specifying income ceilings, normally £5 a week. The only extensive survey available was conducted by the Civil Service Statistical and Research Bureau in 1938-9.[70] The response rate, always abysmal in previous attempts at middle-class surveys,[71] was about 40%; still much lower than in the roughly equivalent working-class inquiry of the year before conducted by the Ministry of Labour.

The pattern of income distribution revealed by this survey was as follows:

Income (£) of head of household, per annum	Percentage of all respondents
250-349	44
350-499	37
500-699	14
700 and over	5

The average household size was 3·27 persons and the number of earners per household 1·22, both lower than for the working class. All these households were spending about 25% of their income on food, including an appreciable expenditure on meals outside the home, compared with 40-50% for typical working-class families, and even higher figures (60% or more) for the very poor.[72] Even so, this lower proportionate expenditure gave all of them higher expenditures per head on food; the £250-350 group for instance spending 66p per head compared with 52p for the working-class average. A sizeable proportion, 64%, owned or were buying their houses, compared with 18% for the working class, and of course their expenditure on other basic items was in every case much higher than the equivalent working-class levels. But it was above all in the category 'other items' that middle-class affluence showed up. On average these middle-class households spent 48·5% of their incomes under this heading, compared with just under 30% for the working class as a whole and of course a very small proportion for the poorest members of society. It was this growth of miscellaneous expenditure on things other than the basics of existence, other that is than food, housing, clothing and fuel, which was the most conspicuous feature of middle-class living standards.

The number of very large incomes had probably declined since before the war,[73] but the expansion of clerical and administrative work in government and industry probably, though no firm figures exist, increased the number of salaried employees at the lower end of the middle-class range. Income tax of course was higher than before the war, the standard rate falling from a wartime peak of 30p in the pound down to 20p in 1925, and then in 1930 starting a climb back to 27½p in 1938. But the burden of income tax on families at the lower end of the middle-class income distribution was very slight. In 1929 for instance a married couple with two children and the man earning £400 a year would have had a personal allowance for the man of £225, an earned income allowance of one sixth (£66·6), and child allowances totalling £110 (£60 for the first and £50 for subsequent children), thus exempting him from tax altogether. If his income had been £500 he would have paid tax of £8. The system of income tax allowances for children meant that middle-class incomes were to some extent geared to family responsibilities in a way that working-class incomes were not.

After 1929 tax rates generally rose, although this pattern was interrupted in 1934 and 1935 when Chamberlain was able to make reductions, including 2½p off the standard rate in the first of those years. In 1935, our married man with £400 a year and two children, whose tax had risen, mainly from Snowden's 1931 impositions, to £9 a year, had his liability cut back again to £3·75. With £300 a year and no children, a married man paid £5·25 a year in 1935, and about £10 between 1931 and 1935. Despite much excited discussion at the time, particularly in 1931, about 'sharing burdens', these tax rates were still clearly not at levels which really hurt the majority of the middle class. Even in the case of the rather extreme example quoted by *The Times* newspaper in 1931, of a married man earning the relatively enormous salary of £1,000 a year, the £35 increase in his tax liability to £141 a year was not exactly crushing by modern standards. Surtax, which steepened the rate of progression above £2,000 a year, affected only a small minority who could presumably well afford to pay it.

The general level of salaries showed very little change in money terms over the whole period.[74] If prices of goods bought by the middle class moved parallel with those bought by the working class this would have represented a gain of about 20% in real terms, as for wages. However as this implies the use of a price index weighted far more heavily with food than was actually the case for most middle-class families, it is difficult to make any positive statement about the movement of real incomes for middle-class families. Anyone living through the twenty years of this period in full employment on a salary of four or five hundred pounds a year must surely have looked back on it as a good time. Of course there are some for whom material prosperity was marred by worry over the threatening international situation after 1932, and others whose social conscience must have been uneasy over the plight of the poor at home. One suspects they were a minority. Another minority experienced unemployment without the benefit of unemployment insurance. How many is not easy to say. Reports of the characteristically anecdotal and alarmist type appeared periodically in the press.[75] The 1931 census was the first to inquire about unemployment, and its results suggest a very much lower rate among professional, managerial and clerical workers than among manual workers. When the rate for 'unskilled manual workers' was 30·5%, that for clerks, typists, and higher office workers was 5·5% and for salesmen and shop assistants 7·9%. The professions, apart from the always irregularly employed musicians and actors, returned only 2%, and proprietors and managers in business 1·3%.[76] Nevertheless, for the fairly small proportion who did find themselves without work life could undoubtedly be hard, with insult, in the form of damaged pride, added forcefully to the injury of material hardship.

But for the luckier majority the interwar years were in many ways something of a golden age. For them, technology had already yielded many of its benefits while, as yet, few of its snags were apparent. The roads were still fairly empty and the ownership of a motor car offered to many both technical interest and efficient and convenient transport.[77] Beaches uncluttered with the proletariat could easily be found, and beauty spots were on the whole still beautiful. Domestic servants, while not as plentiful or cheap as before the war, were certainly a practical proposition for many families with quite modest incomes in the four or five hundred pound range, while electricity, refrigerators, vacuum cleaners, and gas and electric cookers, all appearing in middle-class homes by the mid-twenties, had made a vital contribution to the comfort and ease of domestic management. 'In 1939', wrote a correspondent to the *Evening Standard* in 1947, lamenting the passing of this period, 'I had a salary of £300 a year. We ran a small car, we lived in a modern flat, we threw occasional parties, we danced regularly, we had all the cigarettes we wanted, we could even enjoy an occasional pub crawl.'[78] If not quite paradise on earth, this was certainly not hardship.

VIII *Conclusion*

For the wage or salary earner of the interwar period, the progress of the gross domestic product must have seemed a remote and abstract affair, and indeed the connection between the conventionally accepted measurements of economic growth, discussed in the first part of this chapter, and the quality of life for particular individuals or groups, discussed thereafter, can be tenuous. In the 1960s, despite a tremendous rise in the average level of income compared with the interwar years, it started to seem that economic growth was a doubtful panacea for the ills of society; the basic conflict now in the 1970s is increasingly appearing to be one between those who are still wholly committed to the ideal of economic growth and 'those who are uninterested, except where there is clear evidence, that, as it sometimes has done . . . it improves the quality of men's lives . . . '.[79] The interwar years however would seem to be one of those periods when economic growth was, and was seen to be, clearly improving the quality of the majority of the population's lives. The material goods and services becoming available as incomes rose were close to the basic requirements of life and were almost pure gain; there were no offsets to the better built, better heated houses or to running water or electric heating and lighting. They made positive and obvious contributions to removing some of the drudgery and drabness of working-class life before the war, as did the spread of wireless and the cinema, and the greater possibilities of travel and relaxation. Later expansion in some of these directions was to run into problems, which have led to doubts about the value of the pursuit of growth 'for ever'. But that the growth of the interwar period was a benefit for the majority there can be little doubt.

For the majority: the other snag of the growth process has also commanded more attention since then, but was becoming clear enough. It has proved an extraordinarily difficult social problem to avoid omitting a minority from those benefits. The minority in the interwar period was substantial, and the level at which they were left was often that of real physical hardship rather than one of only relative deprivation.

And the minority included a shamefully high proportion of children. It was concentrated to a quite unreasonable extent on certain areas and occupations through involuntary unemployment.

But the idea of a national minimum and of the state's responsibility to ensure such a minimum was a radical departure from traditional thinking and was only slowly emerging in the interwar period.[80] Although there is no reason for complacency about the plight of many of the unemployed, the young, the sick and the old in this period, for nearly all these categories it is true that they were better off than before the first world war, and they did share to some extent in the rise of the national income.

Notes

1 M. M. Postan, *An Economic History of Western Europe 1945-64* (1967), ch.2.
2 C. H. Feinstein, *National Income, Expenditure and Output of the United Kingdom, 1855-1965* (1972), p.20. Hereafter referred to as Feinstein.
3 P. Deane and W. A. Cole, *British Economic Growth 1688-1959* (1962), and P. Deane, 'New Estimates of Gross National Product for the United Kingdom 1830-1914', *The Review of Income and Wealth* (June 1968).
4 See for instance W. Beckerman, *In Defence of Economic Growth* (1974).
5 Gross domestic product and gross national product are hereafter abbreviated to GDP and GNP. GNP is equal to GDP with the addition of net property income from abroad.
6 All the GDP figures for the United Kingdom in this section are taken from Feinstein and refer to gross domestic product at factor cost at constant 1913 prices. All rates of growth are compound rates.
7 Figures for USA and Germany calculated from A. A. Maddison, *Economic Growth in the West* (1964), tables A2 and B1.
8 Maddison, *Economic Growth*, tables A2, B1 and E1.
9 French and German figures calculated from Maddison, *Economic Growth*, tables, A2, B1 and E1.
10 Gross reproducible capital stock at current replacement cost; calculated from Feinstein, table 46, column 5. If dwellings are excluded the rate of growth is 0·8% per annum. But the rate of growth of the stock of capital invested in plant and machinery was 2·5% per annum.
11 Calculated from Feinstein, tables 55, 56 and 57.
12 The statistics in this section are calculated from Feinstein, tables 55-60.
13 R. C. O. Matthews, 'Some Aspects of Post-War Growth in the British Economy in Relation to Historical Experience', *Transactions of the Manchester Statistical Society* (1964).
14 R. S. Sayers, *A History of Economic Change in England 1880-1939* (1967), p. 68. The chapter from which this quotation is taken (ch. 5) is a survey of these technical developments.
15 M. A. Bienefeld, *Working Hours in British Industry* (1972), ch. 5.
16 These years saw changes in 'normal hours', that is in the standard working day. Increased overtime offset the reduction in normal hours to a

considerable extent after the reductions of normal hours on the last two occasions, in the late 1940s and 1961-4.

17 The London School of Economics, *New Survey of London Life and Labour* (1930), vol. 1, p. 117.
18 *New Survey*, vol. 1, p. 117.
19 Matthews, 'Some Aspects', *Transactions of the Manchester Statistical Society* (1964).
20 D. H. Aldcroft, 'Economic Growth in Britain in the Inter-war Years: A Reassessment', *Economic History Review*, vol. 20 (August 1967).
21 J. A. Dowie, 'Growth in the Inter-war Period: Some More Arithmetic', *Economic History Review*, vol. 21 (April 1968).
22 See for instance R. G. Lipsey, *An Introduction to Positive Economics*, 2nd edn (1966), ch. 45.
23 H. W. Richardson, *Economic Recovery in Britain 1932-39* (1967), p. 312.
24 H. Tout, *The Standard of Living in Bristol* (1938), p. 11.
25 B. S. Rowntree, *Poverty and Progress* (1941).
26 *New Survey*, vol. 6, p. 33.
27 Rowntree, *Poverty and Progress*, p. 453.
28 *New Survey*, vol. 6, p. 38.
29 Tout, *The Standard of Living in Bristol*, p. 29.
30 University of Liverpool, *The Social Survey of Merseyside* (1934), vol. 1, p. 156.
31 The Bristol survey used a more sophisticated method of calculating food needs and in this respect set a higher standard. But its 'standard needs' for a family of five exclusive of rent came to £1·88 compared with £2·18 for Rowntree's 1936 standard, and prices had risen slightly in the intervening period.
32 p. 26.
33 Vol. 1, p. 149.
34 Tout, *The Standard of Living in Bristol*, p. 19.
35 Fenner Brockway, *Hungry England* (1932), p. 14.
36 J. B. Orr, *Food, Health and Income* (1936).
37 Orr, *Food, Health and Income*, p. 49.
38 A. L. Bowley (ed.), *Studies in the National Income 1924-1938* (1944), pp. 118-9.
39 R. M. Titmuss and F. Le Gros Clark, *Our Food Problem* (1939), p. 140. This and the following quotations were all written by Titmuss.
40 Titmuss, *Our Food Problem*, p. 138. The 1855 average referred to was 119·6 per thousand.
41 Titmuss, *Our Food Problem*, p. 140. Figures refer to the 15-24 age group.
42 p. 40.
43 Orr, *Food, Health and Income*, pp. 39-40. But caution is needed in interpreting these results, since many factors may affect growth during adolescence. See J. M. Tanner, *Growth at Adolescence* (1962), p. 137.
44 Titmuss, *Our Food Problem*, pp. 127-8.
45 Titmuss, *Our Food Problem*, pp. 114, 132.
46 A. L. Bowley and M. H. Hogg, *Has Poverty Diminished?* (1925), p. 16.
47 Rowntree, *Poverty and Progress*, p. 461.
48 *A Century of Pay* (1968).
49 E. H. Phelps-Brown, *Pay and Profits* (1968), p. 27.
50 See A. T. Peacock and J. Wiseman, *The Growth of Public Expenditure in the United Kingdom* (1961), p. 27.

51 T. Barna, *The Redistribution of Incomes through Public Finance in 1937* (1945), p. 232.

52 *A Survey of the Social Structure of England and Wales* (1937), p. 12.

53 Cmd 7695 (1949), *Royal Commission on Population, Report*, p. 25. table 16.

54 *Ministry of Labour Gazette* (December 1940), 'Weekly Expenditure of Working-class Households'.

55 This is the average for households where the head of the household was employed; i.e. it excludes the unemployed.

56 Political and Economic Planning, *The British Social Services* (1937), p. 154.

57 An example similar to this is quoted in *The British Social Services*, p. 163. The example given there takes the even more untypical case of a family with five dependent children.

58 The rates given are those of the 1934 Unemployment Insurance Act as amended with regard to the rates for children in 1936. The rates then were: 85p for a man; 45p for his wife and 15p for each dependent child. The rate for children was increased from 10p for each child in 1936.

59 The 25p per week allowed by Rowntree for saving in his calculation of the needs of this type of family has been deducted here to give comparability with the earlier calculation.

60 Margaret Wynn, *Family Policy* (1970), ch. 3.

61 Tout, *The Standard of Living in Bristol*, p. 37 and Rowntree, *Poverty and Progress*, p. 156.

62 Rowntree, *Poverty and Progress*, p. 459.

63 Rowntree, *Poverty and Progress*, p. 66.

64 Political and Economic Planning, *The British Social Services*, p. 144.

65 Political and Economic Planning, *The British Social Services*, p. 144, and Tout, *The Standard of Living in Bristol*, p. 46.

66 Bowley, *Studies in the National Income*, p. 87.

67 In 1911 it was 14%. A. L. Bowley and J. Stamp, *The National Income 1924* (1927), p. 48.

68 D. Seers, *The Levelling of Incomes since 1938* (1950), table 1, p. 34.

69 Barna, *The Redistribution of Incomes*, p. 285.

70 P. Massey, 'The Expenditure of 1360 British Middle Class Households in 1938-9', *Journal of the Royal Statistical Society* (1942), vol. 105, part 3.

71 D. Caradog-Jones, 'The Cost of Living of a Sample of Middle Class Families', *Journal of the Royal Statistical Society* (1928), vol. 91, part 4.

72 Massey, 'The Expenditure of 1360 British Middle Class Households', comment in discussion by Sir John Orr.

73 L. R. Connor, 'On certain aspects of the Distribution of Income in the United Kingdom in 1913 and 1924' *Journal of the Royal Statistical Society* (1928), vol. 91, part 1.

74 Bowley, *Studies in the National Income*, p. 92, table 5.

75 For a sample see R. Lewis and A. Maude, *The English Middle Classes* (1949), pp. 78-9.

76 C. Clark, *The Conditions of Economic Progress* (1951), p. 470.

77 Although road deaths were very high, being at much the same level in the 1930s as in the 1960s, though in the latter decade the number of vehicles in use was about five times larger.

78 Lewis and Maude, *The English Middle Classes*, p. 207.

79 J. Passmore, 'Paradise Now', *Encounter* (November 1970), p. 17.

80 See generally B. B. Gilbert, *British Social Policy 1914-1939* (1970).

Chapter 2

Overseas Trade

I *The International Economy before the War*
British industrial development up to the first world war had produced
an economy that was heavily dependent on world trade for its
survival. At the beginning of the nineteenth century Britain had been
almost self-sufficient in foodstuffs, and even by 1870 imported only
about one fifth of all the food consumed. From then onwards
dependence on imports grew rapidly and by 1913 about half of the
temperate foodstuffs consumed in Britain were imported. In the
interwar years the proportion of imports was to rise still further,
reaching 65% in the late 1930s.[1] The pattern of dependence on
imported raw materials was rather different, with substantial reliance
on imports arising much earlier in the process of industrialisation. By
the 1870s, foodstuffs and raw materials formed roughly similar
proportions of imports and thereafter food drew ahead. But by 1914
the operation of the British economy required the import of a wide
range of raw materials which were not available in sufficient quantity
or not available at all at home. This dependence on imported food and
raw materials was to be heavily emphasised by the German submarine
campaigns in two world wars, in both of which shipping losses were to
bring Britain perilously close to defeat.

Given this dependence on imports, and the corresponding dependence
on the exports needed to pay for them, the reasons for the British
interest in the working of the international economy are clear. British
prosperity and indeed British survival required that trade should flow
freely and that the mechanisms of international finance and payment
should work satisfactorily. This interest manifested itself in two main
ways up to the 1930s; firstly in the policy of free trade and the
attempt, not very successful after the 1870s, to persuade other countries
to pursue a similar policy; and secondly in support of the gold standard

system of international payments. Underlying both policies was a belief in the virtues of the market mechanism, with the minimum possible degree of obstruction to movements of goods, capital and people about the world. Just before the first world war, although most other industrial countries had imposed tariffs on manufactured imports, the international trade and payments situation was one of remarkable freedom. Trade flowed smoothly and with an apparent lack of problems across wide areas of the world. Sterling was freely convertible into almost any other currency in the world and into gold; capital could be exported at will without restraint and personal movement required the minimum of formalities. As Keynes expressed it in more colourful language:

'The inhabitant of London could order by telephone, sipping his morning tea in bed, the various products of the whole earth, in such quantity as he might see fit, and reasonably expect their early delivery on his doorstep; he could . . . adventure his wealth in the natural resources and new enterprises of any quarter of the world, and share without exertion or even trouble in their prospective fruits and advantages. He could secure forthwith, if he wished it, cheap and comfortable means of transit to any country or climate without passport or other formality . . . '[2]

It was thus not surprising that the pre-1914 period came to be regarded as something of a golden age of economic freedom. As Keynes exclaimed: 'What an extraordinary episode in the economic progress of man that age was which came to an end in August 1914'[3]

The problems which the international monetary system has to solve can be categorised as the adjustment problem and the liquidity problem. The adjustment problem is one which arises if a country's earnings of foreign currency combined with its inflow of long-term investments do not match its expenditure of foreign currency plus its outflow of long-term investment. The liquidity problem concerns the arrangements for the holding of international reserves and for the creation of such reserves. Reserves are needed for the day-to-day finance of foreign trade and, if an adjustment problem exists, they are needed to give time for means to be found to correct it. The gold standard was a system which grew up in the last quarter of the nineteenth century and which did provide answers to these problems with a minimum of governmental intervention and a maximum of freedom of movement of goods, capital and labour. This is not to deny that the gold standard involved governments. On the contrary, the decision to adhere to a gold standard is in itself an important governmental decision; and to maintain a country on a gold standard requires a continuing policy of internal currency management. But the policy need only concern impersonal economic matters such as the rate of interest and the money supply and does not involve detailed regulation of such things as the level of imports or exports or the level of prices. Above all, adherence to a gold standard requires that the government be comparatively indifferent to the level of domestic employment, which cannot under the 'classical' gold standard, be regarded as a matter of direct governmental responsibility.

There were three essential elements of the gold standard. Firstly, the commitment to a fixed rate of exchange and free convertibility as between the domestic currency on the one hand, and gold and all other currencies on the other; secondly, the commitment to link the domestic currency to the level of national reserves which were normally held in gold; and thirdly the principle that the total volume of world reserves should be determined not by human decision but by the price mechanism combined with the geological accidents of gold discoveries and the development of gold mining technology. The basic principles of operation of the system are well known and have been described in many textbooks.[4] The gold standard answered the 'adjustment problem' through the link between national reserves, held in gold, and the domestic currency. If there was an adjustment problem reserves would flow out, the domestic currency would contract which would cut domestic prices and incomes and hence tend to correct the outflow. A similar process operated in the reverse direction in surplus countries. This mechanism therefore provided in theory, and to some extent in practice, an example of a 'feed-back' system in which deviations from the required norm provided an automatic correction. The gold standard also provided an answer of sorts to the liquidity problem. The volume of reserves would depend on the world production of gold, and again there was some measure of feed-back since gold production was likely to be stimulated by a fall in prices and the increased production would help to check that fall. A major feature of the gold standard was the way in which it appeared to remove what are essentially political questions which affect people's living standards, and their chances of employment, both within and between countries, from the field of politics to an apparently technical world governed, so it seemed, by something approaching natural laws. In reality this apparent result is achieved by making what are three highly political commitments – to a fixed exchange rate, to a fixed price of gold, and to the use of gold as an international medium of exchange. But in the age of the gold standard between, say, 1870 and 1914, these commitments were not thought of in this way but were regarded as almost part of the natural order. It is impossible to understand the British determination to return to the gold standard after the war without an appreciation of this attitude. And to a considerable extent the apparent smoothness of international monetary relations before 1914 was the result of the unquestioning acceptance of these arrangements. Once people began to realise clearly that the gold standard was a man-made and not a god-given system, that innocent tranquillity was lost for ever. The change could perhaps be compared to the arguments that would certainly arise if it were to be discovered today that it was quite easy to control the weather.

Acceptance of the gold standard principles would not however have been sufficient to provide a smoothly functioning international trade and payments system in the period before 1914. 'That extraordinary episode in the economic progress of man' required other conditions for its fulfilment. First among them was the position of Britain in the international order. That position cannot be explained without briefly anticipating our discussion of the British balance of payments. The main feature of the British balance of payments in the nineteenth century was its great strength. That is British firms and individuals (the government really had very little part in this) regularly acquired abroad a much greater volume of foreign currency than they expended abroad. In short, the British current account was in large and regular surplus throughout the nineteenth century. Other things being equal this would have implied a serious adjustment problem for some other country or countries. This was not however the case since the surplus on the British current account was regularly offset by the fact that British firms and individuals regularly lent abroad on capital account a far larger amount than they borrowed abroad. The long-term capital account was therefore in regular and persistent deficit throughout the period between about 1850 and 1914. And the surplus on current account was very accurately offset by the deficit on the capital account. This fortunate result was probably not just an accident, but the mechanics of the balance are complex and need not be discussed here. But the results were important. Firstly, the very strong British current account meant that sterling was always a currency of great strength. To the person or firm looking for somewhere to keep his international reserves there was always a simple answer: in sterling. Sterling was 'as good as gold' − in fact it was better, since it could easily be made to earn some interest while still being instantly and certainly 'convertible' into any other currency or into gold. Secondly, this result was achieved without any serious adjustment problems since as we have seen the current account surplus was regularly lent abroad, on long term. But the fact that the total balance was achieved in this way gave the monetary authorities in London, that is the Bank of England, tremendous flexibility in their management of the currency. If temporarily there was pressure on sterling, the underlying strength provided by the current account surplus could quickly be mobilised by restricting lending, which could easily be achieved by a rise in interest rates. When the pressure was past, a reduction in rates would lead to a resumption of lending which prevented an adjustment problem developing for other countries. One could well say that the system was a sterling standard as much as it was a gold standard, and that it depended as much on these features of the British balance of payments and on the Bank of England's exploitation of these features as it did on the arrangements of the gold standard itself. It depended in fact on British financial 'leadership'. And the possibility of such leadership depended in its turn on the features of the British balance of payments we have described. A further feature of the British balance of payments frequently stressed is that the balance of visible trade, the balance that is of exports and imports of merchandise, was regularly in deficit. This deficit was always converted into a current account surplus by earnings through exports of services and investment income, and it is this current account surplus rather than any deficit within its components that was important for the world economy. But the visible deficit was significant in that it reflected Britain's free trade policy. Imports were never restrained throughout this period. This undoubtedly contributed to the stability of the system since overseas borrowers could be confident that sufficient sterling could be earned through exporting to service their debts and thus the current account surplus was always kept within the manageable bounds.

There were other aspects of the nineteenth century situation which also contributed to a reasonably smoothly functioning payments system. Prices in industrial countries moved only gently. The size of adjustments which had to be made were relatively small. There were some convenient gold discoveries. The balance of supply and demand between manufactured and primary products certainly changed but never moved drastically. But above all governments generally gave a high priority to the external stability of their currencies and low or no priority to maintaining a high level of employment. If the currency was under pressure, they rarely had any doubt that measures to reduce that pressure, which might result in higher unemployment and a cyclical downswing in production, would have to be accepted. It is true that governments faced with the same problem since 1950 have also accepted increases in unemployment, but they have done so reluctantly and have done everything they could to limit the effects of their measures on employment; and they have been willing in the last resort to devalue their currencies or borrow heavily on short term or impose restrictions on trade to avoid high unemployment. Before 1914, and for some countries right up to the 1930s, the external problem received priority over domestic problems such as the level of unemployment.

II *Changes in the Interwar Years*

The international monetary system in the interwar period presents a striking contrast to the comparative stability of the fifty years or so before 1914. In brief, in the early years of the period strenuous efforts were made to return the system to what was regarded as normal. Prominent among these efforts was the formal British return to the gold standard in 1925.[5] Then for a few years in the middle and late 1920s, it seemed as though these attempts might be successful. In 1929 a major depression got underway, which was to be the largest world depression that the capitalist industrial system had ever experienced. It was at its height between 1931 and 1933, but in addition to being very severe it was also, by the standards of the nineteenth century, exceptionally prolonged and recovery was not really complete by the end of the period. And this depression – a depression which justifies, if any depression does, the adjective 'great' – led to the abandonment of the attempt to restore a nineteenth-century version of normality. It also led to an attempt, after the second world war, to construct a new system, based, unlike the old gold standard, on overtly man-made arrangements and international agreements. Although the post-1945 system has been by no means trouble free, it has shared one feature with its pre-1914 forerunner which sets it and the pre-1914 period apart from the interwar years; that is the rapid growth of international trade which occurred in both periods. By contrast international trade in the interwar years grew very slowly. In the nineteenth century the rate of growth of the volume of world trade had in several decades exceeded 40% and had not been below 25% in any decade since 1830.[6] But between 1920 and 1929 the total growth was only 8½%. World trade then fell steeply between 1929 and 1933, and by 1939 it had only just recovered its 1929 level.

The depression in trade in the middle of our period is the outstanding feature of these years and is one of the most important episodes in the whole history of western capitalism. 'Depressions' had occurred before in that the trade cycle had operated for most of the nineteenth century with a period of seven to eleven years. At the bottom of each cycle there had frequently been increased unemployment, a fall in prices and some reduction in output. But the depression starting in 1929 saw a new order of magnitude in the statistics. Whereas in the nineteenth century the pattern of cyclical change was imposed on a strongly rising secular trend, this was no longer so after the war. But the most striking difference was the extent of the fall in 1929-33. In the forty years before the first world war, the fall in the value of world trade in the year following the start of any downswing had not exceeded 7%. Between the spring of 1929 and that of 1930 the value of trade fell 19% and by 1933 it was down to only 35% of the 1929 level. The volume of trade also fell sharply and at the bottom of the depression, in the second quarter of 1933, was only 72% of the 1929 average. Figures of this sort were altogether outside the range of previous experience. Not only was the fall exceptionally deep; the recovery was quite unusually slow and was barely accomplished by the outbreak of war in 1939. It was this combination of a deep and very prolonged depression which led to the understandable feeling that the international economy had suffered a major breakdown. As the report of the League of Nations eleventh assembly commented: 'When we consider the magnitude of the losses from which the world suffers during a period of economic stagnation such as the present decline, it is impossible not to be impressed by the almost absolute failure of society to devise any means by which such disasters may be avoided'.[7]

The disturbances in the growth of trade were accompanied by an equally unfamiliar and serious disruption of the international financial system. After the attempt to restore the relative stability of the nineteenth century in the 1920s, from 1929 onwards all the old landmarks were swept away. The gold standard was largely abandoned, the price of gold was drastically altered, and all over the world exchange control, devaluations, multiple and floating exchange rates became commonplace. In this atmosphere, the world reverted to what may be described as the 'fortress' principle. Unable to count on the co-operation of trading partners in a worldwide system, countries attempted either self-sufficiency or tried to gather their essential trading partners into a political or military alliance, which it was hoped would enable trade and payments to flow smoothly at least within the boundaries of the 'fortress'. The Germans tried to establish their 'fortress' in southern and south-eastern Europe, where their threat of future military action was effective in persuading small countries to agree to bilateral trade bargains. Italy sought captive sources of raw material in Africa, and also attempted a greater degree of self-sufficiency. Foreign trade played a small part in the largely self-sufficient American economy anyway, but after the onset of the depression, tariffs were raised and the foreign trade proportion fell to an even lower level. Britain was more heavily involved in trade than any of these countries, but in 1932 she headed in the same direction. The policy of free trade, established in the first half of the nineteenth century, was finally abandoned. In 1932 the policy of Imperial preference set out to establish a group of politically friendly trading partners who it was hoped would prove reliable in financial matters.

There have been many interpretations of the 'great depression'.[8] In the views of many leading American politicians, the principal lesson to be learned was that trade restrictions and the development of trade 'fortresses' had led to depression and unemployment, and that in turn had led to fascism and hence to the second world war. The American Secretary of State Cordell Hull remarked, 'For me unhampered trade dovetailed with peace'.[9] In this view, the failure of the interwar years was a failure at the highest levels of international co-operation, which had led to both economic and political breakdown. Implicit in this view is an explanation of the depression as being caused by the growth of tariffs and trading block, rather than the latter being merely a response to the former. Academic interpretations however look further back into the past to try and find features of the period which led to instability and created the great economic downturn in the first place.

Since the break between the gold standard world of the late nineteenth and early twentieth centuries and the upheavals of the twenties and thirties appears to centre round the war, the effects of the war itself are an obvious candidate. The difficulty of any explanation of this sort is clearly the problem of knowing what would have happened if there had been no war. This can never be known. Further, to talk of 'the effects of the war' is implicitly to accept a deterministic view of subsequent events. It assumes that once the war had happened its 'effects' were inevitable. But it would be more reasonable to see the actors in the situation which existed after the war as having a degree of freedom of action. What they made of that situation depended on what they did as much as on the situation with which they were faced. A good example of this is the question of reparations and war debts. The imposition of reparations on Germany by the Allies and the insistence on the payment of inter-allied war debts by the Americans were an important cause of disruption in the international economy. But this destabilising network of debts which bedevilled the whole of the 1920s and was an important contributory factor to the breakdown in 1929, was created not by the war as such but by acts of policy following the war. There was no imperative requiring statesmen to behave in this way; rather they chose to do so. The French took the lead in insisting that heavy reparation payments be imposed on the Germans. They were impelled to do so by the popular hatred which existed in France for an enemy who had humiliated them in 1870 and who had invaded and devastated a great deal of their country again in the world war itself.

And their statesmen were encouraged to believe that payment of a large indemnity was possible because of the success of the French themselves in paying the indemnity which the Germans had imposed on them in 1870. Between 1872 and 1875 the French had paid the Germans, without very much difficulty, an indemnity which amounted in total to 5·6% of their annual gross national product at the time. This was in fact nearly double the proportion of GNP that the Germans were eventually to pay between 1924 and 1932.[10] Further along the chain of debts, the British had made substantial loans to their European allies and borrowed heavily from the Americans. A British proposal that she would only demand payment from her debtors to the extent that the USA demanded payment from her was met by the Americans with insistence on full payment. The Germans in their turn found that effortless payment of the reparations could be made by borrowing from the Americans. But this German borrowing was all of private capital and with the onset of economic difficulties in the USA in 1929 American lending abruptly came to an end. The German economy then adjusted itself to this change along classical economic lines with remarkable speed. But the form the adjustment took demonstrates as clearly as anything the problem with the undiluted market mechanism. The adjustment was accomplished by a drastic reduction of incomes and prices within Germany, thus cutting imports and tending to promote exports. Any classical economist should be delighted with the speed and effectiveness of this reaction; the trouble was the incidental creation of six million unemployed; unemployment at this level has been judged, as Hirsch points out, to have been an important element in Hitler's accession to power. 'This was possibly the most terrible example ever of the price that can be paid for unduly rapid adjustment to balance of payments pressure.'[11] By 1933, the whole network of debt repayment and borrowing had broken down. Debtors almost universally repudiated their debts. There can be no doubt that the reparations and war debts arising out of the war contributed substantially to the instability of the international system. They made the depression much worse in Germany and they weakened the British balance of payments throughout the 1920s.

Commentators have however typically looked for more fundamental reasons for the depression. Three major possibilities are usually considered. First, there is a view that the depression had no single dominant 'cause' but was rather the outcome of a series of circumstances which happened to coincide at this time. The distinguished American economist P. A. Samuelson is a major proponent of this view. Against this another American, Professor Milton Friedman, has blamed the monetary policy of the United States authorities. A third view, supported by W. A. Lewis,[12] places great importance on the unprecedented fall in the price of primary produce.

Milton Friedman and Anna Schwartz see the origins of the depression as lying in the USA and being transmitted to the rest of the world through the fixed exchange rates of the re-established gold exchange standard.[13] The depression, in this view, went on to exceptional depths because the United States, although on the gold standard, failed to operate the domestic monetary policies which commitment to that standard implies. They failed to play the correct 'rules'. Principally this means that as United States gold stocks increased, consequent upon her reduction of imports and óverseas lending, her monetary authorities failed to expand the money supply. 'We did not permit the inflow of gold to expand the US money stock. We not only sterilised it, we went much further. Our money stock moved perversely . . . the result was that other countries . . . had to bear the whole burden of adjustment.'[14] This failure of policy Friedman and Schwartz in turn attribute largely to failures of personal nerve and leadership among the heads of the Federal Reserve System. 'At all times', they continue, 'alternative policies were available and were being seriously proposed for adoption by leading figures in the system.'[15] The depression originated in the USA, the power to control it existed in the USA, but it was not used. This in very brief summary is the powerfully argued view of these leading academics. There is very general agreement about the importance of events in the United States. Although foreign trade played a small part in the United States economy compared with Britain and many other countries, the American economy was by this time so large relative to others that her imports formed an important part of other countries' exports. And the contraction in the USA was extremely severe. At its worst in 1932 the volume of output of consumer goods in the USA was only 75% of its 1929 level and that of investment goods only 31%.[16] Readers accustomed to the typical statistics of the post-second world war period, when so far (1974) declines in output of any sort have been rare, and where a decline of 5% or so is regarded as a major disaster, can form their own impressions of the implications of these extraordinary figures. But W. A. Lewis, while acknowledging the importance of the role of the USA, goes on to seek a further explanation for the prolonged and world-wide severity of the depression. He finds it in the decline of primary produce prices and the extraordinary difficulties this decline imposed on the balances of payments of primary producing countries.

The relationship between the prices of manufactured goods and the prices of primary products used in manufacturing is one that has been, and is, of great importance in economic affairs. In the period between the mid-1870s and 1907 this ratio (the 'terms of trade' between manufactured goods and primary products) had moved in favour of manufactures, that is the price of primary products had fallen relative to manufactures. This trend was briefly reversed in the next phase, between 1907 and 1913, but thereafter the movement in favour of manufactures continued. It not only continued but accelerated. If the ratio in 1913 of British export prices (mainly manufactured goods) divided by British import prices (mainly primary products) is taken as 100, its average over 1921-9 was 127 and over 1930-7 it was 138.[17] This was a very large change and it meant that the export earnings of primary producers were so greatly reduced that in nearly all cases they were in difficulties with their balances of payments by the late 1920s, and suffered severely from reductions of income and employment thereafter. The demand for primary produce from the industrial countries was growing at a slower rate than before the war for various reasons. The rate of growth of population in industrial countries was slowing down. At the same time income per head was rising, at least up to 1929, but the demand for many foodstuffs increased much less in proportion to income (the income elasticity of demand for foodstuffs was low).

Table 2.1 *The Demand for Wheat Percentage Changes (Western Europe and the UK) in the periods shown*

	1881/90-1901/5	1910-38
Population	+16	+13
Consumption per head	+ 8	− 9
Total consumption	+24	+ 4

Source I. Svennilson, *Growth and Stagnation in the European Economy* (1954).

A good example of this is the demand for wheat. Table 2.1 shows how wheat consumption per head, which had risen between the 1880s and 1901/5 by 8%, fell by 9% between 1910 and 1938. Comparing the same periods, population growth slowed down, so that the growth of total consumption was much smaller in the later period. Production however proved unresponsive to price changes, so that the interwar years saw large falls in prices and big increases in stocks. Much productive capacity in Europe and Russia was damaged in the war, so that production was increased by non-European suppliers, such as Canada, Argentina, the USA and Australia, to make good the shortfall. By the late 1920s, however, production was being restored in Europe and in 1930 Russia re-entered world markets as a large-scale exporter. The outcome was a rapid increase in stocks and a collapse of the price, but despite this, there was only a very small reduction in output. By 1929 world stocks of wheat, which had been 10 million tons in 1921, had more than doubled to 21 million tons.[18] The pattern of supply and demand in wheat was repeated with variations for many primary products. All cereals, meat, rubber, tea, coffee and cocoa saw large reductions in price, small reductions or even small increases in output, and large increases in stocks, between the middle or late 1920s and 1931. Too large a proportion of the world's productive capacity was devoted to food and raw materials and too little to manufactured goods. The long-term remedy was the increase of manufacturing capacity, and the reduction of primary produce output, in the mainly primary producing countries. The depression did stimulate the development of industry outside the existing industrial countries[19] but the change was too slow to be of any immediate help. It could not prevent severe hardship in primary producing countries in the 1930s and severe disruption of world trade as these countries struggled to balance their current accounts by cutting imports of manufactures, thus transmitting their problems to the industrial world. Lewis sees this as a crucial factor, not in starting the depression, but in making it so deep and prolonged once it had started. There were the beginnings of what looked like a recovery in early 1930 but this was checked by the problems of the primary producers.[20]

It seems unlikely that there is any possibility of any one view on the causes of the 'great depression' being completely refuted. If any of the factors discussed had been different, the outcome might have been different. Clearly better monetary management and greater willingness to co-operate on an international scale by the Americans could well have helped the situation. In this sense Professor Friedman's view certainly is true. C. P. Kindleberger takes a wider view of American failure.[21] Before the war, the British economy had played an important stabilising role in the international economy through the strength and stability of sterling and the willingness of British entrepreneurs and investors to lend abroad. In the interwar years Britain was no longer able to play this role because her balance of payments was no longer so strong, for reasons that will be discussed in the next section. The obvious candidate for a new 'leader' of the international economy was the United States. The USA had emerged from the war as a creditor nation; her weight in the world economy had now become substantial and her current account remained persistently in surplus throughout the period. But she reacted to this situation in a way quite different from that required of the traditional 'good creditor'. Far from lending extensively abroad, in the 1930s she accumulated a large stock of gold and recalled her loans. Far from permitting a free flow of imports she raised tariffs to ever higher levels. At the height of the depression itself, as we have seen from the Friedman and Schwartz analysis, her management of her domestic money supply was perverse. And in the succession of attempts that were made to arrange international co-operation to overcome these problems, the USA was generally an unwilling partner. Finally, in 1933, President Roosevelt decided to abandon any attempt at stabilising the value of the dollar and to concentrate on domestic measures to overcome the depression. This decision was made in the middle of an international conference which had met in London in the hope of establishing some measure of co-operation between the industrial nations to combat the depression. In a famous message issued to the London conference, Roosevelt destroyed any chance of such co-operation and confirmed the 1930s as an era when each country, or at least each bloc of countries, would have to fend for itself.

In the longer perspective, the problem of organising effective co-ordination within the international economic community is one which today remains difficult and controversial. The failures of the interwar years led after the second world war to a concerted effort to find a solution at the Bretton Woods conference in 1944 and to the setting up of the International Monetary Fund. This marks the start of a new era in international economic co-operation, though that co-operation was by no means an unqualified success. The disruptions of the interwar years have been seen as an accident; a particular conjunction of circumstances which led to difficulty. It might be more realistic to see the pre-first world war period as an accident; a particular conjunction of circumstances, unlikely to be repeated, which led to relatively smoothly functioning trade and payments relationships. In the absence of such a lucky accident, and in the absence of conscious co-operation and planning on the international scale, it seems inherently unlikely that things will work out satisfactorily. Classical and neo-classical economics describe possible circumstances in which the international system might be self-regulating, but these circumstances are unlikely to be realised in practice and certainly were not realised in the interwar years. The factors of production were rarely as mobile as the theory requires for reasonably swift adjustment; or if they were, the process was too painful to be politically tolerable. Production did not respond to price changes, governments did not play in accordance with the rules of the game by lending surpluses or facilitating the flow of trade and capital. In the presence of so many 'imperfections' market forces worked too slowly, uncertainly or painfully to be of much help.

III *The British Balance of Payments and the Crisis of 1931*

The two preceding sections have tried to make clear the nature of the greatly changed international economic environment in the interwar years. Obviously the interwar environment was very much less favourable to a nation heavily involved in trade than the prewar situation. The growth of trade was far slower in the 1920s, and the depression of the thirties was without precedent. Large adjustments were needed; to some extent they were accomplished but the poor record of the interwar economy in Britain with regard to employment is in part a testimony to the difficulty of these adjustments. Further exploration of the problem requires some discussion of the conventions of balance of payments accounting.

A nation's balance of payments is an account of the transactions of its government, its firms and its individuals with governments, firms and individuals outside its own boundary. Certain types of action will lead to the acquisition of foreign currency and others to its disposal. If the total acquisitions and the total disposals are not in balance over a given period then either the national reserves must be reduced, or increased, by a corresponding amount or the government must arrange to borrow, or lend, a corresponding amount from other countries' central monetary authorities. The actions which earn or expend foreign currency are conventionally divided into certain classes. The export and import of goods is classified as 'visible trade'; the export and import of services as 'invisible trade'. The sum of the two plus the net balance of interest on invested capital is called the 'current account'. The balance of lending and borrowing capital on long term is 'the balance of long-term capital', while the sum of the current account and the balance of long-term capital is sometimes called the 'basic balance of payments'. There is also the further important category of short-term capital movements. Short-term capital movements are distinguished from long-term ones by the nature of the transaction. A long-term investment is normally one in physical plant or equipment or in long-dated government stocks or in shares which cannot be converted quickly or certainly into cash without loss. A short-term transaction is one in which there is normally a right to withdraw the investment and convert into cash at very short notice, as in the case of a bank deposit or a trade bill. At the margin this distinction may be uncertain but in principle it is clear enough. If we add to the basic balance of payments the balance of short-term capital movements we get the total balance of acquisitions and disposals of foreign currency, which in modern balance of payments accounting terminology is called the 'total currency flow'. This as already noted has to be offset by an equal and opposite movement of the official reserves or official liabilities. This small excursion into simple theory has been made because of the great difficulty of discussing the balance of payments unless the reader is completely clear about the meanings of the terms used. It should be stressed that the framework is anachronistic in that the terms used are modern.[22] Nobody referred to 'total currency flow' in the interwar years, or to the 'basic balance of payments'. Even the distinction between visible and invisible trade was made with much less certainty than it is today. Contemporaries not only possessed comparatively poor data about most components of the balance, other than visible trade; they also suffered from the lack of a clear-cut analytical scheme into which to organise what data they did possess.

The main features of the British balance of payments in the seventy years preceding 1914 have already been briefly referred to in the first section. In more detail the situation then was that visible trade showed a persistent deficit; invisible trade a persistent surplus, the balance of interest and dividends was in surplus, the current account was also in surplus, the long-term capital account was regularly in deficit and total currency flow was normally very small or nil, all of the above referring to any given year and to almost every year in this period. This adds up to an immensely strong balance of payments situation with persistent export of capital. The importance of this situation in helping to stabilise the international economy has already been discussed. In the interwar years there were changes in the British balance of payments position and these have often been interpreted as a weakening of the accounts. Central to this interpretation is the crisis of 1931, when Britain, having returned to the gold standard with such effort only six years previously, was forced to abandon it and float the pound. However, it is not clear that the actual figures of the economy's overseas transactions in this period do much to justify generalised statements about 'weakness'. It must first of all be stressed that the available figures are not very accurate. C. H. Feinstein writes, 'For all the main items [merchandise, shipping, government, property income] there is a reasonably firm basis for the estimates in all peacetime periods since 1870 . . . it is unlikely that the margin of error would exceed ±10% for the merchandise and ±15% for the other main items'.[23] However annual imports of merchandise in these years ranged between £600 and £1,200 million and ±10% of such figures represents a substantial possible error. Estimates of capital movements, both short and long term, are much less reliable. These inaccuracies are reflected in the large 'balancing item' which has to be included in the accounts if the balance of payments is actually to balance. The 'balancing item' is simply an error term which covers all the errors and omissions which must have been made somewhere in the estimates but which cannot be identified. The 'balancing item' for the nine years 1930-8 inclusive, for instance, totals £784 million, and this is just over twice the central estimate of the total current account deficit for this period.[24]

Considering first the current account, in the 1920s this remained in surplus with an average of £114 millions. This compares with an annual average surplus of £83 million in the ten years 1900-9, but of course it must be remembered that prices had roughly doubled so the surplus was in real terms somewhat lower. Further there was a declining trend. The annual average surplus for the years 1920-5 inclusive was £184 million and for the years 1926-9 inclusive it was £44 million. For the nine years 1930-8 inclusive there was an annual average deficit on current account of £40 millions, and there was a deficit in each of these years except 1930 and 1935.[25] This was a new experience for the British economy. It is unlikely that there had been a decade with deficits of this sort on current account for the preceding 130 years. However, apart from 1931, the deficits were small both in relation to the total of external transactions and to the margins of error in the figures. The possible errors have already been stressed, but they mean that we cannot be completely certain that there was in fact on average a deficit in these years at all; it is only likely that there was. The current account however is only one component of the accounts, and deficits of the size recorded (again excepting 1931) would not necessarily imply weakness if they were satisfactorily covered in the rest of the accounts.

The next major component of the accounts is the balance of long-term capital. In the nineteenth century this had been persistently in deficit, that is to say capital had regularly been exported and to roughly the same amount as the surplus on current account. The best estimates of the balance of long-term capital for the years 1920-9 inclusive suggest a net annual average export of capital of £116 million, which should have been covered by the surplus on current account. For the 1930s net export of capital almost ceases and the average balance of long-term capital works out to minus £12 million, with a range between plus £20 million (1938) and minus £61 million (1930).[26] (The plus here means that there was a net import of capital.) The figures so far discussed would not therefore suggest that there was any serious weakness in the British balance of payments in these years taken as a whole. In the 1920s capital export continued at a substantial rate, equal to about 2% of the gross national product in those years. But this was covered by current account surpluses. In the 1930s the current account surpluses are replaced by deficits, but the deficits are fairly small and capital export ceases. There is one very bad year, 1931, when the current account deficit was £114 million, or about 2½% of

GNP in that year. But the function of reserves is to cover bad years.

The main feature which remains to be discussed, and which turned out to be the most prominent feature of the period, is that of short-term capital movements. Movements of short-term capital across national boundaries are the most complex phenomena of the international financial scene and have, especially since the second world war, been a central element in its most intractable problems. In a classical gold standard world with fixed exchange rates, and unchallenged confidence in the convertibility of leading currencies into each other and gold, movements of short-term capital should not generally occur except in response to interest rate differentials. And the differences in interest rates should in turn correspond to imbalances in countries' basic balances of payments, with high interest rates being adopted by those countries with deficits. The high interest rate both helps to correct the imbalance through income and price effects in the deficit country and also through its attraction of short-term funds from other centres. The world has never been as simple as that, but in the nineteenth century interest rates did exert a powerful and fairly predictable influence on short-term movements into London. Further in the pre-first world war period Britain was regularly a creditor on short term and this reduced the possibilities of pressure on sterling arising from movements of this type, since the scope for an inflow of short-term funds was greater than the scope for an outflow. But the interwar years saw very large changes in these aspects of Britain's international position; larger changes than occurred in other components of the balance of payments.

In the war Britain ceased to be a net short-term creditor[27] due to the financial pressures arising from the conduct of the war and the difficulty of paying for imports and loans to European allies. Secondly, the violent price changes and Britain's and other countries' temporary departure from the gold standard had undermined the essential element of confidence in the fixed rate convertibility of sterling into gold. We have already mentioned the poor quality of information available to contemporaries. The Macmillan Report, published in 1931, referred to the belief that in the 1920s Britain must have been financing some of her long-term lending by an increase, and perhaps a dangerous increase, in her short-term liabilities to foreign centres. Here we come to perhaps the most difficult problem of interpretation of the interwar balance of payments figures. The Macmillan Committee went on to say that they had collected certain information which they thought was of a reassuring character about the extent of British short-term foreign indebtedness. This information, which the Bank of England collected on their behalf by inquiry from

City institutions, showed that the net short-term indebtedness of London was *not* increasing between 1927 and 1931 and that it averaged about £275 million over these years. The Committee concluded that, 'in spite of the reduction of our surplus, the whole of our *net* purchases of foreign securities have been paid for out of our currently accruing surplus on income account. It is possible, we think, that this surplus may be somewhat larger than the usual estimate'.[28] Modern research on the balance of payments in this period suggests that the Committee's estimate of short-term liabilities should be increased by a factor of about 1·6,[29] which means that their estimate of net short-term indebtedness (liabilities minus reserves) needs to be approximately doubled. But their conclusion that net indebtedness was not increasing appears to have been correct, at least for the years 1928 to 1930. The net change in short-term liabilities and acceptances on foreign account in this period, though it can only be estimated very roughly, appears to have been almost zero.[30] And the conclusion that net long-term lending in the 1920s had been covered by current account surpluses has also stood the test of further research. But nevertheless the Macmillan Report was published at almost precisely the moment when a major run was developing on sterling which was, within two months, to drive Britain forcibly off the gold standard.

Table 2.2 *United Kingdom Balance of Payments, 1920-38* (£ millions)

	Trade		Invest- ment Income	Current Balance	Capital Flows		Bal- ancing Item	Total Cur- rency Flow
Year(s)	Visible	Invisible			Long- Term	Short- Term		
1920-9 inc.	−205	+100	+219	+114	−116	NA	+10	+8
1930-8 inc.	−255	+33	+183	−40	−12	−3	+87	+32
1924	−214	+74	+198	+58	−119	NA	+67	+6
1929	−263	+92	+247	+76	−52	−59	+27	−8
1931	−322	+41	+167	−114	−5	−252	+337	−34
1934	−220	+16	+172	−32	−36	+40	+38	+10
1937	−336	+68	+211	−57	−3	+88	+101	+129

NA = not available. Short-term movements before 1928 are included in the balancing item in the absence of separate estimates.

Source Calculated from *Bank of England Quarterly Bulletin* (March 1974), p. 49, table B.

The financial crisis which developed in 1931 can be thought of as the first 'hot money' crisis of the modern type, where currencies are put under pressure by movements of short-term funds motivated not by interest rate differentials but by fears of devaluation or impending exchange control or by speculation on exchange rate changes. Such crises have been frequent since 1950 and have affected sterling on many occasions. In the gold standard period the great strength of sterling and general confidence in its convertibility, plus the short-term creditor position of Britain, made such crises highly improbable. But by 1931 the position had changed. The most obvious change was the short-term debit position. How this arose is not clear. The figures are not good enough to show us. The Macmillan Committee thought the net debtor position may have arisen between 1925 and 1927 when the French were building up large balances. The loss of a creditor position in the war is clearly significant, and the war may even account for a part of the debit. But whatever the origin of this short-term debtor position, it was a new feature in the British situation. The second change was the lack of confidence in Britain's ability to maintain her exchange rate. By 1931, many primary producing countries had already been forced off gold, and financial panic was spreading through Europe. Earlier in the year the Credit-Anstalt bank in Austria had failed, and then the panic had spread to Germany with the failure of the 'Danat' bank. These major bank failures had frozen a substantial proportion of Britain's short-term assets, thus worsening further the short-term debtor position. The Macmillan Report is the first of a long line of official statements assuring holders of sterling that they need not worry since sterling is strong and will not be devalued. In general such statements are only made when there is already substantial doubt about the strength of sterling and their publication always has the opposite effect to that intended. In the case of the Macmillan Report however, Skidelsky has pointed out that there was no mention of it, much less of its crucial table of assets and liabilities, in the French or American press for a week following its publication,[31] by which time (July 1931) the crisis was already under way.

Whatever the precise origins of the panic and the short-term debits, the run developed. International co-operation was poor; the one country with the power to prevent the panic was France, but the Governor of the Bank of England throughout this period, Montague Norman, was a difficult and strongly opinionated man who had quarrelled with the Governor of the Bank of France earlier in the 1920s, and the French were now unhelpful.[32] In any case, the French had long regarded finance as an instrument of diplomacy, were mainly concerned with preventing the spread of German influence in Europe, and might well not have co-operated very much in any case. By August it was clear that British reserves were inadequate to pay all those withdrawing their balances; some credits were sought and given in Paris and New York, but only on conditions which split the minority Labour Government; the loans then proved inadequate and on 21 September the National Government authorised the suspension of gold payments. Britain was off gold. The pound floated, and floated down, in the market.

The political implications of this financial crisis were substantial,[33] the excitement at the time very great. From an economic point of view however, the excitement was, if not unjustified, at least misplaced. The financial crisis in retrospect looks much more like the froth on a turbulent sea, rather than the cause of the turbulence itself. Although the Macmillan Report with its references to British financial strength appeared to be immediately belied by events, the underlying position was basically as they saw it. The £130 million borrowed from Paris and New York was all repaid within twelve months, even though the depreciation of sterling actually involved paying £179 million instead of £130 million.[34] The pound floated down against the dollar in late 1931 but quickly recovered, so that its average level against the dollar in the 1930s was $4·61 compared with the par value of $4·86 from 1925 to 1931. But the underlying turbulence in the international economy was real enough. Unemployment was rising throughout the world; the Nazi regime was soon to be established in Germany and everywhere doubts about the viability of the western economic system were rife.

IV *Britain and the International Economy after the Crisis*

For Britain, the period after the 1931 crisis saw major changes in her relationships with the rest of the world. Up to 1939 the pound sterling remained on a floating rate and was managed through a newly established government agency: the Exchange Equalisation Account. The gold standard was abandoned and the private export of gold prohibited. The long standing policy of free trade was also given up, tariffs were established, and tariff policy discriminated in favour of the Empire countries. The period saw a marked decline in the importance of foreign trade as measured by its proportion in national output, and a marked increase in the share of trade with Empire countries. The export of capital ceased as did also the emigration of British citizens, and there was a return flow of both people and capital. The contrast with the free trade, gold standard, capital and people exporting country of before 1914 was very marked.

Between 1910 and 1913 inclusive British exports of goods had averaged 28% of gross domestic product. The average for 1930-7 inclusive was just under half this proportion, at 12·5%.[35] Figures for the proportion which imports (of goods and services) and property income paid abroad bore to gross national product in current prices are given in Table 2.3. It shows great consistency in the proportion up to

1929, with the actual figure for 1929 being very similar to that for 1873, but the change in the 1930s is clear. From figures which had been regularly around 30% since the 1870s there is a drop to the middle and low twenties. One important feature of the period however is concealed rather than illuminated by these figures and that is the change in the terms of trade. The fall in the price of primary products has already been referred to in the previous section, and it was suggested as a major cause of the disruption of the world trading and financial situation. From a certain rather narrow point of view, this fall in prices brought beneficial effects to Britain in that a given volume of imports now cost less than before, since British imports were predominantly of primary produce. The Macmillan Report offered as an example of this trend the fall in the price of wheat. By 1931 the annual wheat import into the United Kingdom was costing £60 million less than in 1925, and £30 million less than in 1929.[36] Hence this meant that import volumes could be maintained or increased without a proportionate increase in money cost. Therefore the pattern of changes in volume is different from that in total costs, with visible import volumes running in the 1930s about 20% above the 1913 level, but visible export volumes being about 40% below that level. This situation certainly brought cheap food to the British population and cheaper raw materials to industry. The price of a given 'basket' of common foodstuffs fell between 1927 and 1933 by 25%.[37] But the snag was that the resulting depression of incomes in the primary producing countries cut the demand for the products of British industry and contributed to unemployment. Higher primary product prices would almost certainly have increased welfare in the world as a whole at this time, through greater employment in industrial countries and higher incomes in the primary producing ones. Despite this the fall in primary product prices relative to those of manufactured products was not checked.

The second column in Table 2.3 shows how visible exports and re-exports in the 1930s paid for a smaller proportion of a smaller import bill. This is reflected in the halving of the proportion of visible exports as a proportion of GDP already referred to. The share of British manufactured exports in world manufactured exports has generally declined since the mid-nineteenth century, and it fell from 32½% in 1899 to 22½% in 1937.[38] This long standing decline was almost halted in the 1930s, showing the British economy as doing relatively well in this period but only by comparison with a world which was doing very badly by comparison with its own past. The theme of the decline of Britain's share of world manufactured exports is one which has achieved great prominence in the postwar world, where the balance of payments has emerged as a subject of continual discontent. In conjunction with dissatisfaction with the rate of British economic growth, it has led to the view cuttingly satirised by R. E. Caves:

'During the industrial revolution . . . British industry showed a capacity for innovation, growth and change unmatched in economic history . . . [But then] Britain's economic arteries hardened. Custom, leisure and class attitudes triumphed over initiative and enterprise. Amateurish business management took refuge from the rigors of competition and the mysteries of science. Leadership in growth and innovation passed to other nations'.[39]

This might be considered a fair summary of the picture emerging from much discussion of Britain's economic history, though Caves goes on to describe it as a 'dark fable, bardic with years of telling!' Indeed judgements on the total economic performance of large nations over long periods of time seem to be of doubtful status.

Table 2.3

Year	Imports and property income paid abroad as a percentage of GNP (current prices)	Earnings of foreign exchange by source and in total expressed as a percentage of the cost of imports and property income paid abroad			
		Exports and re-exports	Invisible exports	Investment income	Total
1873[a]	29·3	83·8	24·7	14·9	123·4
1879[b]	31·4	68·8	23·6	16·4	108·8
1900[a]	28·2	65·6	20·4	20·6	106·6
1904[b]	28·4	66·2	21·4	22·1	109·7
1913[a]	31·5	79·5	22·3	28·0	129·8
1924	33·8	67·8	17·1	20·2	105·1
1929	30·2	62·8	17·8	24·5	105·1
1931	24·3	46·9	17·0	22·9	86·8
1934	20·2	54·8	17·1	25·2	97·1
1937	23·6	53·0	19·8	23·3	96·1

[a]Peak of trade cycle

[b]Trough of trade cycle

Source Calculated from C. H. Feinstein, *National Income Expenditure and Output of the United Kingdom 1855-1965*, tables 2 and 15.

Certainly it is true that Britain's share of world trade has declined, and there have been a number of attempts to account for this. For some time the major emphasis was placed on the structure of British visible exports, which, it was thought, were predominantly 'old-fashioned' products, the demand for which was growing only slowly, in contrast with products based on recent developments in science and technology for which demand was growing faster. This view derives from an oft-quoted study by the University of Kiel.[40] This finding could be considered in a general way to reinforce the 'dark fable'. Britain's entrepreneurs insisted on continuing to export coal, ships and cotton textiles when they 'ought' to have been developing exports in the new fast growing sectors of world trade like motor vehicles and electrical goods. The Kiel study found that in 1929 42% of Britain's manufactured exports were in the slow growing category, while the USA only had 17% of her exports in the same category. W. A. Lewis commented on this: 'Here we have the clearest proof of the UK's lost leadership in world trade'.[41] Subsequently, a study by Tyszynsky has cast doubt on this interpretation. Using a wider range of countries, Tyszynsky attempted to distinguish between changes in trade shares due to structure on the one hand and to price competition on the other. Part of his results are set out in Table 2.4.

Table 2.4 *Structural and Competitive Effects in Changing Trade Shares*

	Shares of manufactured exports in total of eleven major industrial countries				
				Percentage of change due to	
Country	Actual share 1899 %	Actual share 1937 %	Change 1899-1937 %	Competition	Structure
Japan	1·5	7·2	+5·7	+109	−9
USA	11·2	19·6	+8·4	+40	+60
Canada	0·3	5·0	+4·7	+96	+4
Britain	32·5	22·4	−10·1	−85	−15
France	15·8	6·4	−9·4	−83	−17

Source Adapted from H. Tyszynksy, 'World Trade in Manufactured Commodities, 1899-1950', *Manchester School of Economic and Social Studies*, Vol. 19 (1951), table 10, p. 289.

Between 1899 and 1937 the UK lost 10·1 percentage points of her share of world trade. Of this loss, 85% was due, according to Tyszynksy, to competitive effects and only the remaining 15% to structure. Perhaps more convincing than the actual figures is the way in which the 'successful' exporters of the period (meaning those which increased their shares) actually achieved their successes. If structure really were the important question one would expect those countries which raised their share of world exports to have their exports heavily concentrated in the sectors of trade which grew fastest. This does happen to be the case for the USA, as the Kiel study had shown. However, consideration of two countries not dealt with in that study, Japan and Canada, gives a different picture. Japan, the second most successful exporter of the period, had exports concentrated in the declining sectors of world trade, which included metal manufactures, drink and tobacco, railway equipment, ships, miscellaneous manufactures, and most relevantly for the Japanese case, textiles. Despite this concentration, Japanese competition within these sectors was so effective that she was able to increase her total share of world manufactures exports by nearly 6 percentage points over the period. To complete the confusing picture, Canada, the third most successful exporter, had exports mostly in the 'stable' category, that is in goods which formed a constant proportion of world trade (such as chemicals, non-ferrous metals, and books and films.) This study makes it impossible to assume that Britain's export 'problems' — if problems they really were — were in any simple way the outcome of her industrial structure. Other countries with equally unfavourable structures did much better than Britain competitively.

None of this is to deny that Britain did have a heavy concentration of exports in what have come to be called the 'nineteenth-century staples'. The percentage contribution of certain products to Britain's visible exports at various dates is given in Table 2.5.

Table 2.5 *Principal Items in British Exports, 1911-37*

	Percentage of total exports by value in each category								
Year	Coal	*Iron & steel*	*Mach-inery*	*Cotton textiles*	*Wool textiles*	*Chemi-cals*	*Ships (new)*	*Vehicles & aircraft*	*Total*
1911	8·5	9·9	6·8	26·4	7·0	4·4	1·3	0·8	65·1
1921	6·6	9·0	12·0	25·4	7·4	2·7	4·4	1·4	68·9
1925	7·0	8·8	6·8	25·8	7·4	3·1	0·8	1·8	61·5
1929	7·3	9·3	8·2	18·6	6·9	3·6	2·1	2·8	58·8
1931	9·6	7·8	9·0	14·5	6·1	4·7	2·7	3·3	57·7
1934	8·7	8·9	8·5	14·9	6·5	4·9	0·5	4·3	57·2
1937	8·0	9·5	9·9	13·1	5·9	4·7	0·8	4·7	56·6

Source Calculated from B. R. Mitchell and P. Deane, *Abstract of British Historical Statistics* (1962), pp. 284, 305, 306.

Immediately noticeable is the high proportion of textiles, and especially cotton textiles. Just before the first world war, the latter had formed about a quarter of all visible exports, and wool and cotton textiles together about a third. No other single category exceeded 10%. Of all the changes which affected British exports during the interwar years, and especially in the 1930s, the decline in cotton textile exports is one of the most striking. And the cotton industry, like most of the 'staple' industries, was heavily committed to export markets. Between 1909 and 1913 three quarters of the output of the industry was exported and the British export trade in yarn and piece goods amounted to 65% by value of the world trade in these items.[42] Here we have in fact the predominant reason for thinking of British trade performance in these years as a problem. It was not that British exports failed to pay for imports but rather that the great nineteenth-century exporting industries failed to compete effectively in world markets in this period and hence suffered in nearly every case losses of output and employment which were crucial to the problem of unemployment in Britain.

Two major developments of the 1930s were the use of a floating rate of exchange and the resort to protection and Imperial preference. After the forced departure from the gold standard in 1931, the pound 'floated' until it was pegged again just before the outbreak of war in 1939 at a rate of $4·03 to the pound. In 1932 the government established the Exchange Equalisation Account. Prior to this, in so far as the currency had been managed, this had been done by the Bank of England, and the Bank of England was a private company, not a government agency. This extraordinary situation should not be taken entirely at face value; the Bank of England, the Treasury and the Chancellor of the Exchequer were in fairly close contact. Nevertheless the fact that the currency was nominally under the control of the Bank had an important symbolic value in the gold standard phase, reinforcing the mythology of an automatic system beyond the control of the government. The Exchange Equalisation Account was under the direction of the Treasury, not the Bank, and its establishment marks an important turning point in overt government acceptance of responsibility for the management of the currency. The purpose of the Equalisation Account was to reduce the extent of fluctuations in the value of the pound, by buying foreign exchange when the pound was strong, thus damping any rise in the value, and selling again when sterling was weak, thereby also damping the downward swing.[43] The major problem in this sort of governmental intervention in exchange rates is to distinguish the cycle from the trend. Typically the authorities are prone to regard any change as part of a cycle and are reluctant to admit the existence of a trend. Hence 'smoothing' operations quickly get converted to 'pegging'. This sort of pegged rate has not the advantage of the immutability of a really fixed rate like that of the pound under the gold standard in the late nineteenth century, and it also lacks the flexibility of a genuinely floating rate. For this reason managed floating rates of this type, of which there are several examples apart from Britain's in the 1930s, fell out of favour after the second world war. However, in the short span of its prewar experience, from 1932 to 1939, the British Equalisation Account did not encounter any very severe difficulties, and was quite successful in keeping sterling at a steady rate. Shortly after its inception the pound fell heavily, in November 1932, mainly because of repayments of loans borrowed in the crisis of the previous year. The Account had not had time to acquire adequate reserves and had to stop supporting the pound, which fell briefly to a low of $3·17. Early in 1933 it recovered strongly and the Account was able to acquire reserves, in the process probably keeping the pound at a lower level than it would otherwise have reached and helping British exports, though possibly at the price of diminishing yet further the possibilities of an agreed international settlement. After Roosevelt's decision to force down the gold price of the dollar the pound eventually settled at about $4·95 and from mid-1934 to mid-1938 the Account successfully maintained a rate within about 10 cents of this, while at the same time building up substantial gold reserves. By 1938 the British short-term position was much improved compared with 1931, when as we have seen the excess of short-term liabilities over assets had proved so dangerous. In 1938 net short-term liabilities abroad were about £700 million while reserves averaged £739 millions.[44] On 25 August, 1939, speculative pressures connected with the approach of war led to large movements of funds, and the pound was allowed to fall. By the end of August it was down to $4·27. War broke out at the beginning of September, the sterling rate was pegged at $4·03 and wartime exchange control measures introduced.

The 'managed floating rate' of the 1930s was an interesting episode in currency history but one with comparatively few lessons to offer. The general problem of international adjustment is one which remains unsolved today. The 1930s saw the emergence of that problem in its modern form, and particularly the emergence of the problem of large movements of short-term funds for speculative or other reasons not connected with interest rate differentials. Such movements are always liable to be seriously destabilising. Currency management in the 1930s was much easier than it became subsequently because there was still, in Britain, no serious attempt to overcome the unemployment problem. Had the government wished to pursue a 'Keynesian' policy on unemployment, the job of the Exchange Equalisation Account in the

1930s would have been hard indeed. It was this problem of combining both internal and external adjustment which preoccupied the policy makers during and after the war as they approached the problem of the postwar monetary settlement.

The 1930s also saw the abandonment of free trade, a principle to which Britain had been committed since the middle of the nineteenth century, despite growing controversy on the topic since the turn of the century. But in the elections of 1906 and 1923 the electorate had shown their aversion to tariffs, and in 1930, Britain was still a predominantly free trade country, with over 80% of all imports entering the country free of duty. The election manifesto on which the National Government was elected in 1931 declared that the government would 'give attention' to the question of tariffs, commercial treaties and mutual economic arrangements with the dominions. This threat was enough, as soon as the election result was known, to increase the flow of imports as traders sought to forestall the imposition of a tariff. To stop this, the government rushed through the Abnormal Importations Act and the Horticultural Products Act, imposing a wide range of duties, but exempting imports from the dominions and colonies. Having secured this breathing space the government proceeded to consider its future policy on tariffs and trade. This policy was unfolded during 1932-4. First there was a general tariff of 10% ad valorem, introduced early in 1932, fittingly enough by the Chancellor of the Exchequer, Neville Chamberlain, son of Joseph Chamberlain whose campaigns for the introduction of tariffs had been a major feature of political life thirty years earlier. Exemptions from the general tariff included wheat, meat and bacon, British-caught fish, raw cotton and raw wool, with all colonial imports permanently exempted and imports from the dominions exempted until the Ottawa conference, which was due to discuss the matter in July. Chamberlain made the bargaining potential of the tariff clear. 'We mean also to use it', he said, 'for negotiations with foreign countries which have not hitherto paid very much attention to our suggestions.'[45] And although he said 'foreign countries', the dominions were clearly meant to take notice as well.[46] On top of the general 10% tariff the Treasury had the power to impose further tariffs on the recommendations of an independent tariff advisory committee. This arrangement in fact led to a 20% tariff being established on most manufactured imports, with higher rates designed to protect certain especially depressed domestic industries, for instance iron and steel. The next step was to see what use the bargaining weapon thus gained could be put to and this followed in two stages; the first at the Ottawa conference in July 1932 with the dominions, and the second with a number of foreign countries later in 1933 and 1934.

Ottawa cannot be considered a success from the British point of view. I. M. Drummond describes the concessions won from the dominions as 'insignificant'[47] and to get them it was necessary to impose new or higher duties on imports from non-Empire sources on a whole range of foodstuffs, many of which could not be grown in Britain.[48] Such duties mainly had the effect of replacing foreign imports by dominion imports, since in every case the duty was levied on foreign supplies only in order to give the dominions their preference. This did nothing to solve the problems of British agriculture which was suffering severely from depressed world prices and the glut of food on world markets. Through the rest of the 1930s the government worked slowly towards a solution that would not raise prices to the consumer at home too much, and would provide some support for the farmer while at the same time not provoking dominion or foreign suppliers into retaliation against British manufactured exports. A compromise between these interests was slowly worked out, the main elements being quotas on imports, and deficiency payments, in effect subsidies, to British producers, financed out of taxation. For some products, notably wheat, there were also import levies whose proceeds went to home producers. A typical scheme was that for bacon, an important import item, for which Denmark had been the main supplier in 1932. By 1938 Danish imports had been reduced by negotiated quota to about two thirds of their 1932 level. About a quarter of this reduction was made up by Canadian imports and the rest by increased British production.[49]

The second stage of bargaining over tariffs consisted of the attempt to conclude a number of bilateral trade bargains with certain foreign countries whose position was vulnerable to pressure because they exported more to Britain than they imported from her, which deprived them of much scope for further retaliation. In return for promises not to impose further duties or quotas, these countries were induced to offer concessions to Britain. The most important of these agreements was with Argentina concerning the meat quota, and there were other agreements with the Scandinavian and Baltic states, Poland and Russia.[50] This policy of bilateral agreements negotiated by governments was in the short term very successful as far as Britain was concerned, and much more substantial concessions were won from these countries than from the dominions at Ottawa. Of course a policy of this sort was the complete antithesis of 'free trade' and epitomised the way in which intergovernmental bargaining was beginning to replace the market in international trade in this period.

In resorting to protection and in discriminating through Imperial preference in favour of a particular group of countries, Britain was falling into line with the general trend of economic policies of the time.

The merits of this policy were fiercely debated both then and since. The decision to introduce a general tariff split the National Government, the free traders proclaiming their opposition despite their membership of the cabinet and thus breaking the constitutional convention of collective cabinet responsibility. The Labour Party also opposed protection; Mr Attlee in the Commons thought the Chancellor must have been working on the principle of 'when in Rome do as Rome does and when in a lunatic asylum behave like a lunatic'.[51] And professional economists at the time 'almost unanimously disapproved'.[52] Since then opinion has been more favourable. Given the general trend to tariffs and governmental control of trade through bilateral bargaining and other forms of pressure, it would have been almost impossible for Britain to remain a free trade country without suffering even worse unemployment than she did. H. W. Arndt argued in 1944 that, given the existence of large-scale unemployment, the optimum international division of labour was much less important than a higher level of employment. And it seems clear that as far as Britain was concerned and perhaps as far as the western world was concerned as a whole, the use of tariffs and bilateral and other forms of bargaining did make a contribution to raising the level of employment, if only slightly.[53]

V *Conclusion*

When the United States, Great Britain and the other victorious powers came to consider the question of the new international order after the second world war, the important lesson they drew from the experiences of the interwar years was along the lines followed by Cordell Hull, whose remark that 'for me unhampered trade dovetailed with peace' has already been quoted. The outstanding feature of the interwar years was seen as the failure to allow the market mechanism to work. While it was recognised that some new international agreements would be needed with regard to the monetary system, the main thrust of postwar argument was that trade restrictions, governmental interference at the micro-economic level, economic nationalism and the pressure of vested interests on governments had disintegrated the international economy. What needed to be restored above all was the freedom and confidence of the gold standard era. Low and certainly non-discriminatory tariffs, currencies that were fully convertible at fixed rates, and free movement of capital and if possible also labour, were the ideals which the postwar planners sought. In every case, the interwar years and especially the 1930s were seen as the terrible warnings of what happened if practice departed widely from these objectives. This belief in the effectiveness of the market mechanism if only governments will create the conditions in which it can work is a continuous and vital thread in the history of western economies. It remained dominant certainly up to the end of the 1960s, though never without its critics. In the concluding chapter of his report for the Royal Institute of International Affairs, H. W. Arndt suggested that in future, governments would have to play a far larger role in the management of international trade. He thought that although this might not achieve the optimum international division of labour, what was lost here might be more than repaid in greater stability and lower costs of adjustment. And writing while the war was still on, he even found something good to say about the economic policies of Nazi Germany before the war, whose manipulation of their trade with eastern Europe was generally considered to be the ultimate example of the iniquities resulting from mixing power politics and trade policy. But, commented Arndt, 'the gain the peasants of Rumania derived from the long-term contracts which the Nazis concluded with Rumania cannot be measured in terms of the prices they received for their produce alone. These prices may have been lower or higher than world prices but they were *stable*.'[54] Arndt was perhaps lucky that his sponsors were willing to publish this remark at all in 1944, and they only did so with the addition of a dissenting appendix by two distinguished economists. Yet in the 1970s, Arndt's reflections look once again very topical. The post-second world war attempt to re-establish a free market framework and minimise discriminatory governmental interference in the details of trade seems again to be coming to grief. The role that governments should play or must play in international trade and monetary relations is a question which we seem to be not much nearer solving today than at any other time since that age of economic innocence was ended by the first world war in August 1914.

Notes

1 E. A. G. Robinson, 'The Changing Structure of the British Economy', *Economic Journal* (September 1954).
2 J. M. Keynes *The Economic Consequences of the Peace* (1919), p. 9.
3 Keynes, *The Economic Consequences*, p. 9.
4 e.g. A. C. L. Day, *Outline of Monetary Economics* (1957), ch. 38.
5 The return to the gold standard in 1925 is discussed in more detail in Chapter 4.
6 S. Kuznets, *Modern Economic Growth* (1966), table 6.3, p. 306.
7 Figures from League of Nations, *World Economic Survey, 1933/34* (1934), p. 187, and League of Nations, *Course and Phases of the World Economic Depression* (1931), p. 27. Quotation from *Course and Phases*, p. 7.
8 These various views are well summarised by Professor C. P. Kindleberger in *The World in Depression 1929-1939* (1973), Ch. 1.

9   Quoted in J. L. Gaddis, *The United States and the Origins of the Cold War* (1972), p. 18.
10 F. Hirsch, *Money International* (1969), p. 438 and table 30.
11 Hirsch, *Money International*, p. 436.
12 W. A. Lewis, *Economic Survey 1919-1939* (1949), p. 56.
13 M. Friedman and A. J. Schwartz, *A Monetary History of the United States 1867-1960* (1963), ch. 7. The gold exchange standard was so called because of the use by many countries after the war of convertible foreign currencies as their national reserves instead of gold, on the assumption that such currencies could always if necessary be converted into gold at will.
14 Friedman and Schwartz, *A Monetary History*, p. 361.
15 Friedman and Schwartz, *A Monetary History*, p. 391.
16 Lewis, *Economic Survey*, p. 54.
17 Lewis, *Economic Survey*, p. 202, table 15.
18 League of Nations, *Course and Phases of the World Economic Depression* (1931), p. 39.
19 C. H. Lee, 'The Effects of the Depression on Primary Producing Countries', *Journal of Contemporary History*, vol. 4 (October 1969).
20 Lewis, *Economic Survey*, p. 56.
21 Kindleberger, *The World in Depression*, ch. 14.
22 Also the framework does not correspond exactly to either of the main forms of presentation used in the official balance of payments 'pink books' since 1950.
23 C. H. Feinstein, *National Income, Expenditure and Output of the United Kingdom, 1855-1965* (1972), p. 114.
24 Calculated from *Bank of England Quarterly Bulletin* (March 1974), p. 49, table B.
25 *Bank of England Quarterly Bulletin* (March 1974), p. 49.
26 *Bank of England Quarterly Bulletin* (March 1974). 'Long-term capital' has been taken as the sum of 'official long-term capital', UK new investment overseas', 'repayments on existing issues' and 'other long-term capital'.
27 E. V. Morgan, *Studies in British Financial Policy 1914-25* (1953), p.343.
28 Cmd 3897, pp. 112-13. 'Income account' means current account.
29 D. Williams, 'London and the 1931 Financial Crisis', *Economic History Review* (April 1963), p. 528.
30 D. Moggridge, *British Monetary Policy 1924-31* (1972), p. 118, table 7.
31 R. Skidelsky, *Politicians and the Slump* (1967), p. 340.
32 A. Boyle, *Montague Norman* (1967), p. 260.
33 For further discussion of the political outcome, see Chapter 9.
34 Royal Institute of International Affairs, *The Problem of International Investment* (1937), p. 342.
35 Calculated from C. H. Feinstein, *National Income, Output and Expenditure*, table 15.
36 Cmd 3897 (1931), p. 114.
37 R. S. Sayers, *The Vicissitudes of an Export Economy* (1965), p. 14.
38 H. Tyszynsky, 'World Trade in Manufactured Commodities 1899-1950', *Manchester School of Economic and Social Studies* (September 1951).
39 R. E. Caves and Associates, *Britain's Economic Prospects* (1968), p.279.
40 Quoted in Lewis, *Economic Survey*, p. 78.
41 Lewis, *Economic Survey*, p. 79.
42 G. C. Allen, *British Industries and their Organisation* (1970), p.227 and 229.
43 L. B. Yeager, *International Monetary Relations* (1965), p. 242.

44 Cmd 8354 (1951), *Reserves and Liabilities 1931-45.* Liabilities are given here as £778 million in June and £598 million in December, 1938. £739 million is the average level of reserves for the four quarters of 1938.

45 *Parliamentary Debates, Commons,* vol. 261, col. 287 (4 Feb. 1932).

46 I. M, Drummond, *British Economic Policy and the Empire 1919-1939* (1972), p. 92.

47 Drummond, *British Economic Policy,* p. 102.

48 For instance oranges, grapefruit, peaches, bananas, etc., as well as on basic foodstuffs like wheat, butter, cheese and eggs.

49 H. W. Arndt, *Economic Lessons of the Nineteen Thirties* (1944), p.108.

50 Arndt, *Economic Lessons,* p. 112.

51 *Parliamentary Debates, Commons,* vol. 261, col. 299 (4 Feb. 1932).

52 Lewis, *Economic Survey,* p. 59.

53 Arndt, *Economic Lessons,* p. 270-8 and Lewis, *Economic Survey,* p. 60.

54 Arndt, *Economic Lessons,* p. 302, emphasis added.

Chapter 3

Industrial Development

I *The Growth and Structure of Industry*
In any mature industrial economy the range of manufacturing industry
will probably extend over a number of products so that the economy
will not be entirely or heavily dependent upon any single product or
any narrow group of products. At any point in time some industries
will be growing at a faster rate than gross national product and may
be regarded as leading sectors, compensating for slower growth in
other sectors. Decline in any particular industry or sector must be
more than offset by expansion elsewhere if overall economic growth
and employment of productive resources, including labour, is to be
sustained. Thus it may be argued that sustained economic growth and
full utilisation of productive resources depends upon a continuous
process of structural adjustment whereby new and rapidly growing
industries continue to emerge as existing ones decline or grow at
slower rates.

During the nineteenth century the British economy had become
very heavily dependent upon a group of long established industries
which had pioneered early industrial development. They included
coal, shipbuilding, cotton textiles, iron and steel, and engineering;
railways might also be included. These industries, collectively referred
to as the 'old staples', were highly concentrated in particular parts of
the country. With the exception of Belfast, all these concentrations of
industry were on or near coalfield areas in South Wales, Lancashire,
the West Riding of Yorkshire, Tyneside and the North-east, and
central Scotland. For the bulk of its industrial output, employment and
visible exports Britain depended directly or indirectly upon these
industries and they, in turn, were heavily dependent on export markets.

In the decades before 1914, while new industries and new growth
areas did develop in Britain, they remained relatively unimportant in

aggregate terms. Other countries, including particularly the United States and Germany, developed new industries more rapidly and extensively than Britain. Clearly Britain in this period had the financial and technological capacity to develop new manufactures but, on the whole, did not do so very extensively because the necessary motivation was lacking. There was a heavy capital and labour commitment to the old staple industries, which continued to be profitable, and it was not until the early 1920s that these industries began to encounter very serious long-run economic difficulties.

Before 1914 Britain's savings were channelled into a rising volume of overseas investment and into the traditional industries, rather than into new domestic manufacturing industries. We may assume that this pattern of investment reflected investors' expectations about relative profitability. To what extent it also reflected managerial inertia and institutional bias (including that of the London new issue market towards foriegn investment) are matters for speculation.[1] But on the whole it seems plausible to suggest that the pre-first world war investment pattern was quite rational, given prevailing economic circumstances and short-run expectations. While the old staple industries and foreign securities continued to be reasonably profitable and secure investments, many of the potential new industries were relatively risky propositio,1s in British conditions since they required a prosperous mass consumer market. While such a market was beginning to emerge in the late nineteenth century, between 1900 and 1914 real incomes tended to stagnate and it was not until after 1920 that British incomes began to reach levels which made, for example, the mass production of motor vehicles economically viable. In the United States, where income levels were higher, this industry and others requiring similar market circumstances were able to develop at an earlier stage and on a more extensive basis.

However we may attempt to justify the pattern of industrial investment in Britain before 1914, there can be little doubt, in retrospect, that Britain became overcommitted to the old staple industries. This overcommitment was probably a factor in the economy's very poor performance during the period 1900-14.[2] The first world war gave rise to a dramatic acceleration in the influences which were to cause stagnation in the old staple industries and as a result of the difficulties of these industries, and an overcommitment towards them, the British economy faced severe economic problems during the next two decades. Although the interwar years have often been viewed as a period of industrial decline, they can be more accurately described as a period of difficult, incomplete and inadequate structural adjustment.

There are three possible ways in which we can veiw the origins of the structural adjustment problem which emerged in the interwar period. In the first place it is possible to argue in terms of continuing overcommitment to the old staple industries as a result of a pattern of unbalanced growth in the economy in the decades before 1920. Secondly it is possible to place the main emphasis on an entrepreneurial or institutional failure, both before and after 1920, to develop new growth industries more extensively and rapidly. Both these views tend to carry an implication that non-economic influences (inertia, caution, lack of 'know-how') were inhibiting rational economic decision making. The third possible approach assumes that continued heavy investment in the old staple industries, at least until 1914, was perfectly rational and that new industries, both before and after 1920, developed as rapidly as might reasonably have been expected in prevailing market circumstances. This third view places the main emphasis on influences, largely traceable to the first world war, which caused a sudden decline in the old staple industries in the 1920s. This sudden decline gave rise to a critical problem which might not have emerged in such an acute form if decline had been more gradual.

The problems confronting the export industries, however, were already beginning to become apparent in the later decades of the nineteenth century. New industrial rivals, particularly the United States, Germany and Japan, began to challenge Britain's export trade in industrial goods, forcing British exporters to rely to an increasing extent on Empire markets. In many parts of the world, early industrial development tended to involve import replacement. Goods previously imported from Britain began to be produced locally behind tariff barriers. These developments were greatly accelerated by the first world war. During the war the diversion of industrial capacity to war purposes and the shortage of shipping made it difficult for Britain to continue to supply traditional export markets. While British exports were more than halved during the war, Japan and the United States experienced industrial booms based on rapid expansion of exports. Where traditional customers of Britain did not turn to alternative and rival sources of supply, they began to produce for themselves goods previously imported. Many of these import-competing industries were given tariff protection in the immediate postwar period.

In the 1920s, therefore, Britain's export industries faced much stronger competition from other industrial exporters and from import substitution behind tariff barriers in traditional markets. At the same time, the price competitiveness of British exports was weakened by war and postwar inflation. Between 1914 and 1920 wage-earners in Britain had gained large increases in money wages and a shorter working week. As a result, British export prices tended to be relatively high.

In the period between 1925 and 1931 this situation was made even worse because of the over-valuation of sterling after the return to the gold standard in 1925.

Over the interwar period as a whole world trade tended to stagnate and Britain's share of total world export trade fell from 14% in 1913 to 9·8% in 1937. Most of the staple industries in the period before 1914 had exported at least 40% of their total output, and in the case of cotton textiles up to 80% of output was exported. An increasing proportion of these exports went to primary producing countries. In the interwar period, and particularly from the mid-1920s, these countries faced adverse terms of trade and, after 1929, severe depression. As their capacity to import was reduced these countries turned increasingly to import substitution.

One of the most spectacular and damaging examples of market loss occurred in cotton exports to India. Between 1913 and 1938 Indian output of cotton piece goods quadrupled while British exports to India were reduced to one tenth of their former level. Where India failed to meet its own requirements for cotton piece goods these tended to be supplied by Japan rather than Britain. In the home market also, most of the old staple industries faced serious difficulties as a result of substitution and changes in taste and techniques. Coal was used more economically and gave ground to new sources of power, including oil and electricity. The railways faced severe competition from road transport and the market for cotton was eroded by synthetics. Despite these difficulties it can be argued that the extent of industrial decline has been exaggerated. In terms of output the only basic sector of manufacturing which suffered an absolute decline between 1920 and 1937 was shipbuilding. While cotton also declined absolutely, the textile sector as a whole expanded. The decline of the old staple industries is relative rather than absolute, if we think in terms of output. However, because of improvements in output per worker employed, several old staple industries experienced absolute decline in terms of employment.

In 1928 the Liberal Party's *Britain's Industrial Future* stated:

'There is not to-day, and there has not been for several years, a general trade depression in the sense in which economists are accustomed to use the term. In many directions, on the contrary, there has been remarkable expansion. The broad picture which presents itself is one of long-continued adversity in our leading exporting industries, contrasting sharply with considerable expansion and prosperity elsewhere.'[3]

This view is confirmed by modern quantitative research which suggests that the growth performance of the British economy during the interwar period was quite good in terms of international and historical comparisons.[4]

Measures of the growth of net industrial output (as opposed to measures of total output already discussed in Chapter 1) show the interwar period in an even more favourable light.[5] Between 1920 and 1927 the average annual rate of growth of industrial output in the United Kingdom was 3·1%. This represented a higher rate of growth than that in any comparable previous period since 1860. As a result of a series of quantitative studies there is now a general consensus that British industrial output in the interwar period increased by something in the order of 50%. According to Lomax, total industrial production by 1937 had risen 63% above the 1913 level.[6]

Table 3.1 *United Kingdom: Index of Industrial Production* (1924 = 100).

1913	90·5	1926	98·4
1914	84·8	1927	113·4
1915	86·4	1928	110·2
1916	81·8	1929	115·8
1917	76·4	1930	110·8
1918	73·8	1931	103·7
1919	81·3	1932	103·2
1920	90·3	1933	110·1
1921	73·5	1934	121·1
1922	85·0	1935	130·3
1923	90·0	1936	142·0
1924	100·0	1937	150·5
1925	103·9	1938	146·4

Source K. S. Lomax, 'Growth and Productivity in the United Kingdom', *Productivity Measurement Review*, vol. 38 (1964).

Table 3.1 indicates that there was a temporary recovery to the 1913 (boom) level by 1920. This was followed by a severe setback in 1921, and full recovery to the prewar peak level did not come until 1924. There were further downturns in 1926 and 1928 but growth during the 1920s as a whole was quite rapid, averaging 2·8% per annum over the years 1920-9. The downturn during the 1929-32 depression was far from catastrophic and output had more than regained the pre-depression level by 1934. Between 1932 and 1937 growth was very rapid, followed by a mild downturn in 1938. The average annual rate of growth during the 1927-37 period was 3·3%.

This impressive picture of overall industrial growth is all the more remarkable in view of what has been said earlier in relation to the old staple industries. It follows that certain sectors of manufacturing must have grown very rapidly indeed to compensate for stagnation in the basic industries.

However impressive Britain's industrial performance in the interwar period may have been — and this depends greatly upon the exact period being measured — the fact remains that it was still inadequate since it did not ensure full utilisation of resources. Industrial development, and therefore economic growth, were below potential and an average unemployment level of 14% (for the insured work-force) prevailed. British industrial output did not regain its 1913 level until 1924 (eleven years later). In the meantime productivity had increased, so that fewer men were required to produce the same output, and the labour force had expanded. In these circumstances production was substantially below potential and heavy unemployment was inevitable at prevailing levels of output and aggregate demand.

The story of Britain's industrial development in the interwar period has traditionally been told in terms of the rapid decline of the old staple industries and their gradual and inadequate (in terms of employment) replacement by new and expanding industries. In the last decade the emergence of new quantitative evidence, and modern economic analysis of this evidence, has given further support to the view that this was a period of rapid industrial expansion, but the sources of expansion are rather more widespread, complex and obscure than was previously supposed. There is no simple or single explanation of industrial growth, and disaggregation indicates a complex and changing pattern within particular sectors and important changes in growth performance over time.[7]

In terms of growth in output, manufacturing, construction, and electricity, gas and water, grew more rapidly than gross domestic product, while agriculture, mining and the service sector lagged behind. In terms of employment and capital investment the pattern is rather different in that services absorbed a major share of capital (69% by 1937) and increased their share of employment (from 44% to 49%, 1924-37). Productivity increases were greatest in the primary and secondary sectors of the economy while productivity declined absolutely in services.[8] A major part of the growth which occurred cannot be explained as a result of additional inputs of labour and capital and can only have resulted from increased productivity. This increased productivity was widespread in the primary and secondary sectors of the economy and was not simply confined to new and expanding industries. In aggregate terms the old industries continued to be of great importance, especially in relation to employment, and it would also be wrong to assume that the new industries came to dominate the structure of British industry or employment during the period. While on the whole the new industries led industrial growth, some long established industries including building, building materials, tobacco, furniture, food, paper, printing, utilities, footwear and hosiery also grew rapidly and some of the old staple industries make remarkable advances in productivity. Quite apart from problems of definition, the traditional explanations of industrial development in the interwar period in terms of declining old industries and expanding new industries are less than satisfactory. Some industries, for example, iron and steel, do not fall convincingly into either category. Quite clearly, not all old industries were declining, nor were all new industries expanding. If we think in terms of productivity or output per worker, rather than total output, then the traditional approach becomes even more unsatisfactory. Shipbuilding, a declining industry, had a higher than average rate of growth in productivity, while labour productivity in chemicals, an expanding industry, grew less than average.

Table 3.2 *Employment 1924, 1929 and 1937*

Occupations	1924	1929	1937
		(percentages)	
Agriculture and forestry	8·22	7·39	5·89
Fishing	0·39	0·32	0·25
Mining and quarrying	7·05	5·42	4·22
Manufacturing	33·67	33·48	33·13
Building and contracting	4·70	5·19	5·91
Gas, electricity and water	1·05	1·15	1·33
Transport and communication	8·46	8·22	7·85
Distributive trades	12·03	13·70	14·44
Insurance, banking, finance	2·01	2·09	2·20
National government:			
Civilian	0·99	00·89	1·04
Armed forces	1·88	1·71	1·76
Local government	2·24	2·38	2·54
Professional services	4·77	4·79	5·11
Miscellaneous services	12·55	13·26	14·32
Total	100·01	99·99	99·99

Percentage distribution of persons in employment, self-employed and employers.
Source C. H. Feinstein, *National Income, Expenditure and Output of the United Kingdom 1855-1965* (1972), table 59.

The interwar period was one of rapid technical progress, and this was not confined to any particular group of industries. There were widespread innovations and improvements and some of these affected old and declining industries which were able to make remarkable improvements in output per worker. The hard core of unemployment which persisted throughout the interwar period is traceable to the old staple industries, in particular, mining, shipbuilding, iron and steel, textiles and mechanical engineering. There is quite possibly some connection between falling employment and rising productivity in these industries. Before the war labour had been relatively cheap and was used relatively intensively, and the cheapness of labour may have delayed technical innovation.

Table 3.3 *Changes in Net Output of British Industries, 1924-35*

Industry	Value of net output (£ millions)		Ranking	
	1924	*1935*	*1924*	*1935*
Mines and quarries	226·4	136·2	1	5
Textiles	221·8	156·4	2	4
Engineering, shipbuilding and vehicles	198·4	240·6	3	1
Food, drink and tobacco	172·5	196·6	4	3
Public utilities	165·7	202·4	5	2
Iron and steel	98·6	114·8	6	6
Paper, printing and stationery	93·9	109·7	7	7
Building and construction	80·6	86·5	8	9
Clothing	75·7	77·4	9	10
Chemicals etc.	65·8	87·4	10	8
Clay and building materials	43·6	53·5	11	11
Miscellaneous	41·5	42·7	12	12

Source M. Compton and E. H. Bott, *British Industry* (1940), table 3, p. 28 (based on *Census of Production* and *Board of Trade Journal*).

After the slump of 1921 there began a massive 'shake-out' of labour from the old staple industries. In the changed circumstances of heavy unemployment employers could be more selective and more exacting in improving workforce efficiency. After the introduction of unemployment benefits, employers who had previously been paternalistic were able to adopt a more ruthless attitude towards redundancy. Also, with a constant pool of unemployed workers available, employers were less inclined to maintain their workforces at or near peak production levels. Labour was used more efficiently and it is probable that there was some qualitative improvement in the workforce.

The obvious signs of technical progress were seen in the advent of the motor car, the aeroplane, radio, artificial silk and electrification; but these in turn depended upon a multiplicity of lesser discoveries and applications of technology. Within the motor industry, for example, as H. W. Richardson has pointed out:

'There were continuous improvements in the interwar period: better carburettors, more efficient brakes and combustion chambers, automatic voltage control in electrical equipment, thermostatic control of cooling systems, group lubrication, windscreen wipers, self-starters, besides the more obvious developments such as the diesel engine, pneumatic tyres and generally better coachwork design.'[9]

According to R. S. Sayers, the great technical innovations of the period were the internal combustion engine, ball-bearings, the new alloy metallurgy, welding, the new chemical processes and precision control.[10] However, the list should certainly not stop there, and it should certainly go on to include electrification which had an important influence across almost the entire range of industry, besides constituting an important industrial sector in its own right.

A number of technical developments had been accelerated by the first world war, notably aircraft, heavy motor vehicles, radio, welding, petrochemicals and aluminium. In 1915 the Department for Scientific and Industrial Research (DSIR) was established to carry out scientific research into industrial problems and to assist and encourage private industry to conduct its own research. An increasing number of firms did establish their own laboratories and in some industries research associations were formed. These developments were assisted and supplemented by the expansion of pure and applied science in the universities. According to Sayers, research into particular industrial products was stimulated and guided by new demand, which frequently resulted from the cheapening of complementary goods; by competition from alternative goods; by the desire to economise in use of raw materials and especially fuel; and, occasionally, by argument from basic scientific principles.[11] Technical progress was a crucial factor in keeping the old industries alive as well as in promoting new industries. In shipbuilding, for example, the development of a new hull design just after the first world war represented a major technical breakthrough which may have saved the industry from complete economic disaster.

Capital-labour ratios failed to rise in most industries between 1924 and 1937, and declined in manufacturing as a whole, so the general improvement in industrial productivity which occurred during the interwar period was brought about without any corresponding increase in capital stock. Productivity grew more rapidly than investment, indicating that capital resources were being used more efficiently. There were several reasons for this: industry benefited from better techniques, the employment of a more highly skilled workforce, and from economies of scale. Many of the new industries, and much of the new technology, were well suited to mass production techniques which made considerable improvements in output per worker possible. At the same time investment was gradually shifting into higher productivity areas as it moved from old staple industries into new and expanding industries. Finally, productivity improvements resulted from rationalisation, better organisation of existing assets and from replacement investment.[12]

Table 3.4 *United Kingdom: Rates of Change of Output, Employment and Productivity in Manufacturing, 1924-37* (per cent per annum)

Industry	Output	Employment	Output per employee
Building materials	4·7	2·4	2·3
Chemicals	3·1	1·4	1·8
Ferrous metal	3·0	0·8	2·2
Non-ferrous metals	4·9	2·4	2·5
Shipbuilding	1·2	−1·4	2·6
Mechanical engineering	1·9	1·9	0·0
Electrical engineering	6·3	5·6	0·7
Vehicles	6·2	2·9	3·3
Precision instruments	3·5	0·3	3·2
Textiles	1·6	−0·8	2·4
Leather	1·8	0·6	1·2
Clothing	2·1	0·5	1·7
Food	3·9	1·8	2·1
Drink	0·7	0·8	−0·2
Tobacco	3·5	0·6	2·9
Paper and printing	2·7	1·8	1·0
Manufacturing	3·3	1·2	2·1

Source J. A. Dowie, 'Growth in the Inter-War Period: Some More Arithmetic', *Economic History Review*, vol. 21 (1968), table 3, p. 110.

II *Industries in Relative Decline*

The most spectacular industrial collapse in the interwar period took place in Britain's most important export industry — cotton textiles. Before 1914 Britain dominated the international trade in cotton textiles with 65% of total world exports. Up to 80% of British cotton output was exported and cotton manufacture provided 25% of the total value of British visible exports.[13] During the first world war, cotton was badly affected by manpower and shipping shortages, but the war was followed by a spectacular, if shortlived boom based on demand backlog and sharp price rises. During this boom big profits were paid to shareholders and cotton firms changed hands at grossly inflated prices. The industry was peculiarly vulnerable to the ensuing slump which marked the beginning of a long period of almost continuous decline resulting from loss of overseas markets (home demand continued to increase) and sharp price falls. Between 1912 and 1938, cotton production was halved. Yarn exports fell from 244 million lb. to 123 million lb. and piece goods exports from 6,913 million square yards to 1,494 million square yards. There were sharp reductions in the number of spindles and looms employed and the cotton workforce (in spinning, doubling and weaving) fell from 621,500 in 1912 to 393,000 in 1938.

British cotton exporters suffered heavy losses in most market areas except Africa. The reason for these market losses was competing production by rival exporters, particularly Japan, and more importantly the increasing self-sufficiency of traditional market areas. The most spectacular and painful loss was in the Indian market which had taken approximately one third of British cotton piece goods exports before 1914. By 1938 India's own production of cotton piece goods had quadrupled and British exports to India had fallen to one tenth of the prewar level. India was approaching self-sufficiency in cotton textiles and Japan had captured the major part of the dwindling export market which remained in India.

In the face of market loss, falling prices, dwindling profits and heavy debt, the cotton industry was able to do very little to improve its efficiency, although the high quality section remained relatively prosperous. From the late 1920s attention turned to the need to reduce excess capacity — a difficult operation in an industry which was by tradition highly competitive with many small, independent producers and a low level of integration. After 1927 a number of voluntary rationalisation schemes attempted to reduce capacity and hold up prices in the industry. The limited success of these schemes prompted government intervention in the form of the Cotton Industry (Reorganisation) Act of 1936. Under this Act a compulsory levy was imposed on cotton machinery and the proceeds used to purchase and scrap surplus spindles. By 1938 the Spindles Board had scrapped nearly 5 million spindles. Between 1930 and 1938 the number of spindles was reduced from 63 to 42 million and looms were reduced from 700,000 to 495,000. In 1939 the government made provision for cartelisation in the industry. At the end of the period many problems remained. There was still considerable excess capacity, in spite of drastic reductions, and in comparison with overseas rivals the industry remained inefficient.

The problems of the coal industry were caused by stagnating demand in the home market and heavy losses in export markets. Coal was being used more efficiently and there was growing competition from alternative sources of power and rival coal producers.

World productive potential grew more rapidly than demand, and international competition intensified. By the late 1930s British average annual output was approximately 40 million tons less than the average annual output of 268 million tons between 1907 and 1914. Because of improved productivity, the workforce declined more than output, from the peak level of 1·2 million in 1920 to 702,000 in 1938.[14]

As a result of the 1921 strike, the American coal strike of 1922 and the French occupation of the Ruhr in 1923, the coal industry did not run into serious long-run market losses with declining output, profits and prices, until 1924. During the first world war coal came under state control and the miners demanded nationalisation of the industry after the war. In 1919 the Sankey Commission, which was the first of a series of official inquiries into the organisation of the industry, recommended the nationalisation of coal royalties, but divided on the question of nationalising the industry. Although Sankey's casting vote as chairman went in favour of nationalisation the industry was handed back to private enterprise during the 1921 slump. A bitter strike followed and ended in a partial victory for the miners in the 1921 agreement. In the adverse circumstances which prevailed after 1924 this agreement broke down and the owners attempted to return to local agreements, reduced wages and longer working hours. From their point of view this was the only possible solution given the high share of labour in total costs. A temporary government subsidy delayed the inevitable crisis which came in the General Strike of 1926. The miners continued to strike for periods of up to nine months, but were eventually forced to return to work on the basis of local agreements. Even so sections of the industry continued to make losses and there was a growing realisation of the need to reduce excess capacity. The Samuel Commission in 1925 recommended amalgamation, but this was left on a voluntary basis. There were voluntary amalgamations on a small scale in the 1920s, and area agreements in South Wales, Scotland, Lancashire and the Midlands which attempted to stabilise and maintain minimum prices, and ensure some reduction of excess capacity and export subsidisation. These attempts at market regulation had only limited success because involvement was purely voluntary. Government intervention under the Coal Mines Act of 1930 established compulsory cartelisation on a district basis and the Coal Mines Reorganisation Commission which attempted, unsuccessfully, to introduce amalgamation and rationalisation. The 1930 Act enabled the industry to prevent further falls in prices and profits, but in the 1930s profits remained at approximately half the prewar level. Excess capacity remained and the industry made only modest improvements in efficiency.[15]

The industry most severely hit by depression in the interwar period was shipbuilding. In the period 1909-13 the industry launched an annual average of 1·5 million gross tons. During the war a reduced workforce was unable to make good the losses resulting from German U-boat action and shipbuilding capacity overseas, particularly in the USA, increased during the war and immediate postwar shipping shortage. British output rose to a peak of over 2 million tons in 1920. This level was never regained. Production slumped to 0·6 million tons in 1923 rising to 1·4 million tons in 1924 and falling again to 0·6 million tons in 1926. From this low level production climbed to 1·5 million tons in 1929 but in the ensuing depression the industry almost ceased to operate with an output of only 0·13 million tons in 1933. Recovery in the 1930s was very slow and much of the industry remained idle. By 1938 output had recovered to 1·1 million tons. Between 1913 and 1921 British shipbuilding capacity increased by approximately one third and during the same period total world shipbuilding capacity more than doubled. In the face of this greatly increased capacity, world demand for shipping in the 1920s remained well below prewar levels. There was a world surplus of shipping after 1920 and a large part of shipbuilding capacity remained idle. There were heavy losses in export markets but in absolute terms the most serious damage to the industry resulted from reductions in home orders. To some extent, British buyers turned to overseas sources and naval demands remained low until the later 1930s. Foreign competition was intensified by government subsidies and the overvaluation of sterling in the 1920s. Although there were significant improvements in technology and organisation, British shipbuilding lagged behind foreign competitors.[16]

Labour in shipbuilding fell by a quarter between 1924 and 1937 and there was heavy regional unemployment associated with the industry and substantial financial losses. Drastic reorganisation was required in order to reduce excess capacity and improve technical efficiency. This was left to voluntary action within the industry. In 1930 National Shipbuilders Security Ltd was established with support from most shipbuilders and from the Bankers Industrial Development Company. The latter was formed by the major clearing banks and the Bank of England to rationalise and reduce capacity in depressed staple industries (it was mainly concerned with shipbuilding, steel and cotton). Funds were raised on the basis of a 1% levy on sales and used to purchase and close selected shipyards, which sold at very low prices in the depressed circumstances of the early 1930s. By 1937 a capacity of over one million tons had been destroyed. Even so gross excess capacity remained and relatively little was done to improve the efficiency of the industry.

The iron and steel industry exhibited many features of decline, although it suffered rather less than the industries dealt with so far. While pig iron production declined continuously from 1913 until 1937, this reflected the growing shift from iron to steel and the increasing use of scrap in steel manufacture.[17] Steel output rose by nearly 2 million tons during the war but fell back in the depression of the early 1920s. By 1924 output exceeded the 1913 level and the 1918 level of 9·6 million tons had been regained by 1929. During the depression of the 1930s steel output was almost halved but recovery was fairly rapid and regained the pre-depression level by 1935. There followed a modest boom and the industry reached a peak interwar output of 13 million tons in 1937.[18] Iron and steel lost heavily in export markets and never regained its prewar level of exports. Its growth depended on the home market which was protected in the 1930s from the keen competition of Belgian, French and German producers. In the 1920s the industry faced increased tariffs and other barriers abroad and severe foreign competition in the home market.[19] In 1932 a $33\frac{1}{3}$% ad valorem tariff was introduced and imports fell sharply. This tariff protection was granted on the understanding that there would be reorganisation in the industry and the British Iron and Steel Federation was established in 1934. The Federation gained a temporary increase to 50% tariff protection, and controlled prices, competition and imports in the industry. However, the Federation did little to improve techniques or to promote rationalisation. By the end of the interwar period the iron and steel industry had expanded as a result of government assistance, the armaments boom and growing demand derived from new growth industries such as motor vehicles and aircraft. There was a greater degree of concentration and important advances had been made in technology and productivity. But in comparison with foreign producers the industry remained backward and inefficient.

The brief surveys of industries in relative decline reveal a broadly similar pattern. The misfortunes of these industries resulted basically from a loss of export markets, attributable to intensified overseas competition, import substitution, and trade barriers. The first world war caused disruption and loss of markets, while in the postwar boom expansion was carried to untenable levels and most old staple industries were left with gross excess capacity and heavy debts. Most of these industries had a poor productivity record in the years before 1914 and were relatively inefficient, high cost producers, and remained so throughout the period. Rapid changes in technology proved difficult in circumstances of decline. Export competitiveness was further weakened by sharp rises in wages and unit costs during the brief postwar boom and by government policy on the gold standard. In the 1930s most of the declining industries formed cartels and were given the opportunity to control prices in the home market. The anticipated *quid pro quo* for this was rationalisation, reorganisation and improved efficiency, resulted eventually in increased output and employment. On the whole this was not forthcoming, although most industries improved their productivity performance while discharging labour on a vast scale.

III *Agriculture*

After a brief period of prosperity during, and just after, the first world war British agriculture reached its nadir in the interwar period. The later part of the war brought government subsidies, price guarantees and market and wage controls which continued for a brief period after the war. In 1920 agricultural prices fell sharply and a sudden change in government policy followed. In 1921 agriculture was returned to a free market situation and by 1922 virtually nothing remained of the wartime controls. The gains made during the war and postwar boom were rapidly wiped out by falling prices and increased indebtedness.

Between 1917 and 1921 there was a rush of land sales and speculation in land and it has been estimated that something like a quarter of English land changed hands in these four years.

'Such an enormous and rapid transfer of land had not been seen since the confiscations and sequestrations of the Civil War, such a permanent transfer not since the dissolution of the monasteries in the sixteenth century. Indeed a transfer on this scale and in such a short space of time had probably not been equalled since the Norman Conquest.'[20]

Land values were high in relation to the income from land and the social prestige attached to land ownership was probably less marked than in earlier years. Sales were also precipitated by war deaths, rising taxation and, in particular, death duties. During the war and postwar boom prices and wages rose much more than rents and the returns to landowners fell. The land was purchased mainly by tenants and the owner-occupancy of agricultural land increased from 11% in 1914 to 36% by 1927.

Agricultural prices fell sharply in 1920-2, followed by continued, but slower decline during the remainder of the 1920s; prices fell again by 34% between 1929 and 1932 and then recovered slowly from 1933, but failed to regain the pre-depression level in the 1930s. In general, farm costs fell rather less than prices. Many tenants who had purchased land in the postwar boom were left with debts which (in real terms) tended to rise as prices fell. As a result of state intervention farm wages, although lower than in most other sectors, remained stable from the mid-1920s. Rents also tended to remain stable while prices fell.

It is misleading to generalise about British agriculture because of the enormous regional diversity in land ownership and use. However, it appears that the main pre-1914 trends continued in the interwar period. Production was increasingly concentrated in commodities which were least affected by overseas competition, where price reductions were lowest and where production was relatively less labour intensive. Grain production became relatively much less significant and livestock continued to increase in importance. The major part of farm income was accounted for by milk, meat, poultry, eggs and potatoes. Grain producers in the eastern counties, and hill farmers who could find no feasible alternative to sheep, were most severely affected by falling prices.

Net farm output is difficult to compute because of the growing importance and diversity of inputs from outside the industry – in particular, cheap animal feedstuffs imported from abroad. There does not appear to have been any significant increase in net output between 1918 and 1939. However, labour productivity improved largely as a result of changing structure and improvements in animal husbandry and technology. In the interwar period farm employment fell by nearly one third and the area under plough was reduced by a quarter.[21]

The depression of the 1930s gave rise to a dramatic change in government policy towards agriculture involving a complete reversal of the policy which had prevailed since the repeal of the corn laws in 1846. British agriculture had been sacrificed in favour of free trade. From the 1870s there was an increasing dependence on imported food and by 1914 two thirds of Britain's needs were supplied from abroad and British agriculture accounted for a mere 6% of national income. The rural community had continued to decline and agriculture was compelled to make drastic structural changes dictated by the nature of home demand and foreign competition.

The change in policy dating from 1932 was based on mixed motives and must be seen basically in political terms. The rural community had a much greater significance and influence than its dwindling numbers suggested and there was a real national desire to preserve, and prevent further decline in, the countryside. After the return to protection in 1931 agriculture had a reasonable case, in terms of equity, for assistance. Also there was growing concern about national standards of nutrition and the first world war had revealed Britain's strategic vulnerability by virtue of its dependence on overseas food supplies. From 1932 onwards there evolved a deliberate policy of active assistance designed to maintain farm incomes. The main instruments of policy were the regulation of food imports and marketing, subsidies and price guarantees for farmers.

While the major policy changes came from 1932 onwards, there were precedents in the period since 1917. Control and assistance between 1917 and 1921 has already been mentioned. The Rates Acts of 1923 and 1928 had the eventual result of removing the burden of local rates from farm land and buildings, and the Tithe Act of 1925 reduced debts and standardised tithes. In 1925 an important precedent was created by the British Sugar (Subsidy) Act which granted direct subsidies to beet growers. There were attempts to promote voluntary action and self-help among farmers by the Agricultural Credits Act of 1928, the Agricultural Produce (Grading and Marketing) Act of 1928 and the Agricultural Marketing Act of 1931. The latter empowered two thirds of the producers of any farm commodity to organise marketing schemes which could be made compulsory. The 1931 Act had little effect until provision was made for the control of imports and output in 1933. Gradually during the 1930s protection was extended to a wide range of agricultural products. By 1939 there were seventeen agricultural marketing boards. On the whole marketing schemes were not an outstanding success during the 1930s except in dealing with milk, potatoes and hops, none of which were particularly vulnerable to import competition. However, these schemes together with the Wheat Commission, the Sugar Commission, the Livestock Commission and the Bacon Development Board provided useful precedents for the organisation of agriculture during the second world war.

In 1932 the Import Duties Act and the Ottawa Agreements Act

placed import duties on foreign food and provided for quantitative restrictions and quotas of imports. The intention was to prevent the British market being swamped by a flood of cheap imports and to give home and dominion producers a greater share of the market at the expense of foreigners. Between 1931 and 1935 food imports into Britain declined 12% after a sharp increase prior to 1931. Over the same period imports from Empire countries increased 42% and foreign supplies fell 32%. Import duties and restrictions helped dominion producers to gain an increased share of the British market but did little to raise farm incomes in Britain. By the interwar period only a small part of British agricultural production competed directly with cheap imports. On the whole British farm produce was relatively high cost, and home demand was price elastic. Import controls had to be backed up with agricultural subsidies. There was direct subsidisation of beet sugar and cattle, and from 1932 price deficiency payments (or guaranteed prices involving variable subsidies) were extended over a range of products. By 1939 there were guaranteed prices for wheat, barley, oats, milk, pigs and sheep. The bulk of assistance went to wheat and beet growers in the depressed eastern counties. Direct assistance was also given in the form of relief from tithes, cheap credit facilities, farm services and subsidies for water supply and drainage schemes. Total subsidies (including revenue concessions) reached an interwar annual peak of £19 million in 1938-9.

During the 1930s agriculture made little positive progress in terms of output or income. The fortunes of British farmers tended to be dictated by the buoyancy of demand in the home market for animal products and vegetables, but state measures in the 1930s helped to prevent further decline and paved the way for the distinctive British approach which emerged after the second world war and remained until entry to the European Economic Community in the 1970s. This policy of deficiency payments, or variable subsidies, to farmers from taxation enabled British farmers to share the market with dominion producers who were given preferential treatment over foreign producers while prices to the consumer remained low. In return British exporters were given preferential treatment by the dominions (Canada, Australia, New Zealand, South Africa).

IV Transport and Communications
Transport and communications reveal the full range of industrial experience in the interwar period. Railways, shipping, canals and tramways may be grouped with the declining old staple industries, while at the modern end of the economy, road and air transport, and postal and telecommunications expanded rapidly. The most important

transport development in the interwar period was the rapid rise of road transport at the expense of railways.[22]

After wartime state control of railways the Railway Act of 1921 created four private but regulated rail systems. Before 1914 the railways had enjoyed a virtual monopoly of British long distance transport and the first world war marked the end of a long period of sustained and rapid expansion in railway traffic. In the interwar years rail freight declined, profits failed to regain prewar levels and passenger traffic ceased to expand. This change in circumstances is attributable to growing competition from road transport and stagnation in the old staple industries which the railway network had been built to serve and which provided substantial and profitable bulky freight business.[23]

The new growth industries in the south and midlands were served in the main by road transport which developed very rapidly in the two decades after 1920. Between 1918, when there were approximately 300,000 motor vehicles of all types, and 1938, the number of vehicles in Britain increased tenfold. By 1938 there were nearly 2 million private cars, over 50,000 buses and nearly half a million goods vehicles.[24] The capital and operating costs of motor vehicles fell sharply and they became highly competitive against railways on short and medium distance transporting of passengers and high freight classification goods. It has been suggested that by the mid-1930s the main railway lines had lost half their traffic to the roads.[25] During the interwar period the railway workforce fell by 18% and a large part of the rail network became uneconomic.

The rapid growth of road transport gave rise to an urgent need for government regulation in the public interest. In 1930 the Road Traffic Act made third party insurance compulsory and removed speed limits for private cars. It also introduced general regulations dealing with public transport vehicles which had the effect, *inter alia*, of reducing competition and protecting existing operators. The Road and Rail Traffic Act of 1933 attempted a measure of co-ordination between road and rail traffic. Again the effect was to reduce competition. The Road Traffic Act of 1934 set up the 30 mph speed limit in urban areas and introduced the driving test. In 1933-4 the establishment of the London Passenger Transport Board unified and monopolised the metropolitan public transport system.

Between 1914 and 1938 Britain's share of world mercantile shipping tonnage fell from 43% to 26%. While total world tonnage increased 46% over the same period, there was a 6% reduction in British tonnage. British shipping was adversely affected by the sharp fall in freight rates and profits during the 1920s and early 1930s, which reflected stagnation in international trade and migration (in particular the reduction in British exports of coal and other commodities), and the growing surplus of world shipping and intensified foreign competition, often with government support. British shipping was unable to meet the challenge from foreign competitors who were able to provide cheaper and often more efficient services. Tramp shipping suffered most severely and in 1935 the government introduced an annual subsidy of £2 million to assist tramp shipping. The 'scrap and build' scheme introduced at the same time appears to have been a failure and did little to help modernise the British fleet. Foreign shipping lines were much more successful in developing new and specialised types of shipping and in particular oil tankers.

V *The Growth Industries*
Any list of growth industries between the wars is likely to include electricity generation and supply, electrical and radio equipment, artificial silk (or rayon), aluminium, rubber, synthetic dyestuffs, plastics, chemicals, precision instruments, wireless, aircraft, motor vehicles, and possibly also the canning of foodstuffs, the extraction of oil from coal, beet sugar, films and road transport. Clearly, very few of these industries are in the strict sense new to the interwar period. Most of them existed before 1900 and relied on techniques which were learned and developed during the late nineteenth century. Some, such as rayon, were off-shoots of old staple industries and represented the application of new techniques in traditional areas.

Rayon was an artificial fibre based on wood pulp or cotton lintens. Unlike other textiles, rayon output grew very rapidly during the interwar period rising from 6 million lb. of yarn in 1920 to 58 million lb. in 1930 and 173 million lb. in 1939. This very rapid expansion was based on technical breakthroughs, changes in popular taste in clothing, and continuous reductions in rayon prices and improvements in quality. Rayon's main use was as 'artificial silk', but it also became complementary to other fibres (in mixed fibre production) as well as a substitute for them. The rayon industry was dominated by Courtaulds and, to a lesser extent, by British Celanese. In the late 1920s these two were challenged by a number of smaller firms after the industry was given protection from imports in 1925. The two leaders continued to dominate by their pricing policy and the advantages of size, superior techniques and improvements in organisation.[26]

The motor vehicle industry had made only limited progress in Britain before 1914.[27] Rapid expansion had to await technical improvements, protection, rising incomes and sharp reductions in vehicle prices which could only be achieved by mass production methods. The breakthrough came in the 1920s. From 34,000 vehicles in 1913, production rose to 73,000 in 1922 after a fall during the war. By 1929 output reached 240,000 vehicles of all types and 146,000 motor cycles. Mass production in the 1920s was inaugurated by Austin, Morris and the Ford plant at Dagenham. Nevertheless, Britain's achievement at the end of the 1920s remained very modest in comparison with the American industry. British vehicle production reached an interwar peak of 510,000 units in 1937. Employment in the car industry rose less rapidly than output, from 227,000 in 1920 to 516,000 by 1938. The average factory value of British produced cars fell from £260 in 1924 to £130 in 1935-6, and the demand for motor vehicles proved to be income and price elastic.[28] The number of car makers fell from 96 in 1922 to 20 in 1939, and the industry was increasingly concentrated in the midlands and, to a lesser degree, London and the south-east.[29] By 1938 the six largest firms (Morris, Austin, Ford, Vauxhall, Rootes and Standard) accounted for 90% of total car production. The industry remained competitive despite the elimination of many small producers. As Plummer pointed out:

'In addition to the marked tendency towards the elimination of the smaller units, the large concerns continue to acquire "interests" in units which produce the various accessories they need. Thus the typical motor manufacturer does not actually make the whole vehicle from beginning to end; his principal function is the assembly of parts, many of which are made to his own designs and specifications by specialist manufacturers of accessories and components'.[30]

It was estimated that a motor vehicle might consist of about 7,000 different components, involving a galaxy of backward linkages, in turn involving a wide range of products ranging from steel to glass and rubber. The motor industry accounted for two thirds of British rubber consumption and it consumed about one half of the plate glass produced in Britain. This was one of the most important new industries, not only in terms of absolute size but also through a multiplicity of direct and indirect effects upon economic activity and social life. The motor vehicle was an agent and symbol of modernisation, for better or worse.

What may be said about the importance of the motor car may also be claimed more emphatically for electricity.

'The growth of knowledge relating to electricity is one of the most revolutionary developments of modern times. If we did not know how to generate and transmit electric power for domestic and industrial purposes, many of our newer industries would be non-existent. The economical production of electricity is fundamental to much of our modern scientific and industrial progress'.[31]

Like the motor industry, electricity in Britain made a spectacular breakthrough in the interwar period. Before 1918 development was slow, scattered, inefficient and haphazard. The economy was heavily committed to power derived from steam and coal-gas, which were cheap in comparison, and Britain lagged behind other countries in the use of electricity. The early electrical industry in Britain was dominated by German and American subsidiaries, 'know-how' and exports. Rapid development in Britain had to await the development of cheap electricity supply based on efficient generation and distribution. The important agent of change was government intervention under the Electricity (Supply) Act of 1926 establishing the Central Electricity Board. The Board was given a monopoly of electricity wholesale supply and its main aim was to concentrate output in a smaller number of stations (eliminating large numbers of small and inefficient production units) and to construct a 'national grid' of high tension transmission cables linking these stations. The grid, together with improved technical and thermal efficiency and cheaper coal, helped to halve the price per unit of electricity by 1938. The number of electricity consumers increased from 0·7 million in 1920 to 2·8 million in 1929 and 9·0 million in 1938. The amount of electricity generated quadrupled between 1925 and 1939. However, improvements in the efficiency of generation were not fully matched by equivalent improvements in distribution.

The rapid growth in electricity consumption promoted by falling costs and elastic demand continued unchecked by the 1930s depression. Industry gained in terms of a reduction in total power costs and greater flexibility in location and layout. Domestic consumption also proved to be price and income elastic and was linked with the rapid spread of electric consumer durables. Annual expenditure on these trebled between 1930 and 1938, but a much larger mass market remained unexploited at the end of the interwar period.

Electrical engineering expanded rapidly and its (insured) work force more than doubled between 1924 and 1937 when it employed 367,000. However, the productivity performance of the industry as a whole was very poor, probably as a result of the absence of mass production techniques in the manufacture of heavy equipment. Much of the industry consisted of foreign subsidiaries and it was protected from 1921 and gained additional protection and imperial preferences in later years. Because of the enormous variety of highly specialised products it is difficult to make useful generalisations about electrical engineering and it is probably rather misleading to regard it as a single industry.

Building was not a new industry, but it cannot be ignored in any discussion of interwar industrial development because of its very rapid growth and great aggregate importance. Building and contracting grew more rapidly than any other industry except vehicles, with an average annual growth rate of 5·4% between 1920 and 1938.[32] The importance of building (including housing, industrial and commercial building) in the economy was greater than at any other time in modern history. Its share of total industrial employment rose from 10·4% in 1920 to 15·2% in 1938 when the building trades employed 1·3 million people; and its share of total fixed investment rose to almost 50% in the 1930s. It absorbed labour and capital in a period when factor supply exceeded demand, and tended to have a counter-cyclical and stabilising influence. The various linkage and multiplier effects of the boom in residential building were very extensive. Housing was a labour-intensive industry expanding during a period of rising real wages. On the other hand technical progress in the industry was not rapid and its productivity performance was well below average over the period as a whole. The most rapid growth in building output and employment was in the 1920s when productivity also grew rapidly (3·9% per annum between 1924 and 1929). The poor productivity performance over the whole period is attributable to the fact that there was no improvement in productivity after 1929.[33] It is important to bear these points in mind in attempting to assess the importance of building in promoting recovery from the 1930s depression.[34] In the building materials industry productivity performance was more even over the period and was slightly above the average for manufacturing industry as a whole.

The growth industries did have certain features in common. Most of them were concerned, directly or indirectly, with production of consumer durable goods which were a sign of improving living standards. It is hardly surprising that these industries tended to concentrate on the home market to a much greater extent than the old staple industries. While some of the new industries were able to develop exports these were biased towards the high income dominion markets which granted preferential treatment, and exports formed a relatively small proportion of total output. In motor vehicles, the most successful new industry in the export field, exports during the 1930s were less than 20% of the total output and in other new industries the proportion was usually below 10%. Most of these industries acquired some measure of protection before the introduction of general protection in 1931, and during the 1920s they were regarded as 'infant industries' and deserving exceptions to the free trade policy. In general, they commenced from small beginnings and took time to gain the economies of scale which were possible. As a result most of them grew more rapidly in the

1930s than in the 1920s. In contrast with the old staples, most of the new industries eventually tended to operate in larger units and production was in the hands of a relatively small number of firms. This was particularly true of rayon and chemicals, dominated by the firms of Courtaulds and Imperial Chemical Industries respectively. On the whole the new industries tended to be less competitive than the old staples and even where an oligopolistic or monopolistic structure did not prevail, market control was typical.[35] It will be apparent that between many of these new industries and the growth industries in general there were important economic linkages. Motor vehicles, for example, were based on inputs from a wide range of industries. To some extent the growth industries shared and were products of a new range of technology and their products were frequently complementary.

In choosing their location new and expanding industries were able to exert a much greater freedom of choice than the old staples because of their ability to rely on road transport and electrical power, rather than railways or canals and coal. As a result a substantial shift in British industrial location away from the old industrial areas of the coalfields became possible. Because industrialists were allowed to exercise this freedom of choice without any systematic overall control, Britain developed a very serious problem of regional imbalance, depressed areas and chronic structural unemployment.

The new growth industries tended to establish themselves in the south-east, around London, and in the midlands. London, as by far the largest urban concentration in the country, represented an enormous consumer market which attracted many of the new industries. By being located in the London area industries manufacturing consumer goods may well have gained significant economies in distribution by being able to cheapen the costs of regular deliveries, variable consignments and after sales service. By virtue of its population size and its position as the leading port and communications centre London was an attractive location for most industries which were not dependent upon the supply of bulky raw materials. In the midlands, where there was a long-standing interest in metal-working, new industries such as motor vehicles, which needed skilled labour and numerous ancillary industries to supply component parts, may also have been able to gain significant external economies. In relation to the growth of new industries G. C. Allen has suggested that:

'The south and the midlands benefited from the fact that, before these developments occurred, they already possessed to a greater extent than the north, a nucleus of those industries or, in some cases, particular branches of industry which could easily adapt themselves to the manufacture of the new products'.[36]

While these plausible economic reasons for the southward drift of British industry can be advanced, it also seems possible that non-economic and largely subjective motivations played some part in the process. It is possible, for example, that the preference of the managerial and investing classes for life in south-eastern England, rather than the north, was an influence of some importance. However, there is no substantial evidence to support the suggestion that new industries favoured the south-east because it had a less well-established tradition of working-class solidarity and unionisation; nor is it correct to suggest that the new industries as a whole made substantially more use of female labour than the old.

Once commenced, these developments in industrial location tended to become cumulative and self-reinforcing. In the midlands and the south-east new and growing industries helped to create an atmosphere of prosperity, at least in relative terms, which made these areas even more attractive to new industries. In the traditional industrial areas of the coalfields, dominated by stagnant or declining industries, the general atmosphere of depression tended to discourage new investment. The Special Areas Act of 1934 and other government efforts to assist the depressed areas, did little to change this situation.

From the national point of view the location decisions taken by industrialists in the interwar period gave rise to a situation which caused increasing concern. Chronic depression, catastrophic unemployment and under-utilisation of resources in the old industrial areas contrasted sharply with the prosperity and pressure on resources in the expanding areas. While the developments which produced this situation occurred only on a gradual scale, the results, especially in extreme cases such as Jarrow, were sufficiently dramatic to arouse fundamental criticism of the laissez faire process under which industrial location took place. An inquiry into industrial location carried out in the late 1930s produced the following conclusion:

'It is misleading to speak of a conflict between economic and "social" considerations. The real issue is not between "natural" economic locations for industry and arbitrarily enforced uneconomic locations, nor is it even between economic and social considerations: it is between locations which may be economic for the individual or small group in the short run and those which are economic for the community as a whole in the long run'.[37]

VI *Industrial Organisation*

By the end of the 1930's British industry had assumed a pattern which differed greatly from the pre-1900 situation. The basic influences producing changes in industrial organisation were: growth in the size of firms and the scale of industrial operation, the reduction of competition, and the increasing involvement of the state in industrial affairs. One recent writer has summarised the situation as follows:

'It was not until the 1920s that fundamentally new patterns of company growth began to emerge in their modern form. In that decade, British industry experienced a more intensive merger wave than had been encountered before or than was to be encountered again until the 1960s . . . whereas in 1907 there had been only seven companies with a market capitalisation of over £8 million there were 25 such companies by 1924 and as many as 61 by 1939. This was moreover an age in which the question of the optimum economic organisation of industry was widely debated and in which faith in competition was progressively weakened. Not only did the prosperous "new" industries show spectacular examples of the growth of oligopolies . . . but the old industries were also continually exhorted to emulate them by "rationalisation" . . . '.[38]

While small, privately owned and operated firms continued to be very numerous, an increasing proportion of total industrial output was produced by large firms which made use of modern mass production methods. This was particularly so in the newer industries where the degree of concentration was invariably high. Large companies were usually, although not always, based upon the issue of shares to the general public and their emergence meant the development of a division between ownership and control in much of British industry. Shareholders tended to lose direct control to professional managers. At the same time, a much more complex pattern of industrial ownership arose from financial activities which gave rise to an intricate system of interlocking interests. The incentives behind the increasing scale of industrial operations were, in part, technical, particularly in highly mechanised mass production industries where the desire for economies of scale and smooth flowing input supplies and marketing were important influences. By operating on a large scale industries such as motor vehicles were able to lower unit costs and to sell into a wider market. While there were undoubtedly technical considerations which promoted vertical and horizontal integration in industry, these were probably less important than the desire for market control. Even in industries which did not become dominated by a single firm, or a few large firms, there were widespread attempts to limit competition by controlling output or prices. By the end of the interwar period free competition in industry was possibly the exception rather than the rule:

'The development towards monopoly, combination and association and the application of a variety of methods to prevent competition, apparent even in the early days of the century, have now been so accelerated that organised interference with the free market is almost ubiquitous'.[39]

The conscious removal or reduction of direct price competition was organised by a variety of means which varied from, at one extreme, near monopoly in public utilities and in cement, soap and salt, to loose and unwritten 'gentlemen's agreements' at the other. Between these extremes lay cartels, amalgamations and business associations. In general the aim was to raise or maintain prices either by selling at a fixed price, or by restricting output so that market prices would rise. This is not to deny that many associations did useful work in improving industrial organisation and techniques. Not all associations were successful in attempting market control. Particularly in industries where there were numerous small firms, agreements about prices were likely to break down. In general the pricing policy of business associations had to be restrained since too much variation from the market inevitably increased the possibility of agreements being broken.

State involvement in industry is dealt with to some extent elsewhere.[40] While it is possible to think in terms of a continuum of growing government intervention in industry from the mid-nineteenth century onwards, it is probably more realistic to see the first world war as an important turning point. After 1914 general *ad hoc* involvement in industry became common, whereas before 1914 the state's role was very limited and consisted mainly of general legislation such as the Factory Acts, the Merchandise Marks Act of 1887 or the general regulation of railways. State intervention before 1914 was invariably designed to promote efficiency, to improve safety and to protect the consumer from the abuse of monopoly power. After 1914 these aims tended to lose ground to a desire on the part of governments to promote industry and protect industrial profitability — at the expense, usually, of the consumer.

One important area of state interference took the form of direct attempts to stimulate the development of new industries by means of tariff protection and import control, and, in some cases, by direct financial assistance. In 1914 a loan was given to the British Dyestuffs Corporation. Loan guarantees were also given to shipbuilding, railways and, under a separate heading, to exporters in general, through Export Credit Insurance which commenced in 1919.[41] Shipping, coal, civil aviation, housing and agricultural production were directly subsidised and, under the Special Areas Act of 1934, individual industrialists could obtain financial assistance if they agreed to locate in depressed areas. Apart from direct assistance of this kind, the state also encouraged, and in some cases compelled, cartelisation. Where voluntary control of output and markets failed or was unlikely to develop, pressure was brought to bear through the Import Duties Advisory Committee, the Bank of England and other official or semi-official bodies. Where these efforts failed, in coal, cotton, agriculture and fishing, statutory regulations were introduced. Under the Coal Mines Act of 1930 the production, pricing and marketing of coal was subjected to regulations, The Agricultural Marketing Act of 1931 empowered a majority of producers of any farm commodity to control the domestic market and, from 1933, such control could be reinforced by import controls.

The general effect of government policy and pressure on industry was to reduce competition, and in some cases to promote cartelisation and monopoly. At the same time, successive governments and public authorities paid lip service to the need to promote 'rationalisation', by which they meant the elimination of excess capacity, concentration of output and more efficient organisation and management. In practice, as one recent writer has pointed out, there may have been a 'fundamental inconsistency' in government policy towards industry:

'The control of markets by cartel arrangements, by supporting an existing and uneconomic industrial structure, could greatly impede any move towards rationalisation, which might necessitate the elimination of capacity'.[42]

Rationalisation was invariably sacrificed in favour of more immediate considerations – the maintenance of employment, profits and business confidence. Nevertheless, some reduction of capacity did take place under supervision of public authorities and on a voluntary basis. The inconsistency was not in all cases fundamental and there was an important difference between planned and orderly elimination of capacity and bankruptcy (not to mention the chain of circumstances which ultimately provoked the 'Jarrow Hunger March').

Undoubtedly, the degree of state involvement with industry increased dramatically during the interwar period and there were important changes in the attitude of government towards industry. These developments were accelerated by depression, but even in the 1930s a series of commissions was appointed to examine industrial problems, and legislation which affected a wide range of industry was introduced. Compton and Bott, writing at the end of the period, make the following comment on state intervention:

'It can hardly be called planning. There is no central direction to economic affairs. The State has interfered piecemeal, and as far as possible has left the details to the industry concerned or to independent persons, but has always refused direct responsibility itself. The indirect influence is as important as the direct legislation, but much more difficult to ascertain'.[43]

In terms of general welfare, direct state involvement was probably beneficial, on the whole, particularly where it encouraged the development of new industries and maintained employment in depressed areas. However, several aspects of government economic management may have had detrimental effects. The motor industry may have been hindered by taxation, and industry in general was affected adversely by deflationary economic policies. While some elements of state intervention speeded up the process of industrial adjustment, there were other measures which slowed it down by propping up ailing industries. Above all, it would be wrong to suggest that the impact of direct government intervention was much more than marginal. In the circumstances it fell far short of what was required to meet the problems of unemployment and structural and regional imbalance.

Notes

1 D. H. Aldcroft and H. W. Richardson, *The British Economy 1870-1939* (1969).
2 H. W. Richardson, 'Over-commitment in Britain before 1930', *Oxford Economic Papers,* vol. 17 (1965).
3 *Britain's Industrial Future* (1928), p. 154.
4 D. H. Aldcroft and P. Fearon (Eds.), *Economic Growth in Twentieth Century Britain* (1969).
5 J. A. Dowie, 'Growth in the Inter-War Period: Some More Arithmetic', *Economic History Review,* vol. 21 (1968).
6 C. H. Feinstein, *National Income, Expenditure and Output in the United Kingdom 1855-1965* (1972), table 51, p. T112.
7 For a comparison between the 1920s and 1930s see Dowie, 'Growth in the Inter-War Period', *Economic History Review* (1968).
8 Dowie, 'Growth in the Inter-War Period', *Economic History Review* (1968), table 1, p. 108.
9 H. W. Richardson, 'The New Industries Between the Wars', *Oxford Economic Papers,* vol. 13 (1961), p. 368.

10   R. S. Sayers, 'The Springs of Technical Progress in Bı
     Economic Journal, vol. 60 (1950), p. 27.
11   Sayers, 'The Springs of Technical Progress', *Economic*
     p. 28.
12   D. H. Aldcroft, 'Economic Progress in Britain in the
     Journal of Political Economy, vol. 13 (1966), p. 304.
13   G. C. Allen, *British Industries and their Organisation* (3rd Edn, 1951),
     p. 217.
14   W. H. B. Court, 'Problems of the British Coal Industry Between the Wars',
     Economic History Review, vol. 15 (1945).
15   M. W. Kirby, 'The Control of Competition in British Coal Mining in the
     Thirties', *Economic History Review*, vol. 26 (1973).
16   S. G. Sturmey, *British Shipping and World Competition* (1962); L. Jones,
     Shipbuilding in Britain (1957); Allen, *British Industries.*
17   D. L. Burn, *The Economic History of Steelmaking 1867-1939* (1940).
18   J. C. Carr and W. A. Taplin, *History of the British Steel Industry* (1962).
19   T. H. Burnham and G. O. Hoskins, *Iron and Steel in Britain, 1870-1930*
     (1943).
20   F. M. L. Thompson, *English Landed Society in the Nineteenth Century*
     (1963), pp. 332-3.
21   K. A. H. Murray, *Agriculture* (1955).
22   H. J. Dyos and D. H. Aldcroft, *British Transport: An Economic Survey*
     (1969).
23   D. H. Aldcroft, *British Railways in Transition: The Economic Problems of
     Britain's Railways since 1914* (1968).
24   D. H. Aldcroft, *The Inter-War Economy: Britain 1919-1939* (1970), p. 216.
25   G. Walker, *Road and Rail* (2nd Edn, 1947), p. 128.
26   D. C. Coleman, *Courtaulds: An Economic and Social History, Rayon* (1969)
27   S. B. Saul, 'The Motor Industry in Britain to 1914', *Business History*,
     vol. 5 (1962).
28   Alfred Plummer, *New British Industries in the Twentieth Century* (1937),
     p. 87.
29   Plummer, *New British Industries* pp. 81-2.
30   Plummer, *New British Industries* p. 84.
31   Plummer, *New British Industries* p. 12.
32   Aldcroft, *The Inter-War Economy* p. 202.
33   Dowie, 'Growth in the Inter-War Period', *Economic History Review* (1968),
     table 1, p. 108.
34   See Chapter 6 on Depression and Recovery.
35   Richardson, 'The New Industries', *Oxford Economic Papers* (1961).
36   Allen, *British Industries*, p. 40.
37   Political and Economic Planning, *Report on the Location of Industry*
     (1939), p. 17.
38   Leslie Hannah, 'Managerial Innovation and the Rise of the Large Scale
     Company in Interwar Britain', *Economic History Review*, vol. 27 (1974).
39   M. Compton and E. H. Bott, *British Industry* (1940), p. 252.
40   See Chapter 4 dealing with Economic Policy.
41   D. H. Aldcroft, 'The Early History and Development of Export Credit
     Insurance in Great Britain, 1919-39', *The Manchester School*, vol. 30 (1962)
42   Kirby, 'The Control of Competition', *Economic History Review* (1973).
43   Compton and Bott, *British Industry*, p. 16.

Chapter 4

Economic Policy in the Interwar Period

I *The Nature and Scope of Economic Policy*

In dealing with economic policy in the interwar period we are concerned not simply with developments in economic theory, but with the many influences which may affect thinking about government intervention, or non-intervention, in the economy. Apart from current economic ideas, the economic policy of governments is likely also to reflect the nature of political events and personalities, the influence of important pressure groups, the machinery of policy making, the means of implementing policy and, perhaps also, sheer irrationality on the part of decision makers. The policies which emerge from such a variety of complex influences may be difficult to define precisely in generally acceptable terms, and interpreters will almost inevitably disagree about the exact nature and effectiveness of particular policies. Nevertheless, economic policy in the interwar years has proved to be one of the most fascinating subjects in modern economic history, and one which is likely to receive increasing attention from historians in the future now that the policy documents of the period have become available for study.

The interest in interwar economic policy is not hard to explain: in these years economic events and problems appeared for a time to transcend all others and, by general consensus, acquired an urgency which could hardly be denied. At the same time, and largely in consequence, there were major developments in the field of economic theory as the ideas of Keynes eventually superseded those of the 'classical' economists, and a commitment to a radically different government role involving increasing intervention and 'planning' acquired broader support — in people's minds if not in actuality. As always, economic policy evolved from the constant interplay between ideas and economic circumstances, but the former tended to lag behind the latter and ideas were only beginning to catch up with events when the period ended. The Keynesian view of the economy became acceptable not simply because of its inherent economic logic, but because it appeared to be increasingly relevant to the march of events. The continuation of chronically high unemployment provided increasing evidence for Keynes's argument that the economy, if left to its own devices, would not necessarily tend to stabilise at the full employment level. Also, the first world war had accelerated the rising trend in government economic involvement and responsibility and postwar decontrol did not reverse the trend. Even where governments attempted to deny themselves an economic role, the facts dictated otherwise and a return to nineteenth-century circumstances was clearly impossible. In the interwar years government expenditure was more than double the pre-1914 level. While most of this increase consisted of transfer payments, rather than actual government spending on goods and services, it represented a substantial aggregative increase in the economic importance of government. Qualitatively, as well as quantitatively, there were significant changes in the role of government. New responsibilities were acquired in many areas – albeit often reluctantly. In the Keynesian system governments were to find a means of fulfilling a role which had already been forced upon them by circumstances. But the full realisation of this came only after 1939.

In the modern world two basic aims can be discerned in government intervention: the first aim is short-run economic 'management' designed to smooth out cyclical fluctuations in the economy. Secondly, many modern governments have accepted longer term commitments to run a 'planned' economy, usually with the intention of improving the rate of economic growth. In interwar Britain neither of these aims was clearly understood or attempted. But they were, nevertheless, to be the legacies of the economic turmoil and policy debates which took place in the two decades before 1939.

Apart from its long-run historical significance, interwar economic policy is of interest for the prominent influence personalities played in its making, a feature less evident in more recent times. Policy between the wars involved a small and fascinating group of men: leading politicians – including Churchill, Snowden, Neville Chamberlain and Sir John Simon; leading academic economists – including Keynes, Pigou, Robbins; prominent officials – such as Montague Norman and Sir Otto Niemeyer, and the trade union leader Ernest Bevin. In retrospect a number of writers have been tempted to divide these protagonists of ideas into those who were 'right' and those who were 'wrong', but such divisions can sometimes do less than justice to the complexities of circumstances and argument. The personalities referred to inevitably reflect the institutional pattern of policy making. As the importance of state intervention increased the Chancellor of the Exchequer became a more important political figure and the Treasury emerged as the most important institution in determining policy. At the same time, the Bank of England, particularly during Montague Norman's term as chairman, was an important influence and the role of pressure groups including employer associations and the Trades Union Congress increased. However, the one important attempt at a radical change in policy determination was not a success. In January 1930 Macdonald created an Economic Advisory Council made up of trade unionists (Bevin and Citrine), industrialists (Sir John Cadman, Sir Arthur Balfour, Sir Josiah Stamp and Sir Andrew Duncan) and academic economists (Keynes, Cole, Tawney). The Council was notable only for its continual disagreement, its lack of a clearly defined role, and its failure to make inroads into official policy.

It is natural for historians to seek some relationship between political philosophy and economic policy, but such a relationship is not easy to establish in the interwar years which witnessed the demise of the Liberal Party as a serious contender for power, the failure of the Labour Party to apply socialist principles during two short periods of minority rule, and long periods of dominance by the Conservative Party when it lacked any clearly defined general economic policy. Successive chancellors implemented policies which were determined in the main by Treasury and Bank of England officials who reflected orthodox economic thinking and pressure group influence, rather than political creed. The debates on economic policy which took place had little reference to party lines. Radical policies were urged by individuals and minority groups in all three main parties, but official party policy was swayed only in the Liberal case when, in the 1929 election campaign, Lloyd George failed to impress the electorate with a radical manifesto inspired by Keynes. The transformation in economic policy which was necessary to solve the economic problems of the interwar years did not really begin to come about until Keynes, after years of frustration at the political fringes, set out to convert academic economists with the publication in 1936 of his *General Theory of Employment, Interest and Money*. A few years later the emergency created by the second world war produced new circumstances and brought Keynes himself to the Treasury. For a time at least, ideas were at last able to steal a march on events.

Governments 1916-40

1916-22	Coalition	
1922-24	Conservative	
1924	Labour	(minority)
1924-29	Conservative	
1929-31	Labour	(minority)
1931-1935	National	(basically Conservative)
1935-1940	National	

Prime Ministers

	Assumed office	Party
D. Lloyd George	December 1916	Liberal
A. Bonar Law	October 1922	Conservative
S. Baldwin	May 1923	Conservative
J. R. MacDonald	January 1924	Labour
S. Baldwin	November 1924	Conservative
J. R. MacDonald	June 1929	Labour (until 1931)
S. Baldwin	June 1935	Conservative
N. Chamberlain	May 1937	Conservative
W. Churchill	May 1940	Conservative

Chancellors of the Exchequer

A. Bonar Law	December 1916	Conservative
N. Chamberlain	January 1919	Conservative
Sir R. Horne	April 1921	Conservative
S. Baldwin	October 1922	Conservative
N. Chamberlain	August 1923	Conservative
P. Snowden	January 1924	Labour
W. Churchill	November 1924	Conservative
P. Snowden	June 1929	Labour
N. Chamberlain	November 1931	Conservative
Sir J. Simon	May 1937	National Liberal
Sir K. Wood	May 1940	Conservative

II *Postwar Reconstruction*

During the later years of the first world war the British government, under Lloyd George, accepted for the first time responsibility for the national economy. This dramatic change in governmental attitude was purely temporary. It was followed in the immediate postwar years by a rapid dismantling of controls — a process which is somewhat harder to explain than the acceptance of economic responsibility during the wartime emergency. Despite decontrol, no British government after the war could totally and convincingly deny economic responsibility. Decontrol proved to be difficult and incomplete, but in relation to aspirations which were unleashed during the war, it was devastating. By the early months of 1920 the vision of a 'Land fit for Heroes' had given way to bitter disillusion.

The establishment of wartime economic control came only in 1917-18 after the attempt to mobilise economic and manpower resources by free market methods had proved to be inadequate, inefficient and socially unjust. During the 'Business as Usual' phase of the war strategic supplies were not sufficiently forthcoming and social tensions were created by the taking of excess profits and the erosion of living standards by inflation which aggravated labour relations. Comprehensive control was an essential basis for the government's attempt to increase the production and supply of munitions, food and other strategic materials while minimising, as far as possible, undesirable economic disruption and dislocation. The most essential and important aspect of wartime intervention was price control, which was effective, although incomplete. By 1918 the government had direct or indirect control over all industries of significance, as well as agriculture, and water and rail transport were under direct state management. The marketing of imports and both home produced and foreign food was also subject to direct control. Although relatively brief, the wartime economic experience demonstrated the enormous scope in terms of the production, distribution and redistribution of both goods and income which was potentially at the disposal of government influence. As a result the attitudes of businessmen, trade unions and the general public towards the state changed radically. As a 'national' effort the war demanded sacrifices from all sections of the community and led to a dramatic, if temporary, enhancement in working-class status and aspirations. The imposition of state control gave rise to demands for state welfare. At the same time control fostered the growth and importance of trade unions and established a new role for the government in industrial relations. Businessmen, meanwhile, began to appreciate the possibilities of state assistance to industry. Thus wartime control gave rise to new attitudes which were of long-run significance for postwar economic policy.

The need for a reconstruction policy was realised at quite an early stage during the war, but at first this was little more than a desire to avoid the kind of adjustment problems in the labour market and in the export industries which had followed the Napoleonic and Boer wars. In 1916 the *Committee on Commercial and Industrial Policy after the*

War (the Balfour Committee) was established to consider how Britain might best regain her commercial supremacy in peacetime circumstances. The Committee's report, which was to form the basis of postwar policy, placed a premium on industrial efficiency and recommended rapid decontrol after the war. Also in 1916 a Reconstruction Committee was established by the Asquith Government and in July 1917 this was elevated by Lloyd George into the Ministry of Reconstruction. The Ministry gave particular attention to the demobilisation problem and to the labour market in general, besides considering a variety of other questions ranging from future raw material supplies to Empire settlement schemes. Both the Balfour Committee and the Ministry of Reconstruction are significant in that they represent early, although largely futile, steps towards economic planning. They remained as important examples for the future.

Despite the limited scope and activities of the Ministry, reconstruction under Lloyd George acquired characteristically far-reaching, if vague, connotations which appeared to follow logically from the call for sacrifices on the part of the men in the trenches and the working class in general. As defined by Lloyd George, 'Reconstruction was nothing less than an effort to correct the weaknesses in the British social and economic fabric revealed by the war'.[1] In the general election campaign of 1918 he made specific pledges covering a wide range of social and economic affairs. In part at least, his politicised version of reconstruction must be seen as a not unsuccessful attempt to woo the working-class vote from the Labour Party, which emerged with new vigour from the war. By 1921 decontrol and depression in a general atmosphere of class bitterness made this policy seem, in retrospect, an empty mockery.

The failure of reconstruction policies within such a short time has been attributed to the economic circumstances which emerged after the war: the brief postwar boom which made rapid decontrol not only possible but generally desirable, and the subsequent depression and economy measures which killed or mutilated most welfare schemes. Essentially this view amounts to a condemnation of the deficiencies of wartime administration and planning which failed to foresee these problems. More fundamentally, however, the failure was political and social rather than administrative. Whether we seek an explanation in terms of an absence of political and social maturity or in the peculiarities of the 1918 election, the fact remains that Britain failed after 1918 to generate the kind of national effort that was forthcoming in 1945. The relatively poor showing of the Labour and Liberal Parties in 1918 effectively killed any possibility of a radical reconstruction policy. After the declaration of peace Lloyd George himself was preoccupied with machinations at Versailles and his coalition government was dependent on people who felt they had a vested interest in returning in most respects and as far as was possible to the prewar system. Their conviction and general success were undoubtedly aided by high profit and wage expectations during the postwar boom and the consequent ease of decontrol. In the prevailing political and economic climate, continued general control was neither desirable nor possible.

III *The Gold Standard*

With the possible exception of unemployment, no single issue of interwar economic policy has excited more interest than the gold standard. It is generally agreed that the decision to return to gold after the first world war was the basic factor in determining the pattern of economic policy in the 1920s and it might also be argued that the forced departure from gold in 1931 was a liberating influence which made new attitudes and policies possible in the 1930s. Both contemporaries and more recent writers have presented conflicting views about the exact nature of the gold standard mechanism and the significance for the British economy of the most important policy decision of the 1920s — Winston Churchill's decision that Britain should return to gold at the prewar parity on 28 April 1925.

Under the gold standard system, which became firmly established during the latter part of the nineteenth century, Britain and other countries operating the standard had fixed the prices of their currencies in terms of gold. Central banks were prepared to buy or sell unlimited quantities of gold in exchange for their currencies at these fixed prices (from 1717 the Bank of England's selling price for gold was £2·89 per ounce) and there were no government restrictions on the international movement of gold. In theory at least, this system provided an automatic adjustment mechanism for dealing with international trade imbalances and relative price fluctuations. If, for example, a country experienced an unfavourable external account as a result of an excess of imports over exports, then the market value of its currency became cheap in relation both to other currencies and the official value in terms of gold. If the shift became sufficiently large to cover transfer costs, then speculators would find it profitable to buy gold from the country concerned for conversion into other currencies. The resulting outflow of gold from the country concerned gave rise to an internal chain reaction including rising interest rates, reduced money supply and credit restrictions. This in turn led to a situation of rising unemployment and deflation. The consequences of a relative fall in the domestic price level were likely to be a reduction in imports and an increase in exports leading to an improvement in the external account.

While in theory smooth and automatic adjustments of this kind were possible, the apparent success of the gold standard system in the late nineteenth century owed a great deal to Britain's historically exceptional and temporary international economic predominance. Even so, the adjustments which took place were far from being as simple and automatic as supporters of the system suggested and considerable financial manipulation by central banks was necessary. While the resulting adjustments were relatively smooth in most of the advanced industrial economies, including Britain, primary producing economies experienced more violent fluctuations and tended to bear the brunt of the adjustment process.

Nevertheless, from the British point of view the gold standard system had worked extremely well up to 1914 and, along with free trade, its operation had coincided with Britain's greatest period of relative economic prosperity. At the same time, the growing dependence on invisible earnings, accelerated by the effects of the first world war, meant an increasing reliance on financial institutions and processes which were geared to the gold standard machinery. During the war the system became inoperable and it was necessary to maintain the price of sterling by official market support. In other words, sterling became a 'managed' currency. In January 1918, the *Committee on Currency and Foreign Exchanges after the War* was appointed under Lord Cunliffe, and in August 1918 it produced its *First Interim Report*. There was virtually no opposition to the view of the Cunliffe Committee that Britain should return to gold at the prewar parity as soon as circumstances made this possible. The possibility of returning to the gold standard at a lower parity than $4·86 = £1 was never seriously considered. In effect this meant a policy of returning to gold when the British price level, distorted by wartime inflation, regained its prewar relationship with American prices, which had not risen to the same extent. In immediate postwar circumstances a return to gold at the 1914 parity was impossible because of the depreciation of sterling against other currencies as a result of wartime inflation. Before a return to gold could be considered, the Bank of England had to regain control over the British money market and the British price level had to fall in relation to overseas prices, either as a result of deflation in Britain, or inflation elsewhere, or both. The gold standard was formally renounced in April 1919 and sterling continued as a 'managed' currency, but the long-run aim of returning to gold remained clearly established and conditioned the whole approach to economic policy.

By the early months of 1923 the Bank of England had regained control of the money market and deflation had proceeded sufficiently far to make a return to gold within the bounds of short-run possibility. In the meantime the price of deflation in terms of unemployment, falling money wages and labour market tensions had become apparent. There were signs of divisions of interest between, on the one hand, the City of London which believed it had a vested interest in the gold standard, and on the other organised labour and industrialists who felt themselves to be the direct victims of deflationary policies aimed at making a return to gold possible.[2] Nevertheless, the main weight of opinion remained in favour of the official policy and there was little general support for Keynes's *Tract on Monetary Reform* (1923) which argued against a return to gold because of the high costs which this involved in terms of deflation and unemployment, and suggested a system of managed currencies.

Churchill's actual decision to return to the gold standard in 1925 can be seen, in retrospect, as a mistake, but given the state of existing economic knowledge and expert opinion it was a rational political act. While Churchill, far from being uninformed about the dangers of a return to gold, was aware of alternative proposals, he knew that these proposals had little support from politically significant pressure groups or from expert opinion. As one recent writer has argued:

'The decision to return to the gold standard at prewar par was more or less inevitable, particularly after the rise in the dollar exchange. Successive governments had committed themselves to such a policy goal; the overwhelming majority of opinion accepted it; the specialists in the Bank, the Treasury and the Chamberlain-Bradbury Committee were prepared to force the necessary adjustments. Economic analysis, as such, had little to do with the decision: analysts such as Pigou merely played a "priestly" role, justifying decisions taken for more deep-seated reasons'.[3]

At the practical level, the advice offered to Churchill in 1925 suggested that a return could be achieved relatively painlessly because of the rise in American prices and the expectation that this rise would continue. The price of returning, in terms of deflation, was not expected to be unbearable. At the same time it was suggested that a restoration of the gold standard would promote international economic and financial co-operation which would enable London to regain its prewar position in international finance. This in turn was expected to alleviate Britain's export and unemployment problems and in this sense the policy could be regarded as a general panacea for Britain's economic ills. Essentially however, the momentum emanated from the

City of London which desired an end to uncertainty and a return to a system under which it might be possible to remove restrictions on foreign lending. From the City point of view, these aims clearly took precedence over the export and unemployment problems. In a more general sense, the gold standard offered a solution to the widespread fear of inflation which prevailed in financial circles and it meant a formal restoration of economic control from political to financial hands. By returning to the gold standard mechanism the government was in effect opting out of direct responsibility for economic management.

The anticipated rise in American prices, which had made the return to gold in 1925 seem feasible, did not in fact occur. As a result, sterling in relation to the dollar was overvalued by approximately 10%. Other European countries returned to gold at lower parities, thus depreciating their currencies against sterling. As a result Britain's export industries were at a price disadvantage which compounded their already formidable difficulties. The price of the return in terms of export problems and deflationary pressures, was pointed out by Keynes in his polemical pamphlet entitled *The Economic Consequences of Mr Churchill* (1925).

In the second half of the 1920s the British economy suffered relatively high rates of unemployment compared with other industrial countries. There can be little doubt that the decision of 1925 was a factor in this situation. From Britain's point of view the restored gold standard was not a success. Because of the poor performance of exports, sterling failed to regain its prewar strength. Under the gold standard mechanism a full solution to this situation could only have come through severe deflation involving sharp reductions in money wages. In a situation of already severe unemployment and class antagonism such a solution, particularly after the General Strike of 1926, was politically impossible. After 1925 the gold mechanism proved impossible to operate in the classical sense. While mild deflationary policies, including high interest rates, were implemented, Britain remained on the gold standard as a result of financial manipulation and expedients, rather than by allowing the system to operate in an unrestrained way. Particularly after 1929, when balance of payments problems became more severe, the system became increasingly dependent on short-term funds which had been attracted to London by high interest rates. It was the withdrawal of these funds in 1931 which precipitated the crisis of that year when Britain was eventually forced off the gold standard.

IV *The Role of the Budget*
In the modern economy the raising and spending of money by governments is regarded by most economists as the most important

available means of overall economic management. In the two decades following the second world war it was accepted as axiomatic that in times of depression governments should spend more than they raise in the form of revenue, in order to reflate the economy, and during periods of inflation and pressure on resources they should seek to do the opposite. As a result of these views, first systematically expounded by Keynes, the budget has acquired a significance in modern economic policy which was almost entirely absent in the interwar years. Orthodox economic opinion before Keynes saw no need to make a fundamental distinction between the national budget and the budget of any private company or individual. Like the budget of the private individual, it was believed that the state should always attempt to balance its budget. In so far as any distinction was made it was in favour of minimising state taxation and spending, and achieving a small budget surplus for the purpose of redeeming national debt.

This 'Gladstonian' view of public finance, which appeared to be soundly based in terms of both ethics and political economy, had presented few problems before 1914 when the financial and economic role of government was relatively minor. After 1920 the enormous enhancement in governmental influence, together with the emergence of a massive unemployment problem, rendered this approach singularly inappropriate. Nevertheless it was retained at least ostensibly by most chancellors in the interwar period, and Snowden and Chamberlain followed this line with much enthusiasm. While the arguments varied in emphasis over time, in summary the orthodox approach insisted that balanced budgets were an essential safeguard against inflation and an important factor in sustaining business confidence and in maintaining the faith of foreigners in the value of the currency.

After the first world war the desire to present each April a balanced public account of receipts and expenditure over the previous year became an exceedingly difficult operation which taxed the ability of successive chancellors. The war had been financed in a relatively expensive and inefficient way by relying heavily on internal loans, raised at high interest, rather than on taxation. In the 1920s the legacy of debt left by the war absorbed roughly 40% of annual budget expenditure in servicing and redemption. As the price level fell, the real burden of debt increased, and interest payments and debt redemption from revenue almost certainly meant a transference of funds from consumers with a high propensity to consume to those with a lower propensity, thus tending to reduce aggregate demand. In the long run, the problem was considerably reduced by repayments, funding operations and, after 1932, the cheap money policy; but throughout the entire period public debt management remained a serious budgetary constraint.

Along with the need to service and repay the greatly enhanced national debt, postwar chancellors were also faced with much higher social service expenditure on poor relief, unemployment insurance, health insurance, old age, widows and war pensions and substantial new outlays in housing and education. While a sharp fall (about 50%) in public spending inevitably occurred immediately after the war, public spending remained at roughly double the prewar level and there was no possibility of returning to the 1914 situation.

On the revenue side the war left a legacy of greatly increased direct and indirect taxation which tended to remain although the excess profits duty was removed in 1921 and the standard rate of income tax was reduced in 1922/3 and 1925. However, the standard rate never fell below 20p in the pound in the interwar years and the taxation structure as a whole remained considerably more progressive than in the period before 1914. The heavier burden of direct taxation, together with rising expenditure on social services, promoted some redistribution of income in favour of the poorer sections of the community. Even so, it can hardly be said that the taxation system made significant changes in the extremely uneven distribution of wealth and income. Indirect and regressive taxation remained high, particularly on alcohol and tobacco, and there were further increases with the introduction of general protection in 1932. Apart from protection, there were no major changes in fiscal policy during the period.

The budgetary problem derived from a situation in which chancellors were expected to achieve an annual balance even though, in the short run, revenue and expenditure might move in opposite directions. A downturn in the economy would almost inevitably reduce the yields from direct and indirect taxation; at the same time social service outlays, particularly on unemployment benefits, were likely to increase, while the debt burden, in money terms, remained constant. In fact this was the kind of situation which faced chancellors in most years. The result was a good deal of statistical manipulation, especially during Churchill's period at the exchequer, and a constant, if varying, emphasis on the need for economy in public spending. Severe cuts were made in the early 1920s upon suggestions made by the *Committee on National Expenditure* (1922) headed by Sir Eric Geddes. The 'Geddes Axe' fell particularly severely on social services and education, although almost all aspects of government spending were affected to some degree. From 1924 to 1929 Snowden and Churchill were able to be rather more liberal, but after the downturn in 1929 strict economies again were believed to be necessary. The MacDonald Government disintegrated in 1931 after its failure to agree upon the question of economies, most of which were subsequently imposed by the National Government.

In the absence of detailed studies of the ways in which budget balances were achieved it is not easy to begin to assess the possible economic impact of budgetary policy in the interwar period. Even a strictly balanced budget may, through the 'balanced budget multiplier', affect the level of aggregate demand. There can be no doubt that governments responsible for roughly a quarter of total investment (gross fixed capital formation) and expenditure could, potentially, have had a considerable influence on the level of economic activity. However, because of budget balancing, the influence of fiscal policy was mild. In the first part of the 1920s this influence was most probably deflationary. Between 1925 and 1929 Churchill produced a series of concealed budget deficits which may have given a little stimulus to the economy. From 1929 until 1937 (when defence spending began to rise steeply) Snowden and Chamberlain produced rigidly orthodox budgets which overall were almost certainly deflationary. During the depression Snowden balanced budgets by increasing taxation and reducing expenditure — measures which produced a political crisis and aggravated existing economic difficulties. Nevertheless, balanced budgets were seen as an indispensable element in the recovery programme and during the 1930s British budgets were balanced, at considerable cost, while overseas departures from this practice were ignored. It will be seen that because of the nature of the budget and the obsession with achieving a balance, the direction of budgetary influence during the period as a whole tended to be the direct opposite of what was desirable.

v *Unemployment Policy*

Unemployment will be examined in more detail in the next chapter. The object here is to consider this problem in the general context of economic policy as a whole. In retrospect it may seem obvious that mass unemployment was the most persistent and fundamental economic problem of the interwar years. Many modern commentators on policy have used unemployment as a benchmark against which all policies and aspects of policy can be judged. Measures which increased unemployment tend to be condemned and those which provided some relief are praised. To contemporaries the situation was more complex and it may be misleading to place very heavy emphasis on unemployment. Issues other than unemployment were at various times regarded as being more important and there was never at any time a singular, all-transcending, determination to deal with unemployment as such. The important exceptions to this are Keynes, who had a long-standing concern with the consequences of deflation, and possibly Mosley. This difference in attitude between contemporaries and modern commentators can be explained in terms of different economic concepts and in particular different views about the causes of unemployment. To contemporaries unemployment was merely a symptom, rather than a disease.

Before 1914 unemployment was often viewed as a social rather than an economic problem and as something which arose from essentially abnormal circumstances. Economic theory suggested that the economy would naturally tend towards full employment and that this was the normal state of affairs. This belief rested on the economic doctrine known as 'Say's Law' which suggested that since production created its own consumption, underconsumption or overproduction were impossible. Where unemployment arose it was attributed basically to three sources: first, it was believed that there were social tendencies, including idleness and drunkenness, giving rise to 'voluntary' unemployment which would only be encouraged by generous relief for the unemployed. Secondly, it was recognised that unemployment could arise from casual labour systems in some industries and from technological, structural and seasonal changes causing decline in certain sectors. Thirdly, it was clear that a more general pattern of redundancy periodically arose as a result of trade cycles.

After 1890 there was increasing concern about poverty in general, and about unemployment which was recognised as a basic cause of poverty. An attempt to remedy the inadequacies of the poor law in providing unemployment relief was made through the establishment of the national insurance scheme in 1911. The scheme provided for unemployment insurance in a few industries which were particularly vulnerable to instability and in 1919 these provisions were extended to cover most of the workforce. In 1909 William Beveridge, in *Unemployment: A Problem of Industry*, argued that the problem might be eased by an increase in the mobility of labour. As a means of encouraging mobility he successfully advocated a network of labour exchanges throughout the country. A more direct solution in terms of massive countercyclical public works was strongly urged by the *Minority Report of the Royal Commission on the Poor Laws* (1909), but met with less success. This was not a novel idea. In Britain, and more extensively in Empire countries, local authorities had frequently implemented public works schemes during periods of severe unemployment. On the whole these schemes had been too limited and piecemeal to have an appreciable effect on the general level of unemployment and, from the administrative viewpoint, they were regarded as being wasteful and inefficient. There was little support therefore for a general extension of public works schemes.

Orthodox economics suggested that the solution to the unemployment problem lay in the market mechanism, if only it could be allowed to work freely. Structural unemployment could be solved by mobility of labour, and relief could only reduce this mobility. Cyclical unemployment was the result of excessive rigidity in factor costs and prices caused by trade union pressure and restrictive practices in business. In particular, it was suggested that wage inflexibility was a basic cause of unemployment. This view was rooted in the theory of diminishing returns which stated that the extra output resulting from additional inputs of labour (or any other factor) would eventually begin to decline if other factors were maintained at a constant level. It followed that an employer would continue to employ labour only up to the point where the output of the last man engaged (marginal product) was equal in value to the average wage. When unemployment occurred it was an indication that the level of wages was too high to ensure full employment of the workforce. The solution lay in the reduction of wages. This remarkable line of abstract reasoning, when applied to the real world situation, suggested that the solution to unemployment lay in the workers' own hands. By demanding individual-ly, or collectively through a trade union, an excessive wage he was creating unemployment and becoming, in effect, a victim of his own greed!

At the beginning of the interwar period, the understanding of unemployment was limited and erroneous. While it was accepted that the government should attempt to alleviate suffering by establishing labour exchanges, and through contributory insurance, economic theory suggested that a real solution could only come from market flexibility and not from government action. By the end of the 1920s the official attitude had hardened into what became known as the 'Treasury view'. This was most clearly stated in the White Paper of 1929[4] which was a reply to the Liberal Party's *Britain's Industrial Future* (1928) and Lloyd George's 1929 election manifesto, *We Can Conquer Unemployment*. According to the Treasury view substantial reductions in unemployment could only come as a result of wage flexibility, which meant lower money wages, greater efficiency and structural change in industry. Direct government intervention in the form of massive investment in public works schemes was rejected on the ground that since there was only a fixed amount of savings available for investment in the economy, public works investment would simply divert capital from 'normal' or private channels without increasing the aggregate level of investment and employment. Public works would push up interest rates in the private sector by diverting capital into wasteful and inefficient channels, creating at the same time considerable administrative difficulties. From this point of view, it was believed that the scope for independent action by the British government was very limited and that any drastic action was likely to damage the long-run prospects for British industry, particularly in export markets. The main hope for a solution to the unemployment problem lay in a revival of the international economy.

This rationalisation of inactivity dominated government thinking in relation to unemployment throughout the entire interwar period. In post-Keynesian retrospect the Treasury view is, superficially at least, easily condemned. In the *General Theory*, Keynes rejected the argument that full employment would result naturally from market forces, given factor price flexibility. The level of total output (and employment) was determined by aggregate economic demand (consumption plus investment plus government spending) which might be less than was necessary to ensure full employment. In such a situation, wage cuts were likely to increase rather than reduce unemployment by reducing aggregate demand. The only possible solution was through government intervention to encourage private investment by reducing interest rates, to raise consumption by budget deficits, and to increase public investment through public works and other schemes.

In terms of suggested lines of policy, Keynes and the Treasury were diametrically opposed. We now know that Keynes was right and that the policies of his opponents, far from improving the employment situation, actually made it worse. Unfortunately, although Keynes had consistently urged expansionist policies since the early 1920s, his reasoning was not fully outlined or generally understood until the end of the period and his impact on employment policy was minimal. Keynes was not the only advocate of government spending to solve unemployment. Long before 1914 J. A. Hobson had stressed underconsumption as a cause of unemployment.[5] Ernest Bevin and Sir Oswald Mosley were other prominent figures who suggested action along similar lines. In reviewing interwar economic policy some writers have tended to see the situation as one in which absolute truth and light confronted folly and ignorance, with the Treasury, backed by vested interests in the City of London, clinging to outmoded economic beliefs long after they had been refuted. This view can be given emotional overtones in terms of the human tragedy of unemployment and the intellectual bankruptcy of certain political leaders. It is quite natural that the Labour Party which, theoretically, represented the working class, should be criticised on its record. During the brief period of office in 1924 little was done and nothing was learned about unemployment:

'For the most part, the party emerged little the wiser from the 1924 experience with unemployment. The full price of failure to grasp the inadequacies of Labour's unemployment policy was not paid until the humiliation of 1931'.[6]

Similarly, the 1929-31 Labour administration has been accused of having had no policy for unemployment and its leaders are accused of having been blinded by a mentally stultifying vision of utopian socialism:

'Basically it believed that socialism was the cure for poverty, of which unemployment was simply the most vivid manifestation. It thought in terms of a total solution: but socialism would clearly take a very long time, for it would not be established until the majority of people were ready for it. In the meantime, the Labour Party simply did not know what to do'.[7]

While criticism of this kind is at least partially valid, it has probably gone too far. Failure to solve a problem does not necessarily indicate lack of a policy. In fact, the Labour leadership, together with other interwar administrations, did have policies which were couched in the Treasury view. Snowden, the Labour chancellor, believed himself to be acting on the highest motives of principle and intellect when he wholeheartedly endorsed the Treasury line. His policies, in consequence, were highly unpopular amongst Labour supporters and ruinous to the Party's political prospects. Nevertheless, Snowden sincerely believed that he was acting not only in the national interest but also in the interest of the working class.

The Treasury view survived; first, because it was firmly based in orthodox economic theory which was not successfully challenged by Keynes until 1936; secondly, because it appeared to support the immediate interests of employers and other pressure groups favouring wage reductions; thirdly, because it placed full employment behind other economic priorities including price stability, the free trade system and the gold standard. In the policy arguments leading up to the crisis of 1931, Keynes had insufficient influence. His main institutional connection was with the electorally defunct Liberal Party and he had no position of power to speak from. His influence depended upon the cogency of his ideas which were not fully formed. While the essence of the *General Theory* can be discerned in his earlier policy proposals, these were insufficiently backed by detailed argument to sway academic opinion. There were times when his views were judged to be vague and vacillating. During the financial crisis he did not advocate Britain's departure from the gold standard and suggested a revenue tariff as a means of solving budgetary problems, probably because he believed devaluation to be out of the question. But his proposal for a tariff aroused considerable opposition and was probably a tactical error. During 1931 his line of economic thought was developed to a more sophisticated level in the hearings of the Macmillan Committee where he opposed the Treasury view. In the same year Kahn's theory of the multiplier provided an indispensable analytical tool in the Keynesian system. Unfortunately by this time the opportunity for radical policy changes had been overtaken by events.

While it is not impossible to attempt to defend the Treasury view in terms of modern economic concepts,[8] its best defence must rest at a more lowly level. It can be argued that given certain premises, and the existing state of economic knowledge and political power, the Treasury view was a more coherent, logical and consistent basis for policy than the rival schemes suggested by Keynes, Mosley and others before 1931. These schemes made little sense to the orthodox mind which believed that expansionist policies, by causing wage and price increases, would undermine business confidence and intensify balance of payments problems. A rise in the British price level, relative to international prices, must inevitably lead to higher imports, lower exports, balance of payments difficulties and pressure on sterling. Agreement on a policy of depreciation or protection might have made expansionist policies more acceptable, but this was not forthcoming before 1931. The main aim, in fact, was to preserve the gold standard through improved export performance and a strengthened balance of payments. This could only be done by making British exports more competitive by lowering costs. Given these priorities, the appropriate policy was deflation and the acceptance of heavy unemployment.

The argument between the expansionists and the orthodox related not only to economic concepts but also to economic and political priorities. It is impossible to separate the unemployment problem from the general context of economic problems. Even if the Treasury had embraced Keynesian thinking in 1929-30, it would still have had to make painful decisions about sterling, the gold standard and, possibly, about protection. It is even possible that as in the 1960s, a 'Keynesian' Treasury might still have pursued deflationary policies.

VI *Cheap Money*

Britain's forced departure from the gold standard in 1931, and the subsequent depreciation of sterling, provided immediate relief from external financial pressure and gave scope for new economic policy. Unfortunately, this scope was realised only in a very limited way. In April 1932 the Exchange Equalisation Account was established to buy and sell sterling, as necessary, in order to stabilise the value of the currency. On the whole the Equalisation Account was highly successful in its operations. The establishment of a managed currency gave new flexibility to internal monetary policy which no longer needed to be linked directly to external considerations. It became possible to move towards a sharp reversal of previous monetary policy by a general reduction in interest rates. In the first half of 1932 there was a heavy flow of international funds into London as a result of new confidence in sterling and lack of confidence in other currencies including the dollar. This flow of 'hot' money created upward pressure on the newly established market rate for sterling, making it possible, and indeed desirable, to reduce the official rate of interest. At the same time, the traditional desire to reduce the interest burden on public debt had become more urgent with the general demand for economies and the belief that sacrifices should be borne by rentiers as well as people on the dole. It was decided therefore that the time was opportune for a huge public debt conversion as part of a general reduction of interest rates throughout the money market. In June 1932 Bank Rate was reduced to 2% and it remained at this level until 1939. At the same time £2,085 million of War Loan, about one quarter of the total national debt, was converted from 5% to 3½% interest.

Initially at least, the introduction of 'cheap money' must be seen as a negative and orthodox move which was designed, primarily, to reduce the interest burden of public debt. It was made possible by the strong standing of a newly depreciated currency and a general international tendency towards falling interest rates. However, once 'cheap money' became established more was claimed for it than had originally been envisaged and it was seen by some, including Chamberlain, as a major element in the recovery programme. As it happened, 'cheap money' was in line with the expansionist policies suggested by Keynes and others. Low interest rates might be expected to stimulate increased investment and a rising level of economic activity. In fact there is no evidence that lower interest rates had any appreciable effect on the level of investment in general. Capital was not in short supply and 'cheap money' was less crucial than other factors in restoring business confidence. Industrial investors were far more concerned with the general climate of economic expectations than with the reduction of a few percentage points in the price of capital. While it has been claimed that low interest rates played a crucial part in the housing boom this claim must be sharply qualified. The upswing in the building cycle was already under way before the reduction in interest rates, and building societies and other financial intermediaries were tardy in passing on the benefits of lower interest rates to their clients. While cheaper mortgage and bank credit may have had some influence on the building boom, this was probably less important than reductions in material costs and rising real incomes.

Although 'limited in terms of policy concept and economic impact, 'cheap money' is significant as virtually the only expansionist measure of the early 1930s. After the economic crisis of 1931 Britain had to some extent shed the external constraints which had imposed a dead hand on economic policy in the 1920s. The abandonment of the gold standard, the successful establishment of a managed currency by means of the Exchange Equalisation Account, and the introduction of protection and Empire preference meant that external pressures were no longer a prime consideration in determining economic policy. After the 1933 London Conference it was clear that there was little possibility for successful international economic co-operation. In these circumstances, with a partially insulated domestic economy, an expansionist internal policy was far more feasible than in the 1920s. Yet, with the notable exception of 'cheap money', the orthodox approach continued. While increasing lip service was paid in the 1930s to 'economic planning' along Keynesian and other lines and attention was given to overseas economic experiments such as the 'New Deal' in the United States, British economic policy remained essentially in the 1920s mould. Although some attempt may be made to justify the orthodox economic policies pursued in the 1920s, such justification had vanished after 1931 when the old system had clearly failed.

VII *The Return to Protection*

During the late nineteenth and early twentieth centuries Britain continued to adhere to the free trade system when other countries were turning increasingly towards protection. While free trade did not mean the complete absence of tariffs, only a small proportion of imports were subject to duty. The principal items were liquor, tobacco, tea and sugar, and the duties imposed were designed to raise revenue rather than to afford protection from foreign competition. In the last two decades of the nineteenth century support for the abandonment of free trade in favour of a system of Empire preferences and protection began to gain ground, particularly in the Conservative Party. Nevertheless, both academic and public opinion remained strongly in favour of free trade and in the 1906 election the Conservatives were decisively defeated after putting forward a protectionist programme.

The argument for free trade rested on the theory of comparative economic advantage, which suggested that international output and income would be maximised if all countries specialised in their most efficient areas of production and traded goods freely. Any interference by governments in imposing tariffs or other protective devices, which hindered the free movements of goods, meant a reduction in world efficiency and income. While it rested upon rather unrealistic assumptions,[9] the theory of comparative advantage had a powerful internal logic which was sufficient to defeat any theoretical argument for protection, apart from the special case for 'infant industries'. In the nineteenth century, free trade had been a policy which enabled Britain to take the fullest possible advantage of her commercial supremacy. To some extent the policy must be seen as a rationalisation of this supremacy. It is significant that the countries which began to challenge Britain after 1870 did so to some extent by relying on protection. Nevertheless British free trade was something more than simply a selfish rationalisation. The free trade ethic, as developed by Cobden, Bright, Gladstone and others, was seen as a programme for world peace and prosperity. The more nations became involved in trade, the more they stood to lose from warfare which disrupted trade. At the same time free trade ensured that consumers received the cheapest possible supplies from the most efficient sources. Cheap food was a most important influence in raising real incomes, particularly in Britain.

Although there were moves, on an international basis, towards increased protection in the years before 1914, these were relatively modest and selective. The war was important in promoting the trend towards protectionism. During the war, trade was closely controlled and many of these controls were not relinquished. In postwar circumstances much higher levels of protection were imposed by most countries to protect industries which had developed during the war and to ease postwar problems of unemployment and economic instability. In Britain the war brought the first protectionist measures in more than half a century. The McKenna Duties in 1915 imposed a 33½% duty on 'luxury' items. At the same time a general rise in specific duties and a special wartime import licensing system were introduced to cover a wide range of items. The purpose of these two measures was to preserve foreign exchange by cutting the importation of non-essential goods, to save shipping space, and to aid wartime planning. However after the war revenue and protectionist considerations ensured their continuation. The McKenna Duties were continued on an annual basis (Snowden allowed them to lapse for one year in 1924) and in 1926 they were extended to include commercial vehicles and parts, thus affording increased protection to the motor industry. In the immediate postwar years a series of acts made significant inroads into the free trade system. In 1919 Britain introduced a limited system of Empire preferences, in return for preferences already being given to Britain by

Empire countries. The Dyestuffs (Import Regulation) Act of 1920 was a prelude to the Safeguarding of Industries Act of 1921 which provided protection for 'key industries' (for example chemicals, dyestuffs, glassware, scientific instruments), with a 33½% ad valorem tariff. Under the German Reparations (Recovery) Act of 1921 the Treasury was empowered to impose duties of up to 50% on German goods. In 1925 the Safeguarding of Industries Act was extended to cover cutlery, pottery, lace and other items, and duties were introduced on silk and hops. Perhaps the most overtly protectionist measure of the 1920s came in 1927 when a special system of protection was devised for British films.[10]

By the end of the 1920s some significant precedents had been set in that Britain had begun to protect particular industries and to extend limited preferences to Empire countries. Nevertheless only a very small proportion of imports were subjected to protection; the free trade system remained basically intact and had overwhelming support. In 1924 the electorate had again rejected the Conservative Party when it sought a limited mandate for protection. In the debates on economic policy before 1931 the continuation of free trade was normally assumed, and this assumption was seen as an important argument against the adoption of expansionist policies which might have raised British export prices. If the Labour Party in 1929-31 had been able to agree on the introduction of tariffs, then it might have been more amenable to the employment policies of Mosley and Keynes. But Snowden remained an implacable opponent of protection and made skilful use of the argument that tariffs would inevitably lead to higher food prices and an increased cost of living. When Keynes in 1930 argued in favour of a tariff he was not suggesting protection but simply a device which might offset the overvaluation of sterling and provide revenue to balance the budget. But his proposal was violently attacked in a flood of protest from academic economists and he withdrew the idea once Britain had left the gold standard. At no time during the economic crisis was protection advocated as a general panacea for Britain's economic problems.

Even so, it was the crisis which made it possible for the Conservative Party to introduce general protection. In October 1931, the National Government was returned with a huge majority, largely composed of Conservatives who were committed to protection, even if they did not have a precise mandate for its introduction. The immediate rationale for protection lay partly in the fact that traders assumed it was coming and there was a danger of a flood of imports; the gold standard had been abandoned and free trade now seemed less essential and there was a desperate desire to increase revenue and to balance the budget.

In a broader context, protection was an essential prerequisite to Empire preference in that Britain could hardly give meaningful preferences to Empire countries unless substantial duties were imposed on foreign goods. It was also, quite correctly, believed that in an increasingly protectionist world, a great trading nation such as Britain denied itself considerable commercial and political bargaining power by continuing to adhere to free trade. Britain could only bargain from strength by introducing tariffs. Finally, protection was demanded by industrial interests and was a means of improving business confidence and making the government's industrial strategy more effective. In 1931 protection was introduced on an emergency basis through the Abnormal Importations (Customs Duties) Act and the Horticultural Products (Emergency Duties) Act. The former Act provided for duties of up to 100% on all items previously free of duty. Emergency duties (usually 50%) were imposed under Treasury Order and under the shelter of this emergency legislation, a new tariff machinery was quickly established. In February 1932 the emergency measures were replaced by the Import Duties Act which provided for a general 10% ad valorem tariff on most goods apart from Empire products and certain other specified items. The Import Duties Advisory Committee was established to make recommendations on tariff matters.

The question of Empire preferences was left to the Ottawa Conference of July and August 1932. The overall objective behind the Empire preference movement was free trade within the Empire and a movement towards Empire self-sufficiency. In fact, these were impossible ideals rather than realisable aims. The Empire was made up of widely scattered geographical units specialising in different economic activities. There were parts of the Empire which had developed important links and trade outlets with non-Empire countries. Australia for instance had developed important foreign markets for wool and it was only to be expected that Canada's closest economic links should be with its powerful land neighbour, the United States. The dominion countries were naturally reluctant to jeopardize these important foreign connections. Even more significant was the fact that different parts of the Empire were at different stages of economic development. To take only one example Australia after the first world war embarked upon a policy of building up secondary industries behind tariff walls as a means of providing industrial employment for an increasing population which could not be employed in rural industries. Australian manufacturers had much to fear from any proposal for free trade in industrial goods with Britain. While Australia wanted free access to the British market for primary products, Britain had begun to formulate new policies for the protection of its domestic agriculture. Thus there were fundamental conflicts of interest which made the great aims of Empire free trade and self-sufficiency absolute impossibilities. In these circumstances the scope for agreement at Ottawa was limited. The Ottawa Conference resulted in a series of bilateral agreements in which the United Kingdom and individual dominion countries swopped mutual preferences. In the main these preferences were established by raising trade barriers against foreign goods rather than by reducing inter-imperial barriers. The aim and result of the Ottawa agreements was to divert trade to the Empire and to enable Britain and the Empire countries to capture a larger proportion of a declining volume of world trade.

On the whole economists and economic historians have tended to downgrade the importance of the return to protection and the introduction of Empire preferences, although it is fair to point out that most studies on the subject were done in the late 1930s and 1940s when there was a strong reaction against trade restrictions. While protection did not give dramatic effects and was probably not a major influence in promoting recovery from the depression, it was a useful measure. At a time when Britain had a massive unemployment problem the standard arguments in favour of free trade were less relevant. Britain had continued to operate free trade in an increasingly protectionist world and the example had been ignored. From a free trade standpoint Britain had little bargaining scope; after 1931 it was possible to offer concessions to countries which, in turn, were prepared to reduce their tariff barriers. From the internal point of view, protection provided some stimulus to the economy and helped to improve the balance of payments by reducing imports and promoting import replacements. On the other hand this was to some degree offset on the export side. Protection was of considerable importance in relation to specific industries, notably iron and steel, and must be seen in the general context of industrial policy.

Although on balance protection was probably quite a useful economic measure it was implemented for political rather than economic reasons. The arguments between free trade and protectionist factions revealed major political differences in other areas and especially in relation to the role of the state in economic planning. Many of those who argued in favour of protection saw it as only one step in a general movement towards intervention. Clearly protection did increase the possible scope for expansionist policies but these were not forthcoming. To the Conservative administrators of the 1930s, protection was 'micro' rather than 'macro' economic policy and was designed to counteract the influence of cheap foreign labour and to give aid to particular industries.

VIII *Industrial Policy*

From the end of the first world war onwards the need for industrial reorganisation in Britain was constantly stressed and in the following two decades the attitude towards industrial structure and competition changed radically. Since the late nineteenth century it had become increasingly evident that in certain sectors of industry large enterprises were emerging from the competitive struggle. With the growth of joint stock enterprises, private firms and partnerships became relatively much less significant. Family firms gave way to public companies based on share capital and professional management. Vertical and horizontal integration gave rise to an increasing scale of operations and a much more complex pattern of industrial ownership. Above all British industry was becoming less competitive with the development of oligopolistic and monopolistic structures in industries dominated by a few large firms. Where the number of firms remained large competition also tended to be restricted by agreements organised through trade associations.

While these developments were already apparent before 1914, they were accelerated by the first world war. Wartime planning encouraged the establishment of trade associations and combinations and in many instances they received direct government support. The first report of the Balfour Committee argued that in the postwar period a premium must be placed on industrial efficiency so that British industry could regain its cost competitiveness in world markets. In the 1920s and in particular from 1924 onwards a good deal of attention was given to the elimination of 'wasteful' competition and improvement in efficiency through rationalisation. Inevitably there were many instances of rationalisation which resulted in collusive agreements to raise prices or restrict output rather than in the reduction of production costs. After 1929 and the onset of depression there was a greater urgency in these matters and the government began to assume a more active and direct role. Stagnant and declining markets for industrial goods stimulated a more intensive interest in market control and attempts to reduce capacity and output. Moves in this direction were to some extent sanctioned by the final report of the Balfour Committee, published in 1929. Ostensibly the rationalisation movement of the 1920s gave way to the 'planning movement' of the 1930s, but there was a basic continuity between the two. Nevertheless important new attitudes towards industry did emerge in the 1930s and the government extended its range of activity. Industries were encouraged to form cartels with a view towards reductions in capacity and output and the manipulation of prices. Where industries were unwilling or unable to reorganise themselves in this way pressure was brought to bear. The Import

Duties Advisory Committee insisted in a number of cases upon reorganisation of particular industries in return for tariff protection. In coal (in 1930) and agriculture (between 1931 and 1933) reorganisation was undertaken under statutory provisions. As Pollard has suggested:

'In the course of the 1930s, the State . . . played an active part in the cartelisation of industry. It created favourable conditions for industries, in which combination was easy, and it intervened directly to provide a monopolistic framework where firms were too weak or too scattered, as in the old staples of coal, cotton, iron and steel, shipbuilding and agriculture. For a third type of industry, the public utility, the country groped its way through to a new and significant form of organisation, the Public Corporation'.[11]

In the 1930s there was an almost complete reversal of the nineteenth-century attitude towards industrial competition. The competitive situation was no longer regarded as the most desirable form of industrial organisation and it was accepted that industry would become larger in scale and more monopolistic in structure. It followed from these views that there should be more state intervention to encourage restructuring and to protect the consumer from market manipulation which might result from concentration of business power. Leading exponents of the 'planning movement', such as Harold Macmillan, thus came to believe that the traditional market mechanism was no longer adequate in prevailing circumstances and that the state must provide a substitute. The 'planning' ideas of the 1930s have to some extent been confused with the Keynesian views which began to achieve popularity at about the same time. Keynes however was concerned almost exclusively with macro-economic planning and the management of aggregate economic demand. This was something quite different from micro-economic intervention in industrial and market organisation. The latter type of intervention, where it led to restrictions of output and price increases, may well have tended to increase the level of unemployment. As Donald Winch has pointed out:

' . . . While the Conservative Governments of the thirties may have furthered the idea of a "mixed economy" they did nothing to advance the cause of a "managed economy" as we understand the term today'.[12]

Nevertheless, in moving towards the modern economic order, certain inhibitions on the part of the state had to be overcome and the attitudes and policies of the 1930s can be regarded as part of a movement away from laissez faire attitudes.

Notes

1   S. M. H. Armitage, *The Politics of Decontrol of Industry* (1969), p. 6.
2   L. J. Hume, 'The Gold Standard and Deflation', *Economica* (August 1963).
3   D. E. Moggridge, *The Return to Gold* (1969), pp. 67, 68.
4   Cmnd 3331 (1929), *Memorandum on Certain Proposals Relating to Unemployment.*
5   *The Problem of the Unemployed* (1896).
6   R. W. Lyman, *The First Labour Government 1924* (1957), p. 154.
7   R. Skidelsky, *Politicians and the Slump* (1967), p. 394.
8   A. J. Youngson, *The British Economy 1820-1957* (1960).
9   More recent refinements of the theory have usually assumed uniform factors of production, perfect competition, perfect internal factor mobility, no international factor mobility, identical production functions, constant returns to scale, identical demand conditions and unitary elasticity of demand for all consumer goods.
10 E. B. McGuire, *The British Tariff System* (1939), ch. 17.
11 S. Pollard, *The Development of the British Economy 1914-1950* (1962), p. 172.
12 D. Winch, *Economics and Policy* (1969), p. 218.

Chapter 5

The Unemployment Problem

I *The Extent of Unemployment*
In general the interwar years have tended to be viewed as a bleak and unrewarding period in history; a time of frustrated hopes, bitterness, confusion and disillusionment. Such attitudes are clearly reflected in the literature of the period and in the popular memory of it. Many of the most important social, economic and political experiences of the interwar years are held, in retrospect, to have been mistakes which modern society should seek to avoid. In spite of recent attempts to 'rehabilitate' the period,[1] at least in terms of improving living standards and growth performance, these sombre attitudes remain. They are the result in large part of two indirectly related interwar phenomena: appeasement and mass unemployment. The rise of fascist dictatorships and the long series of forlorn attempts to appease them, culminating with the Munich agreement of 1938, are not part of our direct concern; but it is worth noting that high levels of unemployment in many countries, especially during the 1930s, did play an important part in giving greater scope for extreme views both on the left and right of the political spectrum. We are primarily concerned with Britain where, for almost the entire interwar period, there was a grim background of heavy and continuous unemployment. In the later years of the first world war and during the postwar boom unemployment was virtually non-existent. Suddenly, in April 1921, the situation changed dramatically; the postwar boom — based largely upon accumulated wartime savings and replacement demand — broke, and mass unemployment suddenly appeared and remained a permanent feature until after the outbreak of the second world war.

For many people, the failure to solve the unemployment problem and the failure to maintain international peace and liberty tend to outweigh much of the real progress, especially in living standards, which was made in these years. In Britain the problem of mass unemployment was almost continuously in the forefront of political discussion. To those who supported the existing economic and social order, unemployment constituted a serious threat which had to be countered by what was by previous standards generous provision for the unemployed. For others unemployment, particularly after 1929, was a symptom of an outmoded economic system. While the unemployment problem was very real, it was misunderstood and in some ways exaggerated in statistical terms. The measurement of unemployment is an extremely difficult exercise in social statistics involving the use of concepts which must be, to some extent, arbitrary. In attempting to assess the level of unemployment at any point in time it is necessary, ideally, first to define what is meant by unemployment and then to measure accurately the extent of this phenomenon. Also it is necessary to define and measure the workforce. There is no completely satisfactory definition of unemployment which does not involve arbitrary assumptions. Definitions vary and tend to be affected by methods of measurement, such as registration at labour exchanges, census returns and sample surveys. In Britain in the interwar period unemployment was effectively defined by the method of measurement which was on the basis of registration at labour exchanges. The unemployment statistics normally used, both by contemporaries and historians, rely upon returns which resulted from the operation of the national insurance scheme. These statistics understate the absolute amount of unemployment, while at the same time overstating the percentage rate. Unfortunately there are no satisfactory alternative statistics, either from sample surveys or census returns, and reliable statistical information relating to employment vacancies in the interwar period is very inadequate.

According to the national insurance statistics normally used, at least ten per cent of the British insured workforce was unemployed in any year between 1921 and 1938. During these years the average level of unemployment was over 14% of the insured workforce; that is approximately one worker in seven. The peak levels of unemployment came in April, May and June of 1921, when the postwar boom ended, and during the depression years 1931-33, when unemployment levels exceeded 20%; in the best years unemployment reached its interwar minimum of about 10% of the insured workforce in 1924, 1927 and 1937.

The statistics in Table 5.1 show annual average percentage levels of unemployment among insured workers in the United Kingdom between 1913 and 1939. These annual averages conceal fluctuations in unemployment during each year as a result of seasonal and other influences. In 1921 for example, monthly averages varied from 11·2% in January to 23·4% in May, a sharp cyclical downturn commencing in April, making this an exceptional year. In most years, as a result of seasonal influences, uenmployment was usually higher in the winter months than in summer.

Table 5.1 *United Kingdom: Percentage of Insured Workers Unemployed, 1913-39*

1913	3·6	1921	16·9	1929	10·4	1937	10·8
1914	4·2	1922	14·3	1930	16·1	1938	12·9
1915	1·2	1923	11·7	1931	21·3	1939	10·5
1916	0·6	1924	10·3	1932	22·1		
1917	0·7	1925	11·3	1933	19·9		
1918	0·8	1926	12·5	1934	16·7		
1919	n.a.	1927	9·7	1935	15·5		
1920	3·9	1928	10·8	1936	13·1		

Source Department of Employment and Productivity, *British Labour Statistics Historical Abstract 1886-1968* (1971), table 160, p. 306.

In terms of long-run historical perspective there is no doubt that the interwar period stands out as a time of exceptionally high unemployment. Nevertheless, it is possible to argue that the relative magnitude of the problem has been exaggerated in statistical terms. Average annual unemployment levels in the United Kingdom between 1881 and 1960 were approximately as follows:

1880-1914	4·5%	(Trade union figures)
1921-1938	14·2%	} (Insurance scheme figures)
1945-1960	1·8%	

However this comparison is misleading and gives an exaggerated impression of unemployment in the interwar period, since the statistics quoted are calculated on different bases. Before the introduction of the unemployment insurance scheme in 1911, statistical information about unemployment is available only on the basis of returns from a limited number of trade unions which regularly paid unemployment benefits to their members. The statistics in Table 5.2 reflect returns from trade unions which, before 1900, had less than 500,000 members and less than one million members before 1918. While these trade union returns probably give a reasonably reliable impression of *trends* in employment before the first world war, they do not give an accurate reflection of the *level* of unemployment for the workforce as a whole. Where the statistics in Tables 5.1 and 5.2 overlap it will be noted that those in Table 5.2 are usually lower. Trade unions in industries particularly prone to unemployment were on the whole less likely to pay unemployment benefits. Trade union membership, particularly before 1900, contained a higher proportion of skilled and semi-skilled workers than the workforce as a whole and, as a general rule, skilled workers were less likely to be unemployed than unskilled. It is likely therefore that the only available statistics relating to unemployment before the first world war tend towards serious understatement. The average level of unemployment in the workforce as a whole in the pre-1914 period was probably much higher than the 4½% average suggested by trade union statistics. William Beveridge in his classic work *Full Employment in a Free Society*[2] suggested that the average rate of unemployment in Britain in the three or four decades before 1914 may have been about 6%. Even this may be an underestimate.

Table 5.2 *United Kingdom: Unemployment in Certain Trade Unions which paid Unemployment Benefits, 1881-1926.*
(percentages)

1881	3·5	1894	6·9	1907	3·7	1920	2·4
1882	2·3	1895	5·8	1908	7·8	1921	14·8
1883	2·6	1896	3·3	1909	7·7	1922	15·2
1884	8·1	1897	3·3	1910	4·7	1923	11·3
1885	9·3	1898	2·8	1911	3·0	1924	8·1
1886	10·2	1899	2·0	1912	3·2	1925	10·5
1887	7·6	1900	2·5	1913	2·1	1926	12·2
1888	4·9	1901	3·3	1914	3·3		
1889	2·1	1902	4·0	1915	1·1		
1890	2·1	1903	4·7	1916	0·4		
1891	3·5	1904	6·0	1917	0·7		
1892	6·3	1905	5·0	1918	0·8		
1893	7·5	1906	3·6	1919	2·4		

Source Department of Employment and Productivity, *British Labour Statistics Historical Abstract 1886-1968* (1971), table 159, p. 305.

As a result of the introduction of the National Insurance Act of 1911 a new source of information on unemployment became available and it is this source which is normally used to provide unemployment statistics for the interwar period. The 1911 Act provided unemployment insurance for two and a half million workers in a few industries (the industries concerned were building and construction, shipbuilding, mechanical engineering, iron founding, construction of vehicles and sawmilling). Quite clearly, statistics based on these industries are not necessarily accurate indicators of the level of unemployment in the workforce as a whole. There was a further extension of the national insurance scheme in 1916, affecting about one and a quarter million workers but no major extension until 1920. Under the National Insurance Act of 1920 the national insurance scheme was extended to cover nearly 12 million workers out of an economically active population of approximately 19 million. From 1923 when the scheme began to operate fully, we have employment statistics based on returns made by about 60% of the working population. Workers excluded from the scheme included those engaged in agriculture, forestry, domestic servants, public employees (civil servants, teachers, nurses, police, the armed forces, and local authority workers), railway employees, white-collar workers earning more than £5 per week, workers under sixteen years old and the self-employed. While some of these excluded groups were brought into the scheme in subsequent years, there were no major changes in coverage during the remainder of the interwar period.[3]

On the whole, the workers in the excluded categories were less prone to unemployment than insured workers. The official figures for unemployment, presented in Table 5.1, relate to workers who were more likely to be unemployed than was the workforce as a whole. Apart from the problem of exclusion, it must also be borne in mind that although the national insurance statistics are by far the most accurate available, they do contain some significant inaccuracies. National insurance was not always popular both with employers and employees and as a result of evasion the insured workforce was consistently understated by at least 250,000. On the other hand a number of workers in full or part-time employment may have succeeded in claiming unemployment benefits. The effect of these activities must have given rise to some exaggeration in the percentage level of unemployment indicated in official statistics.

By making use of the 1931 census returns it is possible to get an approximate idea of the extent to which national insurance statistics exaggerate the level of unemployment in relation to the workforce as a whole. According to an estimate by Colin Clark the total workforce in 1931 comprised 21,274 million (male and female) workers. His estimate of unemployment, combining census and national insurance data, is given in Table 5.3.

Table 5.3 *Unemployment in Great Britain, 1931* (Thousands)

	Males	Females
Persons insured against unemployment	1918	598
Domestic workers 16-64	22	95
Agricultural workers 16-64	62	3
Persons over 65	165	29
Persons under 16	23	18
Persons now outside scope of insurance	318	38
Total	2508	781

Source C. Clark, *The Conditions of Economic Progress* (1951), pp. 30-1.

The full extent of unemployment in 1931 according to this calculation was 3,289,000; considerably more than the registered unemployed total of 2,520,000 workers. However the percentage rate of unemployment for the workforce as a whole on this calculation was 15·5% compared with the insured unemployed rate of 21·3% (see Table 5.1). It appears therefore that in 1931 the rate of unemployment for insured workers may have been nearly one third higher than the rate of unemployment in the workforce as a whole. A more recent estimate by C. H. Feinstein suggests a smaller difference of about 20%.

It will be clear that unemployment statistics need to be handled with caution and with a full understanding of the assumptions and methods employed in their compilation. In attempting to assess relative unemployment levels on an international basis the difficulties already referred to are magnified by the different methods and definitions employed in various countries. Table 5.4 gives some approximate comparisons between levels of unemployment in relation to the total labour force in the United Kingdom and three other economies in the interwar period. In this table the United Kingdom workforce is defined broadly on the basis of census definitions. As a result, the recorded levels of unemployment are substantially lower than those in Table 5.1.

The statistics in Table 5.4 represent at best very broad approximations. They suggest that Britain was far from being unique in experiencing a serious unemployment problem in the interwar period. While the problem in Britain may have been rather more persistent than in other countries, particularly during the 1920s and the later 1930s, unemployment in Britain in the early 1930s was lower than elsewhere.

The discussion so far has been concerned with statistics which are simple national averages. These averages conceal some extremely important variations in the incidence of unemployment which varied widely according to age, sex, occupation, industry and region, and within regions. Generally it can be said that female and older workers were more severely affected by unemployment, although there were many exceptions to this in particular occupations, industries and regions.

Table 5.4 *Unemployment as a Proportion of Total Labour Force,*
        1920-38

	UK	USA	Germany	Canada
		(Percentages)		
1920	1·8	3·9	1·7	—
1921	9·6	11·4	1·2	5·8
1922	8·1	7·2	0·7	4·4
1923	6·6	3·0	4·5	3·2
1924	5·8	5·3	5·8	4·5
1925	6·4	3·8	3·0	4·4
1926	7·1	1·9	8·0	3·0
1927	5·5	3·9	3·9	1·8
1928	6·1	4·3	3·8	1·7
1929	5·9	3·1	5·9	2·9
1930	9·3	8·7	9·5	9·1
1931	12·6	15·8	13·9	11·6
1932	13·1	23·5	17·2	17·6
1933	11·7	24·7	14·8	19·3
1934	9·9	21·6	8·3	14·5
1935	9·2	20·0	6·5	14·2
1936	7·9	16·8	4·8	12·8
1937	6·7	14·2	2·7	9·1
1938	8·1	18·9	1·3	11·4

Source A. Maddison, *Economic Growth in the West* (1964), table E.1, p. 220.

Men over the age of 45 did not necessarily run a higher risk of being unemployed than younger men; but if an older man became unemployed he found it harder to obtain a new job. Older men therefore faced longer periods of unemployment. With female workers the situation is complicated by the fact that there is no way of knowing how many unoccupied women would have been willing to seek paid employment, at prevailing wage levels, if it had been available. There is no doubt that many married women, who were not entitled to unemployment benefits, did not trouble to register themselves as unemployed. In some industries and areas there were social pressures which dictated that married women should be the first to lose their jobs, but this did not always make economic sense from the point of view of employers when women were paid lower wages than men for equivalent work. Many of the industries dominated by female labour, especially in the tertiary sector, suffered rather less from unemployment than some of the basic, male-dominated, manufacturing industries. In consequence, there were many families which relied on female rather than male earnings. Perhaps the most striking variation in unemployment rates is by occupation. Unskilled manual workers were twice as likely to be unemployed as skilled and semi-skilled workers, who in turn were much more vulnerable than white-collar and professional workers.

Table 5.5 *Unemployment by Occupation, 1931*

The figures show the percentage of the total male labour force unemployed in England and Wales.

Unskilled manual workers	30·5
Skilled and semi-skilled manual workers	14·4
Agricultural workers	7·6
Forces	0·0
Personal service workers	9·9
Salesmen and shop assistants	7·9
Clerks and typists	5·5
Higher office workers	5·1
Professions	5·5[a]
Retail traders	2·3
Farmers	0·5
Other proprietors and managers	1·3

[a]Swollen by unemployed musicians. Average for other professions was about half this level.

Source C. Clark, *The Conditions of Economic Progress* (1951), p. 470.

These variations in unemployment in relation to occupation are a reflection of education and social class as well as immediate economic circumstances. Workers in the higher occupational categories were in relatively short supply because the vast majority of the population had failed to obtain even a rudimentary secondary education. By virtue of their small numbers and higher social status they were able to enjoy a position of relative privilege in the face of economic adversity. As might be expected, there was a considerable degree of variation in unemployment rates between industries as a result of labour immobility and varying degrees of vulnerability of particular industries to market influences. Table 5.6 gives unemployment rates in certain selected industries in two years which differed widely in terms of economic circumstances: 1932, in the trough of depression, and 1937, which was the peak of the upswing.

Table 5.6 *Percentage of Insured Workers Unemployed in Selected Industries, 1932 and 1937*

Industry	1932	1937
Coalmining	34·5	16·1
Chemicals	17·3	6·8
Pig iron	43·8	10·7
General engineering	29·1	5·8
Electrical engineering	16·8	3·1
Shipbuilding	62·0	24·4
Cotton textiles	30·6	10·9
Hosiery	13·5	8·1
Dressmaking	11·5	7·5
Boots and shoes	18·0	12·1
Drink industries	14·4	7·7
Furniture	21·7	9·8
Printing	11·0	6·7
Building	30·2	14·6
Gas, water, electricity supply	10·9	8·3
Railway service	15·7	6·5
Trams and buses	5·9	3·3
Docks, harbours, canals	33·3	27·5
Distributive trades	12·6	8·9

Source Department of Employment and Productivity, *British Labour Statistics Historical Abstract 1886-1968* (1971), table 164, p. 315.

II *Regional Unemployment*
During the interwar period a severe problem of regional depression emerged and this problem, although much reduced, is still a matter for concern at the present time. Over the years a depressed area has usually been defined as a locality or region which has a rate of unemployment which is substantially above the national average. The main areas which came into this category in the interwar years were the north-east, and the north-west, Scotland and Wales.

Table 5.7 *Regional Unemployment Rates, 1930*

	(Percentages of the insured workforce)
National average	16·1
London	8·1
South-east	8·0
South-west	10·4
Midlands	14·7
North-east	20·2
North-west	23·8
Scotland	18·5
Wales	25·9

Source W. Beveridge, *Full Employment in a Free Society* (1944), p. 61.

Regional variations in unemployment can be explained by the adverse market circumstances which affected a small group of old staple industries (textiles, shipbuilding, coal, and iron and steel), the heavy concentration of these industries in coalfield areas, the location of growth industries elsewhere and the immobility of the industrial workforce. It has been suggested that in the two decades before 1920 the old staple industries had become hoarders of labour, being to some extent 'overmanned' and that during the war and postwar boom they were 'overexpanded'. It is probably more accurate to say that in the period before 1914 these industries used labour in a manner which, in terms of postwar technology, was relatively intensive; and that during the war and postwar boom they were expanded in response to highly unusual market circumstances which could not be maintained. After 1920 rapid changes in technology, rising productivity and contraction from exceptionally high levels of output and employment led to a massive 'shake-out' of labour in the old staple industries. These influences provided powerful reinforcement to the unemployment problems which arose from the failure to regain prewar markets. In the old industrial areas economic deceleration was diffused by linkages between basic and other industries so that regions as a whole slid into persistent depression with unemployment rates well above the national average. In the midlands and south-east new and expanding industries produced an opposite effect leading to prosperity and expansion. In this way the prosperous south and the depressed north emerged and Britain became, in some ways, two nations. In general coal was the most badly affected industry and Wales was the area which suffered most. The regional unemployment rates already quoted are averages for large geographical regions. They conceal phenomenal rates of unemployment in certain industrial areas where dependence on declining industries was very heavy and where structural decline was reinforced by cyclical depression. In January 1933 in the north of England, 91% of the insured labour force was unemployed at Saltburn, 77% at Jarrow and 64% at Cleator Moor; in Scotland, 70% at Stornoway, 60% at Wishaw and 54% at Clydebank; in Wales, 82% at Taff Wells, 72% at Pontycymmer, 68% at Merthyr and 66% at Abertillery.[4] It would be possible to extend greatly this list of industrial blackspots. While industries declined and industrial expansion shifted elsewhere, people tended to remain immobile. Despite wide differences in unemployment rates and relative prosperity between regions there was no large-scale migration of the industrial population. In the interwar period as a whole only about 4% of the workforce moved from the depressed north and west to the expanding south. Between 1920 and 1935 the south-east of England made a net gain of about one million workers as a result of migration from all other regions. This migration, which accelerated during the 1930s depression, must have had some influence on relative unemployment rates, but enormous differences remained. In aggregate terms the largest population movement was from the north-east to the south, but in proportionate terms Wales lost more heavily. Writing in 1937 Brinley Thomas pointed out, 'Wales is outstanding in that almost 7% of its insured population has been absorbed by the south-east; and the bulk of this movement has probably occurred during the past decade'.[5]

In relation to total population the amount of inter-regional migration which occurred was small.[6] The major part of the workforce continued to live in depressed industrial areas with heavy unemployment. In South Wales, Scotland, Lancashire, Tyneside and Northern Ireland generations of men left school, married, and in some cases reached middle age without being in employment. While these areas soon became familiar with the sight of the dole queues, idle men gathering in the streets and obviously underfed children, the most serious effects of unemployment were not always immediately apparent. It was particularly tragic that unemployment struck most severely in areas which were the most vulnerable. The industrial revolution had produced clusters of highly specialised and regimented industrial communities with a pronounced 'work ethic', strong working-class solidarity and a way of life which was geared to regular work and weekly wage income. In such communities, heavy and persistent unemployment was the ultimate tragedy in both social and economic terms. Men without work lost not only income but also social standing and individual self-respect. [7]

It should also be borne in mind that even for those who remained in employment, the threat of redundancy represented a constant anxiety which conditioned attitudes in a manner difficult to comprehend from the postwar standpoint. Unemployment in the interwar period must be seen as a moving stream with the majority of people being unemployed only for relatively short periods. The most tragic consequences of unemployment related to a substantial minority, mainly concentrated in the depressed areas, who were without employment for long periods. Long-term unemployment, defined as unemployment lasting more than a year, was essentially a post-depression phenomenon. In 1929 out of an (insured) unemployed total of 1·2 million, only 53,000 had been unemployed for a year or more. By July 1933 this figure had leapt to 480,000 and in the upswing from the depression a hard core of long-term unemployment tended to persist.

According to a study carried out in the later 1930s many men simply 'went to pieces' after long periods without work. They experienced:

'A subtle undermining of the constitution through lack of physical exertion, and the absence of physical stimuli, insufficiently varied diet and worry, and the emergence of abnormal psychological conditions characterised by disabling fears, anxieties, and sympathetic physical conditions, functional disorders and the like'.[8]

Unemployment affected families as well as individuals:

'In most unemployed families the parents, and in particular the wives, bore the burden of want, and in many instances were literally starving themselves in order to feed and clothe the children reasonably well. But the indirect effects on the children are of course very great. They are inevitably growing up to accept low material standards and growing up in an atmosphere of strain. Both these factors are going to play an important, though as yet not precisely calculable part in their lives. It will not be surprising if many of them feel that their future . . . is to stand behind their fathers in the queue'.[9]

It has already been pointed out that the high degree of variation regionally in levels of unemployment resulted, in part, from the immobility of labour. Inter-regional migration in the interwar period was much less than might have been anticipated. There are several reasons for this, in terms of both weak 'push' and 'pull' factors. Wage differentials were not sufficiently large enough to attract large numbers of workers into expanding areas. Workers who considered moving from depressed to expanding areas had to face economic costs arising from loss of earnings, transit and the need to purchase or rent accommodation in a more expensive area. For some there was a possibility of a loss of status. A miner, for example, who moved to the London area was likely to find employment only as an unskilled labourer. Skilled or semi-skilled workers in textiles, shipbuilding and other basic industries had little to gain in terms of job status by moving south. Above all, the fact remained that unemployment was high even in the expanding areas and migration did not necessarily offer any guarantee of permanent employment. Undoubtedly there were some very powerful social deterrents to mobility. People were reluctant to withdraw from close-knit working-class communities and strong family connections, particularly in conditions of economic adversity when these were most highly valued, in order to move into an alien environment. Despite these powerful economic and social restraints on labour mobility it is probable that much more extensive migration would have occurred had it not been for radical changes in the social security system. The unemployed were offered the 'dole' which prevented them from being faced with a forced choice between migration or starvation. Although the 'dole' was introduced for political and humanitarian reasons, there were highly important consequences for economic policy. Once it became clear that movement of labour on a large scale was not likely and that full recovery in the declining basic industries was out of the question, it followed that policies must be devised to create employment in the depressed areas.

In practice this kind of conclusion was never clearly drawn by interwar governments. Before 1934 government efforts in relation to depressed areas were confined to measures designed to encourage the mobility of labour by offering information, advice, retraining and financial assistance to those willing to move. In 1928 the Industrial Transference Board was established to retrain labour and to assist movement to other areas. A regional policy aimed at creating new employment opportunities in the depressed areas did not commence until 1934 with the Special Areas (Development and Improvement) Act, which was introduced as a temporary measure. Under the 1934 Act four Special Areas — Central Scotland, South Wales, West Cumberland and the North-east — were designated and two commissioners were appointed. It was apparent from the outset that the powers provided under this Act were far too limited. The initial sum of money available to the commissioners amounted to only £2 million; major cities in the Special Areas were specifically excluded and the commissioners were not empowered to assist any private profit-making activity or any activity which received government funds from other sources. In 1936 the Bank of England established the Special Areas Reconstruction Association with the aim of offering loans to small businesses in the Special Areas. In 1937 the Treasury was empowered to make loans to similar and larger undertakings. Under these two arrangements a total of approximately £2 million was advanced between 1937 and 1940. Later in 1936 Lord Nuffield established a private Trust which by 1940 had provided over £2 million to industries in the Special Areas. By 1938 a total sum of £21 million had been advanced under the Special Areas Acts of 1934, 1936 and 1937. Virtually all of these funds were directed towards the improvement of public amenities. Any stimulus to private industry was mainly indirect and, in aggregate terms, negligible. In Trafford Park (Salford), Welwyn Garden City and at Slough, private enterprise had successfully pioneered trading estates as a means of attracting industry to particular localities. In the later 1930s this idea was adopted by the Commissioners for the Special Areas. Between 1937 and 1940 ten trading estates and over 300 factories were established with government encouragement and assistance. During the same period under its rearmament programme the government attempted to assist depressed areas as far as possible in placing orders for military equipment and in deciding the location of defence establishments.

By the end of the interwar period a useful range of measures designed to attract industry into depressed areas had been developed. Unfortunately, these measures proved to be too little and too late to have any appreciable impact upon the regional unemployment problem. It was not until after 1936 that really effective policy measures began to be introduced and the efforts made were simply insufficient. While unemployment remained a serious problem in the country as a whole it was particularly difficult to promote expansion in the depressed areas and it seems doubtful that a more active regional policy could have been highly successful. There was not much industrial expansion in the late 1930s. Firms which were willing to expand usually had no difficulty in finding labour in the more prosperous parts of the country. In these circumstances it is not surprising that regional policy made little impact.

III *The Nature and Causes of Unemployment*
It has already been pointed out that any attempt to define and measure unemployment is likely to involve arbitrary assumptions which reflect social attitudes and statistical conveniences as well as economic realities. In discussing unemployment at any particular time we tend to make assumptions about the obligation and willingness to work of particular social groups. In the modern context it is usually assumed

that the under 15 and over 65 age groups ought not, ideally, to be employed and should be thought of as being outside the workforce. In the interwar period large numbers of people in these age groups were employed and it is possible that unemployment affected the extreme age groups most severely. In relation to female employment, social attitudes are undoubtedly very important in determining participation rates, particularly for married women. In the interwar period it is possible that the employment of married women was becoming socially more acceptable. Female employment had played an important role in the national effort during the first world war; families were smaller and the relative status of women in society was changing. But economic circumstances militated against a more enlightened social attitude in relation to female employment. If more women were willing to work (we cannot be sure of this in the absence of extensive sample surveys) and were prevented from doing so by the high level of unemployment, then it would follow that the real rate of unemploy-ment for women was much higher than is suggested by official statistics.

In attempting to analyse unemployment economists have defined several different types. Commonly used categories are: seasonal, frictional, technological, structural and cyclical. In any economy certain activities such as harvesting, building and retailing will be subject to seasonal influences which give rise to temporary redundancies or 'seasonal' unemployment. At any time a number of workers, for a variety of reasons, will be in the process of transferring from one job to another and the resulting unemployment is classified as 'frictional'. Where, as a result of changes in technology and innovation, one industrial process is superseded by another process which requires less labour or a different type of labour, this may produce 'technological' unemployment. If entire industries contract as a result of technical and economic changes the resulting unemployment is defined as 'structural'. Finally, where the economy as a whole experiences a 'cyclical' downturn this may give rise to high levels of unemployment on a temporary basis. While all these types of unemployment were present during the interwar period, the unemployment problem was largely a result of structural and cyclical influences. As a simplification, it is possible to think in terms of a hard core of structural unemployment, involving on average approximately 6% of the insured workforce, which persisted throughout most of the interwar period. If we add to this the fairly persistent levels of seasonal and frictional unemployment, which may have amounted to 3% or 4% of the insured workforce, this would explain the interwar minimum unemployment levels of about 10%. Superimposed upon these types of unemployment were varying levels of cyclical unemployment which was most intense in 1921 and during the depression period 1929-33.

While the above simplification may help to explain the nature of the unemployment problem, it fails to do justice to the full complexity of the situation. The different types of unemployment referred to reacted upon each other. For example, during periods of high cyclical unemployment, other types of unemployment were likely to be more severe. Cyclical depression had a severe impact upon industries already suffering structural decline. Workers changing jobs during periods when the economy was depressed were likely to take longer in finding new employment. Above all it is in practice impossible to distinguish clearly between the different types of unemployment which have been defined. While it is obvious that cyclical unemployment was very severe at certain times, it is impossible to estimate with any precision the proportion of total unemployment attributable to cyclical influences. It should be borne in mind also that unemployment is defined in relation to existing wage rates, markets and currency values. Structural unemployment resulted mainly from exporting difficulties faced by the staple industries. These difficulties are partly attributable to protection in overseas markets, the overvaluation of sterling in the 1920s, and to Britain's high cost structure relative to other countries. It is possible to argue, as indeed many pre-Keynesian economists did, that unemployment was the result of an inflexible wage system. If the traditional export industries had been able to pay lower wages then it is possible that they may have regained many of their foreign markets and employment capacity so that the problem of structural unemployment might not have arisen in such an acute form. According to classical economic theory, employers would continue to recruit labour up to the point where the output of the last man engaged was equal in value to the average wage. In a flexible market situation wage levels would adjust to ensure full employment. Attempts to reduce money wages were strongly resisted by the trade union movement and this resistance came to a head with the General Strike in 1926. During the 1920s it became clear that the country had to face a choice between wage inflexibility and political crisis. Once the choice had been made, in terms of wage inflexibility, it followed that there was a need for new economic theory and radical changes in government policies. These changes did not materialise until after 1940 and as a result unemployment remained a serious problem.

While wage inflexibility may have had some influence in giving rise to the problem of structural unemployment, this influence was probably exaggerated by opponents of Keynesian policies. The theory relating average wages to marginal product was based on restrictive assumptions (including constant factor costs and an absence of economies of scale and multiplier effects) which were probably unrealistic. While a reduction of wages in the export industries might have assisted those industries in selling into foreign markets, reduced purchasing power in Britain would have aggravated cyclical unemployment and may have retarded the development of new consumer goods industries which were the main hope for future growth in the economy.

Britain's unemployment problem between the wars was both cyclical and structural. While the distinction between the two is abstract and imprecise, it is nevertheless useful. Cyclical unemployment, while very severe, was largely confined to the years 1921 and 1929-33. In post-Keynesian retrospect we know that cyclical unemployment might have been considerably reduced by government measures designed to raise the level of aggregate demand during the downswing of the trade cycle. Over the period as a whole structural unemployment presented a much greater problem, particularly in its regional manifestations. While regional unemployment might have been reduced by 'pump-priming' at the national level it could have been removed (in the absence of mass migration or wage flexibility) only by the development of new industries in the depressed areas.

In the interwar period Britain suffered not from one unemployment problem but from two. While cyclical and structural unemployment were mutually reinforcing and difficult to distinguish clearly, they were fundamentally different in nature and causes. The duality of the unemployment problem was a complicating factor in policy debates aimed at seeking a solution to unemployment. In the opinion of many manufacturers and some economists, the expansionist policies advocated by Keynes and others were likely to have intensified structural unemployment by raising production costs in the export industries. At the same time it might be argued that the expansionists, including Keynes himself, did not give sufficient attention to the need for *ad hoc* regional policies as a means of easing the structural unemployment problem.

IV Conclusion

While unemployment is very much a part of the image of the interwar period, the unemployment problem has been to some extent exaggerated and misunderstood. This judgement does not in any way detract from the cruel waste and tragedy, the irony and futility of a situation in which at least one million workers were, at any point in time, suffering the pain and deprivation of unemployment. Nevertheless, the fact remains that the existence of widespread unemployment does not appear to have had any fundamental impact upon the direction of economic or political development during the interwar period as it appears to have had in certain other countries. Over the period as a whole the economy grew more rapidly than it had done since the nineteenth century and the overwhelming majority of the population enjoyed a higher standard of living than ever before. While there was hunger and much suffering, this was no new development and in the 1930s at least, Britain was in a relatively fortunate position compared with most overseas countries. It might even be argued that Britain's unemployment problem was not serious enough. In Sweden, the United States and Germany the magnitude of the crisis gave rise to a search for radical political solutions under new leadership. In Britain there was no such development and never any serious possibility that an equivalent of Hitler or Roosevelt would emerge. If the situation had been more serious, then extreme political solutions and charismatic leaders such as Lloyd George or Mosley might have gained more attention and there might have been a greater willingness to listen to the new economic views advocated by Keynes. But the unemployment problem in Britain proved to be limited and containable. It was possible therefore for the majority of the population to accept unemployment as an inevitable misery which had to be tolerated by an unfortunate minority at least for the immediate future. Historians have invested much energy in attempting to allocate blame for the unemployment problem. There is no doubt that most economists, the Treasury and the Bank of England were misguided and offered bad advice to successive governments; influential pressure groups, including City of London financial interests, were narrow-minded, selfish and short-sighted; and many, if not most, of the leading politicians lacked ideas, ideals and courage in the face of the unemployment problem. Yet in the final analysis it was the people themselves who rejected Lloyd George in 1929 and in 1931 gave the National Government a massive mandate for retrenchment. The majority of the British electorate accepted the existence of unemployment with fatalistic resignation. The unfortunate minority made do with the 'dole'.

In attempting to understand the attitude of the majority of the British people towards unemployment in the interwar years it is important to bear in mind that in the decades before 1914 unemployment probably affected an average of 6% of the workforce and during times of crisis much higher levels were common. Also many people were employed on a casual basis. Although the average level of unemployment in the interwar period may appear to have been catastrophic when viewed from the post second world war viewpoint, the impression is rather different in terms of pre-1914 experience. While there is no doubt that unemployment was appallingly high in a number of areas where declining industries were heavily concentrated, and throughout the country during the world crisis of 1929-33, in much of the country during most of the interwar period unemployment may not have been very much higher than in the pre-1914 period.

It has been pointed out that the national insurance statistics tend to overstate the percentage rate of unemployment in relation to the workforce as a whole, while at the same time understating the absolute amount. In terms of international comparisons Britain suffered relatively severely during the 1920s and was relatively fortunate during the 1930s. However, the fact that heavy unemployment was much more persistent in Britain than elsewhere indicates the magnitude of the structural unemployment problem. Above all it is important to note that there were two mutually reinforcing unemployment problems rather than one. Cyclical unemployment arising from the world depression affected Britain severely, but for a relatively short period confined mainly to the years 1929-33. The long-term unemployment problem, which was the more tragic and intractable, was essentially structural and regional and it affected areas which before 1914 had been relatively highly developed and prosperous. Structural unemployment had a particularly damaging impact upon these areas because of their specialised employment structure. In other parts of the country such as London , Bristol and the midlands the industrial and occupational structure was much more varied and was therefore less vulnerable to structural unemployment. Workers in the south and midlands had before 1914 been relatively less well paid, more dependent on casual labour, more prone to unemployment, and more mobile between industries than workers in the old industrial areas. Ironically, these pre-existing disadvantages enabled the south and midlands to avoid the horrors of mass unemployment after 1920, and they may well have been an important factor in attracting new and expanding industries.

By the 1930s the depressed areas in Wales, Scotland, Ireland and the north of England had become, to some extent, separate enclaves in a comparatively prosperous country. While a new, relatively affluent, working class was being created in the south and midlands, the depressed areas were dominated by introversion and bitterness. Protest became institutionalised in a long and futile series of marches, including the 1936 Jarrow march which became a focus for publicity and a lasting symbol of the unemployment tragedy at its most extreme. Government efforts to deal with the problem of regional unemployment were both too little and too late and were largely ineffective.

Notes

1 D. H. Aldcroft, 'Economic Growth in Britain in the Interwar Years: A Reassessment', *Economic History Review*, vol. 20 (August 1967).
2 W. Beveridge, *Full Employment in a Free Society* (1944), p. 73.
3 In 1928 people over 65 who were entitled to state pensions were excluded. Workers under 16 were included in 1934 and agricultural workers in 1936.
4 G. McCrone, *Regional Policy in Britain* (1969), p. 91.
5 B. Thomas, 'The Influx of Labour into London and the South-east, 1920-1936', *Economica*, vol. 4 (1937), p. 328.
6 For further discussion of migration see Chapter 8.
7 For graphic descriptions of the effects of unemployment on working-class communities see George Orwell, *The Road to Wigan Pier* (1937), and W. Greenwood, *Love on the Dole* (1923).
8 Pilgrim Trust, *Men Without Work* (1938), p. 137.
9 Pilgrim Trust, *Men Without Work* p. 112.

Chapter 6

Labour in the
Interwar Period

I *Labour in Modern British Industrial Society*
In the century before 1914 Britain had developed into the world's
most highly industrialised society. In consequence the majority of the
British people became, during their working lives, industrial wage
earners. At the other end of the social scale there existed a small,
relatively highly privileged social and economic elite which benefited
from a grossly uneven distribution of national income and wealth by
virtue of its ownership of land, capital and 'know-how'.

The emergence of an industrial working class under capitalism, and
the consequences of this, have for many years been matters of major
concern for historians and social scientists. There can be little doubt
that this concern owes a great deal to the impact of the ideas put
forward by Karl Marx and Friedrich Engels during the third quarter of
the nineteenth century. According to Marx and Engels, the working
class would eventually become conscious of the fact that capitalism
was a basically immoral system which operated against the material
interests of the masses through its exploitation of labour. They further
predicted that a series of cumulative crises in the capitalist economy,
increasing working class deprivation, and the development of
working-class organisation would eventually lead to a breakdown of
capitalism and a violent and revolutionary overthrow of the established
order. In subsequent British history there does not appear to have
been any development of this kind, and we must assume therefore that
either the theories of Marx and Engels were fundamentally wrong and
have been disproved by subsequent events; or that 'external' influences,
not fully anticipated by Marx and Engels, have entered the historical
situation, giving rise to a different pattern from that predicted.

The extreme polarisation of society foreseen by Marx and Engels
did not, in fact, occur. While there was indeed gross inequality and a

strong sense of working-class identity in Britain, wage earners were far from being an undifferentiated mass. There were enormous differences in status, material situation and political opinions within the working class and working-class solidarity was an ideal rather than a reality. During most of the period after 1870 the majority of workers were tending to become better rather than worse off, although the Edwardian period is an important exception to this generalisation. From the late nineteenth century the state began increasingly to assume an ambivalent role as, on the one hand, a traditional instrument of 'capitalist oppression', and on the other, a means of liberation for the working class through the extension of suffrage, the development of civil rights and extensions in social welfare. The powers of the state were extended and limitations were imposed upon the economic power of private property. While the working class and working-class organisations continued to distrust law and government as tools of their 'oppressors', they began to place an increasing faith in gradual political change as their ultimate means of salvation. The structure of power in modern British society was far from being a simple reflection of the ownership of private property or capital. To an increasing extent constitutional and institutional political power became rivals to direct economic influence, and changes in the occupational pattern and distribution of income produced a new social structure in which private ownership was relatively less important.

The British working class failed to realise its supposed revolutionary potential, despite the fact that the privileged minority made remarkably few concessions in terms of redistribution of income and wealth. This failure has been attributed by Marxists mainly to three influences: the *embourgeoisement* of sections of the working class, and particularly the working-class leadership, the wide diffusion in Britain of the material benefits and ethos of imperialism, and the new role and concept of the state in modern society.

It might be argued that the interwar period provides the best opportunity in modern British history for an empirical examination of the Marxist theory of history. In this period there is no doubt that working-class consciousness appeared to be greatly enhanced and class conflict became more violent, harsh and intense. Labour organisation became for a while much stronger and appeared more militant. Class conflict was symbolised above all in the General Strike of 1926. At the same time capitalism appeared to be in a state of crisis during most of the period and experienced an apparent breakdown in the early 1930s. This approach to the fulfilment of Marxist predictions did not give rise to any widespread revolutionary tendencies on the part of the British working class. While organised labour was certainly willing, at least in theory, to challenge capitalism, it deliberately chose to work through non-revolutionary methods. In the light of this we must conclude either that the British working class really did not have the revolutionary potential defined by Marx, or that, despite the apparent historical fulfilment of certain Marxist predictions, other circumstances operated against the realisation of a revolutionary potential. During the interwar years there were factors which tended to make the working class both more and less politically radical, but the latter appear to have been by far the more effective in the long run.

Increasing working-class militancy during the interwar period can be attributed to a wide range of influences. These include the first world war, the Russian revolution of 1917, syndicalism, the growing strength of labour organisations and the apparent failure of labour interests, and the Labour Party in particular, to make much progress in constitutional politics. During the immediate postwar period labour had very strong bargaining power in the industrial arena and substantial gains were made in increased wages and reduction of working hours. The war and postwar boom periods gave rise to a sharp enhancement of working-class expectations. After 1921 with the commencement of mass unemployment, these improvements and expectations were threatened by a counter-offensive from the employers. This counter-offensive came to a head in the General Strike, which apart from the depression of 1929-33, was the most serious crisis of the period. During every crisis of the interwar period there was a marked absence of revolutionary tendencies in the working class as a whole, or even in particular sections. The unemployed were, perhaps, the most obvious group which might have wished for a radical alternative to the established order. In fact mass unemployment failed to act as a basis for the immediate radicalisation of British politics. In the circumstances which prevailed, it weakened and exposed the labour movement and strengthened the forces of reaction. Labour was at its strongest and most militant and radical during the short period between the end of the first world war and the beginning of heavy unemployment in 1921. At this time the trade unions were highly successful in gaining major concessions. During this period, and for a few years after 1921, there was a genuine fear of revolution in government circles.[1] Whether or not these fears were justified, they disappeared altogether after the General Strike of 1926.

There were a number of influences which tended to reduce working-class militancy or political radicalism. Some of these have already been mentioned. They include real improvements in the standard of living and quality of life for large sections of the working class. In the interwar period cheap mass-produced consumer goods came increasingly within the reach of working-class incomes. The benefits of imperialism were widely diffused in the form, particularly, of cheap foodstuffs. In political terms, nationalism and imperialism confused and divided the working class and diverted attention from the class struggle within British society. Where working-class organisation was successful in bringing pressure to bear, vested interests made marginal concessions and skilfully diverted working-class leadership into non-violent and relatively harmless channels. The established order never lost its nerve or sense of purpose and was always willing, in the last analysis, to maintain itself by force if necessary. The threat of military measures was a factor in a number of industrial disputes, including especially the General Strike. Responsible working-class leaders were left in no doubt that the price of direct physical confrontation with established interests was too high to be contemplated. Instead, they were persuaded to accept the gradual progress of political reformism through established constitutional channels. In attempting to operate by constitutional means working-class organisations were compelled to compromise their ideals and to accept conventional attitudes and ideas. Labour leaders who entered Parliament and who, as ministers, received the advice and influence of civil servants, had to compromise more than leaders at lower levels. When the Labour Party formed governments in 1924 and in 1929-31, its leaders felt that they had to act in the national interest rather than simply on behalf of the working class. As the labour movement enhanced its power and status the gap between leaders and rank and file tended to widen.

By a skilful combination of minor concessions and persuasion, backed ultimately by a resolve to use force if necessary, the vested interests in British society were able to perpetuate and adapt themselves. During the interwar period organised labour never felt able to challenge the legitimacy of the established power structure enshrined in the law and the constitution. The irony of this situation was illustrated in an interesting manner during the hearings of the Sankey Commission when leading mine-owners, such as the Duke of Northumberland, were challenged to establish the basis of their claim to the mines. Even symbolic challenges of this kind were rare. Over the period as a whole organised labour was attempting to adjust to, and to accept, the established legal and constitutional order and doing what it could to make modest progress within it. Far from being 'alienated', the masses developed their own sub-culture, which was separate and divorced from the main avenues of power and prestige. For the aspiring few there were safety-valves in the form of better educational opportunities and the ability to rise in working-class organisations. In areas where tension was most likely, such as unemployment, state bureaucracy and the dole had a numbing influence on militancy. In more general terms, unemployment placed labour on the defensive both collectively and as individuals. In the long run unemployment may have had an important influence in producing new and more liberal ideas, but in the short run it strengthened vested interests and the forces of reaction rather than producing left-wing militancy on a large scale.

Finally we should note the importance of mass communications which reached new levels in the interwar period. The extension of mass communications went hand in hand with the rise of urbanisation, affluence and democracy. As incomes rose and leisure increased, more and more people were willing and able to buy cheap entertainment on a regular basis. The communications and entertainments revolution of the twentieth century was based on the adaptation of a cluster of inventions of the late nineteenth century, including radio, the telephone, the gramophone, electric lighting and moving pictures. In the interwar period the cinema, radio and the popular press became mass entertainments on an unprecedented scale. Communications became big business, subject to profit considerations and the dictates of financial power. Control of communications media passed into fewer and fewer hands, as a few press barons and film magnates emerged from the financial struggles. In radio, where an attempt was made to remove commercial considerations, a state monopoly, in the form of the British Broadcasting Corporation, was established. A monopoly or quasi-monopoly in the mass media was something far more serious than the ordinary business monopoly, in that the mass media were not only a means to financial power, but also a route to political power. They could be used to mould mass opinion, whether they were in private or state hands. One private extreme produced the Beaverbrook-Rothermere press. In Germany, state influence was carried to extreme lengths through the Goebbels propaganda machine. The BBC, an independent public corporation, was a not unsuccessful attempt to avoid these extremes.

Those who controlled the mass media were able to determine what was to be communicated in the form of programmes, features, news and information. In general terms, three main types of media control emerged. In the first place there were authoritarian controllers, such as Beaverbrook, who communicated strictly in terms of their own political and financial interests. Secondly, there were paternalistic outlets, of which the BBC under Sir John Reith is the best example, presenting material which they believed to be in the best interests of the people, society and the state. Thirdly, there were controllers who pandered simply to popular taste as expressed in sales turnover. In general, the mass media tended either to divert attention from serious political matters, or to provide continued support for the status quo, and a belief in progress through constitutional means.

During the interwar period genuine fears of revolution or class upheaval, which prevailed until the early 1920s, gave way to a situation in which almost the whole of organised labour adopted a constitutional and reformist attitude in its attack upon the established order. At the same time, the establishment accepted that organised labour had a rightful and permanent place in the power structure. By the late 1930s it had become obvious to labour leaders that capitalism was not going to break down and that progress could be made through the continuation of the private enterprise system modified to some extent by state intervention. At the same time, the owners of wealth had accepted that there had to be a continuing compromise with organised labour. They also became increasingly aware that there was an important distinction between organised labour and labour as a whole. In terms of membership, at least, the trade unions usually spoke and acted on behalf of a minority of the labour force. The Labour Party failed to gain a parliamentary majority during the interwar period and large sections of the working class continued to vote for other political parties.

Table 6.1 *Union Membership and Industrial Disputes: Selected Years and Periods*

Year or period	Total membership of trade unions (millions)	Working days lost due to strikes (millions)	Percentage of total days lost which were lost in coal mining
1900-1910	2·2	4·1	39
1912	3·4	40·9	77
1920	8·3	26·6	66
1921	6·6	85·9	85
1922-1925	5·5	11·7	16
1926	5·2	162·2	90
1927-1930	4·9	3·8	16
1931-1938	5·0	3·6	29

Source Department of Employment and Productivity, *British Labour Statistics Historical Abstract 1886-1968* (1971), tables 196 and 197. Where a period is shown in the first column the figures are given for the average of inclusive years.

II *The Pattern of Industrial Relations*

For a brief period during the first world war 60% of the workforce were union members, but during the interwar years the unions always represented a minority of workers. Union membership reached a peak in 1920 and fell to a trough in 1933 before rising again to a figure well below the 1920 level. Over the period as a whole it fluctuated between a quarter and one third of the workforce. However there was a high turnover in membership and a much greater proportion of the workforce were union members at some stage of their working lives. While the trade unions consistently claimed to speak for the working class as a whole, their membership remained a minority and only a tiny proportion of union members played an active part in union affairs. The majority of unionists almost certainly did not feel themselves to be a part of a political movement or social class organisation. According to one observer of working-class attitudes in the 1930s:

'The trade union is valued most as a protective society . . . The appeal is present that as a member of a trade union one is a participant in the labour movement. The main object, however, is protection and a sense of security on the job'.[2]

The basic aims of trade unions were to defend and to improve the conditions and rewards of work. However it would be quite incorrect to assume that these functions were carried out only by officially organised trade unions. Labour history is far from being simply the history of formal labour organisations, and industrial relations inevitably existed where trade unions were absent or ineffective. Informal dealings conducted by individuals and work groups were of tremendous importance both in unionised and non-unionised areas of industry. Work group patterns also had an important influence upon the origins and development of official trade unions.

From the point of view of general economic history the formal record of official labour organisation is not particularly relevant in its own right. What is relevant is the extent to which labour organisation may have influenced the pattern of economic development, and the extent to which the pattern of economic development may have influenced labour organisation. Obviously, the extent of each of these influences is highly debatable. The main impact of trade unions on economic development results from the extent to which wage levels and costs of production are influenced by union activities. It appears that wage trends were determined, overwhelmingly, by general economic conditions rather than by trade union activity. Money wage rates for all sections of the workforce show a direct correlation with the level of economic activity, and an inverse correlation with the level of unemployment. Money wages reached a peak during the postwar boom and fluctuated at lower levels during the subsequent period of heavy unemployment. It is impossible to estimate the extent to which unions were successful in accelerating wage increases (and reductions in hours) during boom periods and in preventing wage cuts during slack periods. In relation to the latter, at least, most commentators would accept that they did have a considerable influence, although the general pattern was determined by the level of economic activity.

Economic development clearly had a major influence on the whole area of union development and organisation. Union membership fluctuated in accordance with the level of economic activity, which also had a direct effect upon union bargaining power and the incidence of strikes. Apart from the obvious direct relationship between union activity and the short-run economic situation there were important long-run economic influences. The unions faced serious organisational problems as a result of the decline of the old staple industries and the emergence of prolonged depression in traditionally solid working-class areas. Organisation in the expanding industries in the south and midlands proved to be a difficult long-term process. Other problems resulted from the relative decline in status of skilled workers and the narrowing of wage differentials between skilled and unskilled workers, largely as a result of changing techniques and the emergence of new 'white-collar' groups which did not usually embrace union activity in this period. The increasing pace of technical innovation gave rise to a more complex wages system with a growing tendency towards piecework payment on a fragmented basis. Demarcation disputes became a serious problem in a number of long established industries. In a period when unemployment was very high and money wages tended to fall, the unions also faced severe financial difficulties which undoubtedly had some influence upon their attitudes and activities.

Trade union methods and policies reflected a changing pattern of economic circumstances. On both sides of industry the strongest weapons were used when bargaining power was at its greatest. Strikes were most frequent during periods of relatively high employment (the General Strike of 1926 is an important exception) and lock-outs were most frequent when unemployment was relatively high. Within the union structure the level of economic activity had an important influence upon the relationship and distribution of power between national and local leaders. The latter tended to diminish in importance during periods of heavy unemployment. During the interwar period the strike was gradually being eliminated as a normal union method and being replaced by national negotiation and arbitration. For a time, however, in the early part of the period national strikes were a prominent feature of the industrial relations system. Over the period as a whole industrial stoppages became less frequent and strikes became increasingly local and unofficial.

From the late nineteenth century collective bargaining gradually shifted from the local to the national level and during the interwar period nationally negotiated agreements became the general rule in most industries. This development became possible only as a result of the establishment of nationally organised employers' associations as well as trade unions. National collective bargaining placed power increasingly in the hands of full-time officials. Between 1914 and 1921, with full employment, local officials and work groups were able to assert themselves. Workshop organisation developed rapidly during the war, especially in engineering, and shop stewards gained a new stature. However in the period of heavy unemployment after 1921 these local groups and leaders were usually integrated into the official union structure and national negotiations tended to become more important than local. One result of these developments was a reduction in trade union militancy.

The structure of British trade unions developed to meet a complicated range of changing industrial circumstances. There were basically three types of trade unions: craft unions, industrial unions and general unions. From the late nineteenth century the exclusive craft unions which dominated the labour movement were forced to adjust to changing technology, which threatened the status of many skilled workers, and they widened the range of their intake to include the less skilled. Some, including the Amalgamated Engineering Union, became in effect general rather than craft unions. Nearly one quarter of unionists were organised into industrial unions, of which the most important were in coal, railways, and iron and steel. However over much of industry organised workers were divided between craft and general unions rather than being organised on an industrial basis. General unions had been growing in stature and numbers since the late nineteenth century. Under the Trade Union (Amalgamation) Act of 1917 it became possible to arrange amalgamation on the basis of 50% ballot and a 20% majority (before 1917 two thirds of the membership had to vote). There were several amalgamations between 1917 and 1924 and two giant general unions emerged: the Transport and General Workers Union, with its basic strength in the docks and road transport, and the National Union of General and Municipal Workers, which relied on well organised groups in public utilities. Despite the development of industrial and general unions the craft influence on British trade unions remained strong.

In the early 1920s the TUC was reformed in a manner which had the effect of making it less political. The Parliamentary Committee, which had acted as the TUC executive since 1871, was replaced with a General Council of thirty members. Individual unions did not surrender any of their autonomy and there was no attempt to establish central direction. While the new TUC was given the power to co-ordinate industrial action, to promote common action and to mediate and settle disputes between member unions, its authority was subject to the approval and authority of individual unions. While many left-wing unionists supported this apparent strengthening of the TUC for syndicalist and possibly revolutionary reasons, the General Strike provided clear evidence that centralisation was likely to reduce rather than enhance militancy. In the immediate postwar years the TUC failed to grasp its opportunities and there was an absence of overall strategy and leadership. While the unions advocated full employment policies, public works, minimum wage legislation, nationalisation of coal and other industries, and the extension of Whitley Councils, they had insufficient power and organisation really to press these aims. By the time the new TUC was established in 1921, industrial circumstances had placed the entire union movement on the defensive. During the first world war the unions had become virtually an agent of government and in the immediate postwar period they clearly had the potential to exercise enormous political as well as industrial power. These opportunities were largely wasted. After 1921, with the onset of heavy unemployment, successive governments of all parties found it possible to ignore the attitudes and opinions of trade unionists to a much greater extent. Public opinion influenced by the mass media and academic argument was persuaded, to a degree, that trade union militancy constituted a fundamental threat to society. In some quarters the unions were seen as potentially revolutionary organisations which were bent on the destruction of the British constitution and the established order. In a more general sense the trade unions were criticised by orthodox economic theory which suggested that high and inflexible wages created unemployment and jeopardised export markets. In the interwar period trade union militancy was contained by economic circumstances and the moulding of public opinion, rather than by any form of direct repression.

III *The Origins of the General Strike*

The first world war gave rise to a long period of full employment and rapid growth in trade union membership. Government control was a powerful factor in raising union membership and in promoting co-operation and amalgamation. The growth of employers' associations and organisations was encouraged and national as opposed to local bargaining became general. The Federation of British Industries, which became the industrialists' equivalent to the Trades Union Congress, was established in 1916 and the National Confederation of Employers' Associations in 1919. As a result of the war the unions made great gains in status, membership and potential power. At the same time a large section of the British working class was in the armed forces undergoing experiences which in many cases destroyed traditional attitudes. Raymond Postgate has commented:

'The immense and useless slaughter made the most stupid doubt the intelligence of the generals responsible for Passchendale and the Somme. The belief, deeply inherent in most Englishmen, of the fitness of the aristocracy of birth and money to rule, was seriously shaken and in many cases destroyed. The sight of clergymen, exempt from danger, urging others to die and kill, and on both sides of the front calling on the same god in similar terms, ended for hundreds of thousands . . . any real confidence in Church and Chapel. At the end of the war great masses of the male population had become cynical and semi-revolutionary in political belief, and agnostic in practice if not in theory'.

The years 1917-20 were a period of social crisis in Britain with a real, though probably exaggerated, danger of revolutionary activity. The Russian revolution of October 1917 had created ripples throughout Europe. In Britain there was a questioning of traditional authority and of pre-existing social and political patterns. The labour movement had been radicalised and greatly strengthened by war, and hopes for better conditions in peace time were based on inflated expectations. The Labour Party, despite being taken by surprise, greatly increased its vote in the 1918 General Election and, in the same year, it adopted a socialist platform by embracing a policy of public ownership. The Communist Party of Great Britain was formally established in 1920.

In the immediate postwar period the British government had to face this situation of social tension at a time when there was serious dissatisfaction, verging on mutiny, in the army, navy and the police force. After the demobilisation crisis, during which there were several instances of open rebellion and defiance of orders, the government experienced a serious shortage of military manpower in relation to its commitments in Ireland, Russia, Germany and the Empire. There were police strikes in August 1918 and in May 1919. British intervention against the Russian Bolsheviks gave rise to the *Jolly George* affair in which British dockers took a political stand by refusing to load supplies destined for Poland. In August 1920 when the Red Army threatened Warsaw the labour movement threatened a general strike to prevent British intervention.

There was a very high degree of industrial militancy between 1918 and 1921 which is clearly reflected in the strike statistics. According to one commentator: 'The force behind this sudden outburst of industrial conflict derived not so much from particular claims over hours and wages (most of these were soon met) as from a pent-up, passionately felt demand for drastic change, an angry refusal to return to prewar conditions'.[4] At this time the unions were demanding the nationalisation of the mines, railways and land, workers control of industry, a capital levy and measures to promote a more equitable distribution of income. However, these demands were not pressed in a systematic and co-ordinated way and the opportunity of the moment was missed. No attempt was made, for example, to link civil and military discontent. The labour movement, and in particular the revolutionary element of it, was too immature and badly organised to take advantage of the situation. The ruling elite was only too well aware of the inherent dangers and handled the threat with relative ease and confidence. By late 1920 the boom was over, the first signs of mass unemployment began to appear, and the labour movement was rapidly forced into defensive action designed to preserve the gains which had been made. By 1921 the employers were gaining successes in most negotiations. The employers' offensive aimed at longer working hours, lower money wages and local rather than national bargaining. Increasingly the employers argued that they could meet foreign competition and make a 'reasonable' return on capital only if wages were reduced. High wages, it was argued, were squeezing the profitability out of British industry and creating unemployment. It is hardly surprising that the struggle was at its fiercest in the declining industries and it was here that the employers had most success. However over the interwar period working hours tended to remain shorter than previously; money wage rates did not, on the whole, fall as much as prices, and national bargaining remained the general rule throughout most of industry.

In January 1919 the miners voted by an overwhelming majority in favour of strike action to back their demands for shorter hours, higher pay and nationalisation of the mines to prevent their return to private hands. Threatened with a national coal strike and the possibility that the Triple Alliance, between the miners, railwaymen and transport workers, might be invoked, Lloyd George played for time and a Coal Industry Commission (the Sankey Commission) was appointed. When it eventually reported, the Sankey Commission, on which unions and mine-owners were represented equally, divided evenly, but the chairman's casting vote went in favour of nationalisation. However the main danger had been averted and the government was able to ignore the Commission.

To some extent, the struggle in the coal industry became symbolic of the general struggle between labour and capitalism. On repeated occasions coal was seen as a test case in determining wage movements. Coal had helped to pioneer the industrial revolution and had become the major employer of industrial labour. Despite declining productivity, coal output continued to expand right up to 1920 before running into severe economic difficulties resulting from loss of markets. The miners were particularly well organised and militant, largely as a result of their living and working conditions, but they also had real immediate grievances resulting from the relative decline of their wages during the war years and their fears that coal would be handed back to private ownership after the war. In September 1920 the miners secured a partial victory in the form of increased wages in return for higher output after a three week strike. Although during this strike the miners' attempts to use the Triple Alliance were not successful, the threat was enough to induce the government to introduce the Emergency Powers Act of 1920. Under this Act the government was empowered to declare a 'state of emergency' and to govern by decree if vital supplies were threatened. These powers were put to use in the coal dispute of 1921 and during the General Strike.

In 1921 the mines were returned to private hands at a critical time when the economic tide had turned, and the owners immediately tried to impose wage cuts and longer hours. An attempt was made to revive the Triple Alliance so that the miners could call upon the railwaymen and transport workers for support. On 15 April 1921 (subsequently known as 'Black Friday') the Triple Alliance failed to function and the other unions withdrew their support from the miners. The miners attempted to defy the owners' lock-out, but were eventually forced to return to work on the employers' terms under the 1921 agreement, which involved lower wages and a return to local agreements. 'Black Friday' may be seen in certain ways as a dress rehearsal and a preliminary for the General Strike. The breakdown of the Triple Alliance occurred because the other unions feared government intervention and were far less committed to the issue than the miners. Also there appears to have been a failure in communication about negotiations, if not an actual betrayal of the miners by the other unions. This feeling of betrayal on the part of the miners helped to prepare the ground for the General Strike of 1926. It was a factor in the reform of the TUC and played some part in the sense of obligation which the TUC felt towards the miners in 1925-6.

In 1924 there was a temporary revival in the fortunes of the coal industry, mainly as a result of disruption of overseas supplies by the French occupation of the Ruhr and strike action in the United States. In these temporary boom conditions, and with support from the first Labour Government, the miners were able to change the 1921 agreement, securing a reduction in working hours and higher wages. In the subsequent year foreign competition revived and the mine-owners once again faced falling prices and profits. When they demanded that there should be a return to the 1921 agreement the miners responded by calling upon the TUC for support. As it happened, the TUC was temporarily under strong left-wing influence and the miners had a powerful reserve of sympathy dating from 'Black Friday'. The TUC agreed to give its support and threatened a total embargo on the movement of coal. In the face of this threat the government, on what became known as 'Red Friday', agreed to give the coal industry a temporary subsidy so that existing wage rates could be maintained. At the same time yet another official inquiry into the coal industry was announced in the form of a royal commission headed by Sir Herbert Samuel. This was the fourth official inquiry into the coal industry in six years, and, like its predecessors, it was largely ignored by the government. The Samuel Commission favoured eventual nationalisation and made some useful suggestions for reform of the industry. While it favoured wage cuts, these were not as drastic as the owners proposed and many shades of opinion, including some trade unionists, saw the Samuel proposal as a reasonable compromise. The miners, however, stood firm on Cook's slogan: 'Not a penny off the pay, not a second on the day'. The harsh attitude of the mine-owners was matched by the miners' leaders, who represented stubbornness in the case of Smith and fanatical extremism in the case of Cook.

The granting of a temporary subsidy gave the government nine months to complete its preparations for just the kind of national stoppage that had been anticipated since the early 1920s. However, it would probably be wrong to assume that the Baldwin Government sought such a stoppage. By May 1926 the government was well prepared. Emergency stocks had been accumulated and an emergency organisation had been prepared. An Emergency Committee for Supply and Transport was established and ten Civil Commissioners with wide emergency powers were appointed. With government approval, the unofficial Organisation for the Maintenance of Supplies was founded to organise volunteers who were willing to work during a national strike. The TUC, on the other hand, made no elaborate preparations. At the 1925 Conference right-wing leadership was reasserted and the new General Council was left with a commitment to support the miners by strike action, for which its support was half-hearted. The main hope of the TUC was that some reasonable compromise, such as that suggested by the Samuel Commission, could be reached and that strike action could be avoided.

When the temporary subsidy ran out and the owners, with apparent government backing, insisted upon wage reductions, the TUC had no alternative but to support the miners who were locked out by the mine-owners at the end of April 1926. The TUC called a general sympathy strike for 3 May. Workers in printing, transport, iron and steel, gas, building and electricity were asked to strike and on 11 May workers in engineering and shipbuilding were also called out. The strike involved one million miners and one and a half million others. Despite the TUC's half-hearted attitude and lack of organisation, local organisation was on the whole very effective and there was a very high response to the strike call. Local organising committees showed tremendous initiative and enthusiasm, despite the lack of liaison, co-ordination and direction from above. While a large part of normal industrial activity was brought to a standstill, the elaborate government preparations were successful in ensuring that essential supplies were maintained and the strike was, in effect, turned into a stalemate which meant ultimate defeat for the strikers. There was little actual use of force by the government, but the threat of force, especially in breaking the closure of the London docks, was a crucial factor in deciding the issue. Undoubtedly the TUC made a mistake in preventing normal newspaper publication by calling out the printers. In the propaganda battle the *British Gazette*, a temporary government newspaper, was more successful than the TUC's *British Worker* and, to some extent at least, the BBC was forced to bow to governmental influence.

During the strike it appears that the more militant element of the cabinet, who desired a showdown with the unions, were able to gain the ascendancy. Churchill, Birkenhead and Joynson-Hicks were among those who believed that the strike could be broken and that there should be no negotiations until the strike had been called off. Negotiations between the government and the TUC were apparently terminated on rather flimsy grounds and the TUC found itself in an invidious position; the strike could not be won by normal industrial methods and the government refused to negotiate. Rather than seeking to extend the strike the TUC was anxious to contain it and to terminate it as soon as possible. While members of the government accused the TUC and the strikers of seeking to challenge the constitution, members of the General Council feared that their powers and authority could be challenged and possibly seized by more militant and revolutionary elements within the labour movement. After nine days the General Council called off the strike on the pretext of a compromise formula put forward on a private initiative by Sir Herbert Samuel. At first it seemed that certain assurances had been given and that the government had accepted the Samuel compromise. Eventually it became clear that the TUC had called off the strike without securing any guarantees and without securing the agreement of the miners' leaders. Naturally the miners, and many of those who had gone on strike in their support, felt betrayed. The miners continued on strike until the winter of 1926 when they had to admit total defeat, returning to work on the basis of local agreements.

The General Strike was a costly defeat and a blow to the morale of British trade unions. However, it would probably be wrong to see the strike as a major turning point in trade union history since most of the subsequent developments were already under way before 1926, and the real turning point in interwar trade union history almost certainly came in 1920-1 with the onset of mass unemployment. Nevertheless it is true that after the General Strike the incidence of strikes was extremely low and there was a greatly diminished faith in mass industrial action as a political and industrial weapon. After 1926 union membership continued to decline and cautious leadership continued to prevail. In 1927 the government consolidated its victory by introducing the Trade Disputes and Trade Unions Act which made general sympathy strikes illegal and attacked the legal position of trade unions in other ways. Under the same Act, contributions made by the unions to the Labour Party were attacked by making it necessary for union members to 'contract-in' to the political levy. But though the unions had suffered a serious defeat, they were by no means crushed and both employers and government were as anxious as the TUC to avoid any future major conflict of this sort.

In 1927 G. Hicks, the General Secretary of the TUC, suggested a series of talks between labour leaders and industrialists on the future of industry and the economy. This suggestion was taken up on an unofficial basis by Sir Alfred Mond and a group of leading businessmen. The Mond-Turner Talks of 1928-9 achieved little of practical consequence and were subject to left-wing scorn. The official employers' associations were not prepared to accept what was agreed or to contemplate a National Industrial Council. However, the talks were symbolic of new attitudes of compromise on both sides of industry and they did enable the TUC to gain valuable new prestige.

IV *Labour in the 1930s*

During the early 1930s the labour movement reached its lowest point of the period in terms of strength and membership, largely as a result of the depression which brought unemployment to a new peak. In 1931 the Labour Government disintegrated and shortly afterwards the Party suffered a devastating electoral defeat. Trade union membership continued to fall, reaching its nadir in 1933, before recovering in the relatively prosperous period between 1935 and 1937. The British trade union movement, unlike its counterparts elsewhere, was able to survive the setbacks of depression relatively unscathed. While membership fell, the union structure, the system of collective bargaining and the pattern of leadership survived; the TUC retained its leadership of the movement and even managed to consolidate its position; above all the employers won few major victories during the depression. While unemployment gave rise to deprivation for many and became a cause of anxiety for most workers, the majority experienced a rise in real income as prices fell to a greater extent than money wages.

The 1930s ranks as one of the least militant decades in modern industrial history. Between 1927 and 1939 an annual average of 3 million working days were lost in strikes. This compares with an annual average of 28 million working days lost between 1919 and 1925. The changing pattern of industrial militancy owes something to the defeat the unions suffered in the General Strike of 1926, to rising unemployment in the early 1930s and the continuation of high unemployment throughout the decade; it may also be that there was less need for wage adjustments in the 1930s than in the 1920s since in the 1930s prices were relatively stable and real wages tended to rise. Thus, although the unions were weakened, they had rather less to fight for in the industrial arena than in the 1920s. The major exception to this was the textiles industry which faced severe depression. Textiles from the late 1920s replaced coal as the main area of industrial dispute.

While it is possible to advance several reasons for Britain's quieter industrial history during the 1930s, the main factor appears to have been a gradual change in the pattern of industrial relations. National collective bargaining had become well-established in most industries. Between 1910 and 1926 national strikes had been relatively frequent, adding considerably to the number of working days lost through strike action. In the 1930s the national strike became very infrequent and ceased to be regarded as a normal union weapon. Both unions and employers came to regard it as a clumsy and costly procedure which should be avoided as far as possible by reaching negotiated settlements. The majority of strikes which occurred in the 1930s were local and unofficial.

During the 1930s moderate leadership of the trade unions, represented in particular by Bevin and Citrine, consolidated its control and came to dominate the movement. The threat from the communist Minority Movement was finally destroyed by 1932 and left-wing elements suffered defeat in most sections of the official labour movement. While moderate leadership paid lip service to a vaguely defined concept of socialism as a long-term aim, it believed in coming to terms with capitalism in the present and accepting gradual progress and reformism as the way forward. Leaders like Bevin appreciated that capitalism was likely to persist for many years and could not be defeated by industrial action. They believed that the working class should compromise and seek an accommodation with capital while at the same time seeking to control it by means of increasing government intervention in the economy. Increasingly the TUC sought to establish a right to be consulted on major issues affecting its members, although no such right was clearly established before 1940. Nevertheless it may be argued that the TUC and the trade union movement as a whole made a more successful attempt than the Labour Party to come to terms with economic reality during the 1930s.

During the 1930s new technology began to have a major impact upon the pattern of work and way of life of industrial workers. In many ways conditions improved: individual employers began to pay more attention to personnel problems and the physical health and mental well-being of their employees. Personnel management of a specialist kind developed rapidly and there were improvements in factory hygiene, and in canteen and social facilities, particularly in the new industries. On the other hand increasing mechanisation, electrification and the regimentation which went hand in hand with mass production and the increasing scale of operations gave rise to a speeding up of work processes. Work tended to become faster and more intensive and individual workers became subject to greater stresses and strains, both mental and physical. During the 1930s the number of industrial accidents tended to increase rapidly and this reflected the changing pattern of work as well as better reporting. The changing location of industry meant that new kinds of working-class communities were established in the expanding areas. These were less homogenous and more physically dispersed than the traditional working-class areas which had developed around the old staple industries. In the new areas class consciousness and solidarity were less pronounced and new groups of relatively affluent workers began to emerge.

For the trade unions the changing pattern of industrial location posed severe organisational problems. The expanding industries were more difficult to organise because of their lack of solidarity and the absence of traditional union organisation. The greater geographical dispersal of industries and of workers' dwellings made organisation difficult both inside and outside the factory. In some new industries there was a relatively high proportion of female, juvenile and unskilled workers who were notoriously difficult to unionise. Above all the new industries developed in a general context of heavy unemployment which was not conducive to the growth of union membership. The TUC and the official union leadership in general failed to launch any large-scale and concerted effort to organise the new industries and the main effort was left to local and individual initiative. It is hardly surprising, therefore, that there was little general success in extending trade union activity to the new industries until the upswing of the 1930s. Throughout the interwar period the main strength of British trade unionism remained in the traditional areas. Union organisation in the new areas remained limited and, on the whole, weak. At the end of the interwar period very large groups of workers amongst the unskilled, female and white-collar groups, and in the tertiary sector in general, remained unorganised and unrepresented.

V *Labour and Politics*
In the words of Henry Pelling: 'The Labour Party . . . was in large measure a weapon of the trade union leaders devised for the reversal of the Taff Vale decision'. In its early years the Labour Party was simply a loose federation of trade unions and socialist societies which supported parliamentary candidates as political representatives of the working class. The early Labour members of parliament were heavily dependent on the informal alliance which they were able to develop with the Liberal Party. Before 1918 the Labour Party was not committed to socialist policy and it aimed simply at a gradual amelioration of working-class conditions through the influence which it was able to exert upon the larger political parties. In the interwar period Labour emerged as a rival and replacement for the Liberal Party; it adopted a socialist platform and came to command majority support from the working class.

Because the Labour Party emerged relatively early in Britain it was able to develop pre-emptive support from the working class and this tended to reduce the impact of more revolutionary organisations, such as the Communist Party, which developed later. On the whole the British political left remained relatively united and left-wing intellectuals and leftist organisations, including those with Marxist leanings, tended, at least to some extent, to work through the Labour Party and the trade unions, rather than by establishing their own rival organisations. The Independent Labour Party, the Communist Party and the communist-inspired Minority Movement all attempted to operate through the Labour Party and the official trade union movement.

Within the labour movement there was an almost constant confusion and conflict between the immediate demands of labour, such as higher wages, more welfare benefits, better housing and improvements in education, and the long-run aim to establish a socialist society. At its simplest this conflict became one between a commitment to gradual reformism within the capitalist system, or to revolutionary change. There were alternating periods of radicalism, notably just before and immediately after the first world war and in the late 1930s, interspersed with longer periods when a more moderate attitude prevailed. Overall however, the Labour Party remained firmly committed to reformism and it never really looked like becoming a revolutionary organisation, despite the efforts of minority leftist groups. Right-wing influence remained firmly in control and in the early 1930s the communists and the Independent Labour Party were forced to sever their formal connections with the party.

In 1929 Britain had its first general election based on universal adult suffrage. With the extension of suffrage, power came to depend increasingly upon institutional control rather than upon the actual ownership of property or capital. The ruling classes gradually realised and accepted the fact that the labour movement could not be crushed. However, by a skilful combination of marginal concessions and persuasion it became possible to absorb the labour movement into the existing system and to ensure its deradicalisation. The mass media played an important part in establishing the legitimacy of the existing constitutional and economic order. Gradually the Labour Party dropped the ultimate socialist ideal of strict equality and became committed to the concept of equality of opportunity or meritocracy. In education policy, for example, the party pinned its hopes on a massive extension of free grammar and secondary school places, without realising that such a policy would tend to compound rather than remove many existing inequalities. At the same time the party became increasingly bureaucratic and moved away from the democratic intentions expressed in its formal constitution. Control drifted into the hands of professional organisers in the parliamentary party and the TUC. To an increasing extent these people were either middle class, or highly susceptible to middle-class influence.

While the Labour Party came to command the support of the majority of manual workers in the interwar period it never gained a parliamentary majority. Many working-class voters continued to support the Liberal Party until its eclipse in 1929, and the Conservative Party continued to win a massive working-class vote. At least one third of the British working class did not vote Labour during the interwar period and the Labour Party was never able to form a government with majority support in the House of Commons. Clearly a very large number of British workers and their wives were influenced by anti-egalitarian and deferential attitudes. They did not accept the egalitarian philosophy of the Labour Party and believed that others were better fitted and more competent rulers of the country.

Although the Labour Party won only fifty-nine seats in the general election of 1918 its share of the vote was 24%, compared with only 8% in the previous general election held in 1910. It was, nevertheless, a considerable surprise when in 1923 the Labour Party suddenly found itself called upon to form a minority government. MacDonald's aim in 1923 was to establish that the Labour Party was capable of taking its place within the constitutional framework as an alternative party of government. In MacDonald's cabinet of twenty there were only seven trade unionist members and in its attitudes towards trade union affairs the first Labour Government behaved in much the same way as other governments. It considered for example the use of emergency powers, including military measures, against strikers. To trade unionists and Labour voters in general the first MacDonald administration was a disappointing experience during which the party achieved very little and learned nothing. In particular, the problem of unemployment was not tackled and the party failed to develop any effective policy for dealing with unemployment.

While the first Labour Government was at best a mild disappointment the second, between 1929 and 1931, proved to be little short of disastrous. During this government there was a lack of consultation with the TUC and serious differences arose with regard to economic policies. The opposition of the TUC to deflationary measures, and particularly to cuts in unemployment benefit, was a crucial factor in the cabinet split of 1931. In the subsequent battle for party loyalty with MacDonald the TUC had a relatively easy victory and for a time during the 1930s the party was under strong trade union influence. Recovery from the debacle of 1931 was slow and the party remained in eclipse throughout the 1930s.

In political terms the British labour movement during the interwar period became firmly committed to democratic socialism, that is to the establishment of a socialist society through constitutional means and by gradual progress. It was during the interwar years that the difficulties and fundamental conflicts involved in this approach first became apparent. The failure of the 1929-31 Labour Government has attracted a good deal of attention in recent years and the record of that government has been examined in great detail by Robert Skidelsky in his book *Politicians and the Slump*. Skidelsky's account of incompetence and muddle leads him to a rather remarkable conclusion:

the Labour Government, dominated by MacDonald, Snowden and Thomas, was blinded from reality by its utopian vision of socialism:

'Basically the Labour Government believed that socialism was the cure for poverty, of which unemployment was simply the most vivid manifestation. It thought in terms of a total solution: but socialism would clearly take a very long time, for it would not be established until the majority of people were ready for it. In the meantime the Labour Party simply did not know what to do . . . without any adequate theory of transition, the Labour Party was bound to be defeatist in the circumstances of 1929. Socialism was impossible and capitalism was doomed: there was nothing to do but govern without conviction a system it did not believe in but saw no real prospect of changing. It struggled to defend the working class as long as it knew how, and when it could defend them no longer, it resigned'.[5]

In other words, Skidelsky suggests that the belief in ultimate socialism was a reason and excuse for doing nothing and for rejecting new ideas such as those put forward by Keynes and Mosley. In fact a more fundamental explanation for the failures of 1929-31 must be sought, first, in the Labour Party's commitment to constitutionalism and in the influence which this had upon the party, and secondly, in the complex and deeply entrenched structure of British capitalism.

Within the framework of the British constitution and party system there was a fundamental conflict between the circumstances which had to be met if the Labour Party was to attain office, and those which had to be met if it were to retain office, once elected. In order to get elected into office, Labour had to raise the expectations of the under-privileged by promising a redistribution of income and wealth within society. In making such promises, which were necessary in order to win office, the Labour Party either directly or indirectly threatened business confidence and the confidence of overseas financiers. It was almost inevitable, therefore, that the establishment of a Labour government would produce a crisis by its impact upon capitalist confidence. In 1929-31, this political crisis was superimposed upon severe problems produced by the economic system.

Any democratically elected Labour government when faced with a crisis of confidence on the part of capitalists both at home and abroad had basically two choices. On the one hand, it could proceed with determination through a protracted series of crises towards a radical social and economic transformation along socialist lines. Or, on the other hand, it could go to extremes to try to reassure the business and financial communities. In 1929-31 the nature of the Labour leadership and the nature of the British capitalist system dictated the latter course of action. To pursue the former course of action might have meant a departure from constitutionalism and a possible complete breakdown of the economic system in which the working class, at least in the short run, would have suffered most of all. Leaders such as MacDonald and Snowden were simply not prepared to consider such possibilities. In other words, the Labour Government found it impossible to reach any working compromise with capitalism which was acceptable to the labour movement; at the same time, in the interests of the working class, it feared any threat of a breakdown in the economic and political system. It was forced, therefore, to betray its elemental ideals and to pursue unfair and divisive policies which eventually forced its own destruction.

The basic influence in the situation was the peculiar and almost unique nature of British capitalism which dictated economic policy and placed the Labour Government in impossible circumstances. The financial interests of the City of London exerted a level of influence which was not paralleled in overseas economies. The City had developed primarily as an international financial centre, rather than as a centre for raising capital for British industry. Britain had become heavily dependent not only on international finance, but also on overseas trade, and during times of crisis this dependence enabled financial interests, both at home and abroad, to impose deflationary policies on governments. The scope for radical economic reform in Britain within a constitutional framework was extremely limited by an unavoidable dependence upon overseas trade and finance. It was this situation, rather, than the depression and the unemployment problem, which produced a crisis and caused the downfall of the Labour Government in 1931.

The conceptual problems of how to achieve a socialist society in Britain within a democratic and constitutional framework were not even seriously considered, let alone solved, by the British labour movement during the interwar period. The Labour Party after 1931 continued with the pious hope that its established methods and policies were practicable, blaming its earlier failures upon the inadequacies of its leaders and the extreme nature of the short-run problems which they faced.

Notes

1   B. B. Gilbert, *British Social Policy, 1914-1939* (1970), ch. 2.
2   E. Wight Bakke, *The Unemployed Man: A Social Study* (1933), p. 17.
3   R. Postgate, *A Pocket History of the British Working Class* (1964), p. 69.
4   A. Bullock, *The Life and Times of Ernest Bevin*, vol. 1 (1960), p. 99.
5   R. Skidelsky, *Politicians and the Slump* (1970), pp. 394-5.

Chapter 7

Population

1 *The Pattern of Population Change*
The interwar years saw the completion of the 'demographic transition' in Britain. The 'demographic transition' is the name given by demographers to the change from an approximately stable or slowly growing population with fairly high birth and death rates, typical of pre-industrial societies, to an approximately stable or slowly growing population with low birth and death rates, typical of modern industrial societies. This transition is a major preoccupation, perhaps the major preoccupation, of modern demography. In particular, many attempts have been made to find causes, or at least correlates, of the fall in the birth rate which is a feature of the later stages of the transition. This fall in the birth rate, which occurred in Britain between the 1870s and the 1930s, brought to an end the high rates of population growth typical of the middle phase of the transition. This middle phase in Britain ran from about 1760 to the 1860s and includes the period of the classical industrial revolution.

Whether or not the high rates of population growth experienced in western Europe and the USA in the century after 1760 were a necessary or even a sufficient condition of industrialisation has been much discussed but is outside the scope of this book. Certainly by 1900 rapid population growth had been continuing for long enough for most people to regard it as part of the normal state of things, and the adjustment to the prospect of a slowly growing or stable population was likely to cause problems, if only psychological ones. The ending of the era of rapid demographic expansion in the West also marked the beginning of a new era in its relations with the rest of the world. Between 1750 and 1900 Europe's population growth had been faster than that of Asia or Africa.

Table 7.1 *Population Increases between 1750 and 1900*

Europe	186%
Asia	96%
Africa	27%

Source Cmd 7695, *Royal Commission on Population, Report* (1949), table 2, p. 7.

Great Britain's population growth had also been faster than that of the rest of Europe, and the British population had risen from about 6% of the European total in 1800 to 9% by 1900. Thus in the nineteenth century, the predominance of Europe in the affairs of the world, and of Britain within Europe, had both been reinforced by demographic developments. By the interwar years, the beginnings of a change in this situation were apparent. British and western European population growth was slowing down, but growth in eastern Europe and in Russia was continuing at a high rate, while in many countries today referred to as 'under-developed', there was the beginnings of a large acceleration in the rate of growth. The first phase in the industrial history of the world was coming to an end. This first phase had given an extraordinary but inevitably temporary importance to Britain and western Europe. The demographic patterns emerging in the interwar years marked the beginning of a new phase in which the population balance, and much else besides, was to change dramatically. In 1900 Europe's population was 34% of the world total; a proportion probably never exceeded before and unlikely ever to be exceeded again. By 1971 the European total had fallen to 12·6% of that of the world.[1]

The rate of population growth in England and Wales between the census of 1801 and that of 1901 was 1·3% per annum compound. In historical perspective this is a much faster rate of growth than anything that is likely to have occurred before the onset of industrialisation. Between 1650 and 1750 the world's population had probably grown at about 0·3% a year,[2] and the English population at a slower rate than this, whilst a growth rate of 1·3% per annum is only half the rate reached by some Latin American and 'under-developed' countries in the 1960s. Between 1871 and 1881 the excess of births over deaths in Great Britain was 3,895,000. Net outward migration was 257,000 leaving an increase over ten years of 3,638,000 or 13·9%. Such rates of increase were typical of nineteenth-century Britain. The rate of increase since 1881 had fallen but the absolute increase in numbers continued until the decade 1901-11, which saw the largest excess of births over deaths recorded in any ten-year period of British history: 4,587,000. Compared to these pre-first world war figures, the interwar figures look very different.

Table 7.2 *Population Increase in Great Britain, 1921-41*

	Natural Increase (millions)	Migration (millions)	Population Change (millions)	(per cent)
1921-1931	+2·591	− ·565	+2·026	+4·7
1931-1941	+1·160	+ ·650	+1·810	+4·0

Source Cmd 7695 (1949), table 4, p. 9.

The percentage rate of increase for the interwar years was about a third of that typical of the nineteenth century and the absolute excess of births over deaths in the 1920s about half that of the last two decades of the nineteenth century, falling to about a quarter in the 1930s. The 1930s saw the reversal of the flow of emigrants which had been leaving Britain in varying but substantial numbers since the middle of the nineteenth century. Between 1902 and 1921 net emigration from Britain totalled about 1·6 million persons. The flow continued in the 1920s and in all between 1871 and 1931 net emigration amounted to about 3¼ million people, or 15% of the natural increase of just over 22 million in this period. By contrast net immigration in the 1930s added 56% to the natural increase in these years. This change was mainly due to the declining opportunities in overseas countries relying economically on primary products, whose prices were low in the 1930s, and to immigration restrictions in the USA. Depressed primary product prices, leading to world-wide distress in agriculture, appear to have persuaded many former migrants to return to Britain. The outcome was a rate of increase of population in Great Britain in the interwar years of 0·4% per annum compound (1921-41). Britain had reached the end of the 'demographic transition'. Her rate of population increase was now reduced to the sort of figures typical of pre-industrial revolution societies, but this new comparative stability was characterised by the far lower birth and death rates typical of modern industrial societies.

II *The Pattern of Birth and Death Rates*
The increase of population in the third world or 'under-developed' countries, the first signs of which were manifest in the interwar years,

has since reached the point at which it is a major problem of policy and topic of discussion. Many economists and most governments of the countries concerned would like to be able to offer some prescription for lowering the birth rate, and demographers faced with this question have turned to the experience of countries such as Britain to see if there are lessons to be learned. It is this more than any other factor which accounts for the strong modern interest in the falling birth rate in industrialised western countries between about 1870 and the 1930s. Unfortunately it cannot be said that any firm conclusions have been reached. G. Hawthorn summarises the position as follows: 'The more research is done the less confident must any general description of the mechanics of transition be'.[3]

The main facts of the change are clear. Women married around the 1860s each had about 5·7 children during the course of their married lives. The number of children born on average to each married woman declined steadily from that figure. For marriages of the 1880s it was about 4·6 and for marriages between 1900 and 1909 3·37. From then on the figures are as follows:

Table 7.3 *The Fall in Fertility in Great Britain*

Marriages in the years	Number of live births per married woman
1910-1914	2·90
1915-1919	2·53
1920-1924	2·38
1925-1929	2·19

Source Cmd 7695 (1949), table 16, p. 25.

In historical perspective this is a large change in childbearing practices to have occurred in a period of only seventy years. It can be emphasised by considering how common large families were for the marriages of the 1860s compared to the marriages of 1925-9. At the earlier date 63% of all marriages produced five children or more, and 10% had ten children or more. By 1925, only 12·3% of all marriages produced five or more children and only 0·3% of all couples had ten or more children. At the other end of the scale the one-child family had occurred in only 5% of the 1860s marriages, but was 25% of those of 1925-9.[4] The decline in the number of children born to married couples is the central fact of interest in debates on this stage of the 'demographic transition'. What caused it? It is clear that the question in this form cannot be directly answered, since to answer it would be to assume that human behaviour is determined rather than a matter of choice. Even if it could be shown that changes in the number of children born to married couples in the past had always been associated with the same factors it would not follow that this was an explanation or that the same factors repeated in the same form in the future would be bound to cause similar results. People may, in fact, very often respond to social pressures or circumstances, but even if they do, they are not logically bound to do so, and may respond differently in the future.[5] This does not make it uninteresting to discover what social pressures or circumstances people did actually respond to in any particular case. However, even this is not very easy to discover. Many features of the period in question have been seen as candidates for the fall in the number of births. A list of every factor that has ever been offered would more or less amount to a social history of the period. This of course explains nothing at all.

The first factors to be considered here are the age at marriage of women and the availability and social acceptability of contraception. Over most of the world and for most of human history marriage has usually followed quickly after puberty. The great exception historically to this generalisation is what has been called the 'European marriage pattern'.[6] In western Europe between the seventeenth and nineteenth centuries, women married much later. From the mid-nineteenth century onwards, the age at marriage started to fall, but at the same time fertility within marriage started to be controlled by contraception. On this view there is some aspect of the European or perhaps protestant Christian attitude to life which leads to a desire to control fertility. This was expressed by delayed marriage before the general availability of contraceptives. Since contraceptives have become more available and more acceptable, they have enabled more effective control of fertility to be practised within marriage and this has in turn permitted a reversion to a more natural age of marriage. There are objections to such a view in general; control of fertility within marriage was quite widespread before the industrial revolution, and contraceptives were hardly generally available at any time in the nineteenth century. However the historical importance of the European marriage pattern is sufficient to justify mentioning this view. Apart from any general objections however, the British data in particular do not fit very well into this scheme. Britain certainly shared in the European marriage pattern with a late age of marriage in the eighteenth and nineteenth centuries. But in the second half of the nineteenth century the British age of marriage was actually rising, and although it fell slightly after 1900, it was much the same (at 25½ for spinsters marrying for the first time) in 1931 as it has been in 1860. Subsequently it fell, to reach 22½ years in 1970, but certainly the idea of a replacement of fertility control through late marriage without contraception, by early marriage with contraception, does not fit well into the British data for our period.

Clearly contraceptive practices of various sorts were increasingly used and this provides a proximate cause for the fall in family size, though it leaves open the question of the influences which persuaded people to use these contraceptive techniques. The 1949 Royal Commission conducted its own inquiry into contraceptive practices and their report provides almost the only source of information which has any statistical backing.[7] Even here the sample of women questioned was not very satisfactory by modern standards, and the commission approached this aspect of its work somewhat nervously. 'It was clear because of the intimate nature of the questions that only by means of a very tactful approach could the co-operation of the women in the enquiry be expected.'[8] The results for what they are worth – and they are all we have – showed that of women married between 1910 and 1919, 40% used some form of birth control at some time in their marriage, and for those married between 1935 and 1939, 66% had done so by the time of the inquiry. Further, at the earlier date about a quarter of the women who were involved in any form of birth control used a method other than withdrawal, but by the later date 57% of the 'controllers' had used some form of appliance. In short birth control within marriage was more extensive and more effective in form. The change is more marked still if we consider the proportion of women using some form of birth control at the start of their married life, as opposed to some period within it. For the marriages of 1910-19, only 8% of women used birth control at the outset, but by 1935-9 the proportion was 25%.[9]

Impressionistic evidence supports these figures for the increasing use of contraception. The attitude of the Roman Catholic Church remained of course implacably hostile to contraception by 'artificial' means throughout the period, though in 1932 J. Latz published a popular account of the demonstration in 1930 by Ogino and Knaus of the existence of a 'safe period', which was accepted by the Roman Catholic Church as a permissable form of birth control in certain circumstances.[10] But during this period the Church of England was in the course of a major change of attitudes. In 1916 a church body called the National Birth Rate Commission considered the matter and expressed outright opposition to any form of birth control other than abstinence. The Bishop of Southwark stated what was the general church view when he said that 'sexual intercourse was only justified if the procreation of children was intended — otherwise it was mere gratification'. He further thought that abstinence might have to be practised even if it risked the break-up of the marriage, if the circumstances of the couple made it impossible to accept the arrival of children.[11] From this apparently immutable hostility at the start of our period, the Church of England had moved by the 1958 Lambeth Conference to acceptance of family planning as the responsibility of parents. Some part of this shift in attitude took place in the interwar years. The 1930 Lambeth Conference allowed, rather grudgingly, some recognition of birth control by methods other than abstinence. There was by this date a substantial group of churchmen with more liberal attitudes. Thus after 1930 the Church was uncertain in its attitude, which must have at least reduced the discouragement offered by its earlier position on the subject.

Also during this period the pro-birth control or 'neo-Malthusian' movement started to extend its influence. Books giving details of contraceptive techniques had circulated fairly widely in Britain since the 1880s. H. A. Allbutt's *The Wife's Handbook*, first published in 1884, had sold half a million copies by 1929. R. T. Trull's *Sexual Physiology and Hygiene*, of 1886, was still being published in 1937. Marie Stopes, the author of many books on this topic with a wide circulation in the interwar years, brought a new style to birth control literature, relating it to marital adjustment and happiness, and emphasising the planning of families rather than the mere mechanics of the sexual act and contraceptive technique.[12] Her first birth control clinic was established in 1921. In 1930 the Family Planning Association was established and by 1939 it had sixty-six voluntary birth control clinics. Such activities are mostly of interest as symptoms of changing attitudes rather than for their actual effect. By 1939 it seems very unlikely that more than a small fraction of the population were attending or had ever attended such a clinic, or had ever received any form of outside advice about birth control, whether from doctors, clinics or anywhere else. The subject was still very largely taboo, and the typical working-class married couple would have found out by gossip, common sense, and perhaps through a book. Their contraceptive technique was likely to be withdrawal, or male sheaths bought from a barber's shop. But of course that is not to belittle the importance of the change. The effect of their contraceptive knowledge and practice, simple as it might seem from certain points of view, was a very large and historically important fall in the birth rate.

What social or economic pressures led them to wish to limit their families? This is the question to which we must now return. The report of the Royal Commission does not offer any model of the processes involved. Rather it points to a number of factors which have often been invoked as 'ex-post' explanations of the facts. Children were becoming more 'expensive' in that they had to be maintained for longer than in the nineteenth century. 'As the nineteenth century advanced more and more people were being thrown into the struggle for security and social promotion.' In these circumstances, 'it paid to travel light'. Fewer children could be given a better chance of success in life, a better start. Higher standards of parental care were becoming a normal requirement. The growth of science, the debates on evolution and the change in the status of women had all in some way affected people's attitudes. In summary, 'powerful economic, social and cultural forces were tending against the acceptance of an uncontrolled birth rate'.[13] If more specific reasons are to be sought, the most obvious correlate which suggests itself is income per head. The acceleration in the growth of personal incomes after the 1870s occurred at roughly the same time (though the timing is not exact by any means) as the start of the fall in the number of children born to married couples. Unfortunately there is no convincing empirical evidence to support such an idea, and *a priori* it is most unconvincing. The most plausible *a priori* link would be that, other things being equal, a rise in income would raise fertility. There is a lot of pre-industrial evidence to support such an idea. Good harvests and in general 'good times' tended to produce increases in the number of births.[14] But an increase or decrease in the number of births over a period of a few years may be due to accelerated or postponed conceptions rather than a general change in attitudes to desirable family size. And in pre-industrial conditions there had never been a prolonged secular rise in living standards such as occurred in Britain after about 1850. Nevertheless, the most convincing model would probably be a 'utility model', which attributed a positive utility to children (though a declining one with increasing numbers). Thus other things being equal, higher incomes would mean more children. The principal factor which did not remain equal in our period would be expectations in relation to material living standards. The processes which generate higher living standards also generate expectations of higher living standards, or to put it in other words, they provide an increasing range of opportunities for expenditure. Children thus come to be seen as alternative forms of 'consumption' and provide utility like other goods and services. Like some other goods, children also have 'running costs' which have to offset against the utility they provide, and the 'running costs' of children were increasing. Partly this was due to the same process of rising expectations already referred to. For instance, rising incomes made it possible to provide most children with shoes by the interwar years. But as well as becoming possible, it

had also become socially essential. Before 1914 children could be sent
to school without shoes without this calling for comment, but by 1930
it was considered essential for children to wear shoes at school.[15] In
addition to involving costs and providing utility, children are also
potential earners on behalf of their family. It could be argued that the age
at which they would make a useful contribution to the family budget was
postponed by the increase in the school leaving age. In the middle of the
nineteenth century children could be earning a wage by the age of 7 or 8
or even earlier. By the interwar years, they had to stay at school until they
were 14. Although this may be a factor, perhaps not too much weight
should be put on it. Very young children did not earn much in the
nineteenth century, and interwar children could and often did earn
something before they were 14. Anyway what matters is the balance
of earnings and costs. The increase in the socially acceptable minimum
expenditure on children could have been more important than the
change in the children's earning capacity as such.

An influential hypothesis which is in some respects an alternative to
the 'utility model' briefly outlined above is the 'diffusionist thesis'.
This suggests that the practice of family limitation started in the upper
income groups of society and spread downwards through the social
spectrum and also outwards from the largest city centres to provincial
and eventually rural areas. This hypothesis requires two steps. First an
account of why the upper income groups themselves adopted family
limitation, and then a further account of how this practice was
diffused outwards to other social groups. It is certainly true that the
fall in the number of children born to each married woman started first
in the upper income groups. This effect was well-established by 1900
and, in the marriages of the period 1900-9, the wives of professional
men had an average of 2·33 children while the wives of labourers had
an average of 4·45 children.[16] For the marriages of those years the
wives of manual workers had on average 1·41 times as many children
as the wives of non-manual workers. From this period on however, the
divergence between social classes in the number of children born
ceased to change very much. The ratio between manual and non-manual
workers' wives remained within a small margin of the 1900-9 figure of
1·41 up to and including the marriages of 1925-9.[17] Thereafter the
margin has narrowed, and the picture has been complicated by changes
within broad social groups.

Although he does not make the theory very explicit, J. A. Banks's
book *Prosperity and Parenthood*[18] is a principal source for the
diffusionist thesis. Banks resorts to what is in fact a utility model to
explain the fall in fertility of the upper income groups. The middle
class was under the pressure of rising expectations. To maintain their

standard of living in relation to these expectations they reduced the number of children they had. The economic advantages which this conferred then led the manual working classes to copy the practice of family limitation. In doing this, they were helped by the changing climate of opinion in relation to the acceptability of contraceptives, their increasing availability, and the diminishing taboos on discussion of the subject.

Although the above account appears plausible at a common sense level, it is still not without its problems. There is no model or hypothesis currently available which in any satisfactory way 'explains' the onset of family limitation. For instance the diffusionist idea assumes that the manual working classes were lacking in the knowledge or ability to practise family limitation within marriage, but there is little evidence for such a view. Research on pre-industrial population patterns has made it clear that birth control within marriage has been a possibility for all classes for hundreds of years.[19] The birth rates of a number of French and English village communities which have been deduced by family reconstitution studies show sharp fluctuations in response to economic conditions, which can only have been due to conscious use of birth control. Further it is clear that neither instruction through books nor contraceptive apparatus is a necessary prior condition of such family limitation. People will, and in the past frequently have, limited their families without instruction or apparatus, presumably through withdrawal or abortion, or less probably, abstinence. However they did it – and there can be almost no direct evidence on this – the point is that they did do it. The mere fact that apparatus and knowledge was more available after 1870 is thus not an adequate explanation for the fall in family size, and the example of the middle classes cannot be a convincing explanation for changes within the working classes, because the working classes had shown that they did not need such an example. They were quite capable of managing it on their own.

Further the theory that the middle classes were experiencing pressure on their living standards through rising expectations is not entirely convincing. Middle-class incomes probably rose steadily through the period up to 1900, but by contrast there does seem to have been a shift in the distribution of income after the war; this distributional shift has already been discussed in Chapter 1. Thus if there was a period when the middle class was experiencing pressure on its living standards in relation to expectations one would expect it to have been in the 1920s rather than at an earlier period. Yet the differential between working and middle-class fertility rates opened up in the earlier period, and thereafter remained stable. This does not dispose of the idea that expectations and standards were running ahead of income in the earlier periods and Banks adduces a lot of descriptive evidence to support this idea. The impossibility of any secure measurement of expectations so long after the event means that this proposition is hardly susceptible to proof one way or the other.

Finally any convincing explanation would have to take into account the complex variations between specific occupations and regions. E. H. Phelps-Brown suggests a relation between conservatism and resistance to new attitudes, and the type of work in which a person was employed. The suggestion is that the rougher and heavier the work, the greater the resistance to change, and in particular, the greater the resistance to the adoption of birth control. 'The biggest families were those of men doing rough muscular work in the open air . . . such as dock labourers, dustmen, coal heavers, building labourers and agricultural labourers.'[20] But some wage earners, as Phelps-Brown also points out, were having no more children than the middle classes; for instance domestic servants, men in the textile trades, caretakers and waiters. It is not easy to account for these variations; to start to do so it would first be necessary to standardise for the effects of differing age structure, though the variations are so large in many cases that they are unlikely to be entirely accounted for by one occupation employing on average younger people than another. A possible connection might be between the heaviness of the most commonly available manual work in any given area and the opportunities in that area for female employment. Textile workers had a notably low birth rate and notably good opportunities for the employment of wives. The reverse is true of mining districts. Even if this connection could be more firmly demonstrated, it would still not explain the general decline in the birth rate in these years, but only the differences between certain occupations.

Hence it seems necessary to return to a very open verdict on the reasons for the fall in the number of children born to each married woman which started with the marriages of the 1860s and culminated in the marriages of the 1930s. Possibly the question is being put the wrong way round. Perhaps what really needs explaining is the period of rapid population growth rather than the periods of lower growth. Historically, fairly low population growth has been the norm, that is until the population 'explosion' of the developing world after the second world war. The exceptional state of affairs was the rapid growth associated with the transition to an urban industrial society. Although outside the scope of this book, it might be easier to explain how the normal tendency to control the rate of growth was disrupted by industrialisation but reasserted itself when the new social forms were stabilising after 1870, and when the flow of migrants from rural areas was drying up and the towns were increasingly populated with second and third generation urban dwellers.

Turning now to mortality, death rates in the age groups between middle childhood and middle age, that is between about 5 and 45, started to fall at much the same time as the birth rate, in the late 1870s. They had been approximately constant for the preceding forty years, since the start of registration in 1837 had made it possible to calculate them. The fall in these middle age groups, once under way, continued steadily until it levelled out at what are probably irreducibly low rates in about 1960. Thus for instance the death rate for the 25-34 age group which was 10·5 for males in the UK in 1870 fell to 6·6 in 1900, to 4·5 in 1920, to 2·8 in 1939 and to under 1 by 1960.[21] All these central age groups show a similar pattern of prolonged and regular fall in death rates, persisting for about eighty years after the late 1870s, apart from increases due to casualties in the two wars. This decline has almost certainly very little to do with medical progress but is due to general improvement in nutrition, clothing, housing and public health.[22] The major cause of death in these age groups in the mid-nineteenth century was the infectious diseases; various forms of tuberculosis were by far the largest single cause of death, and measles, scarlet fever, enteric fever, diphtheria and dysentery were prominent.[23] It is not possible to analyse the causes of death as early as this with much confidence, as diagnosis was poor and large numbers of deaths were certified as being due to 'convulsions' or 'diseases of the nervous system' which in most cases simply meant that the doctor did not know why the patient died. However the prominence of tuberculosis and of other infectious diseases is not in doubt. Nor is there any doubt that the conquest of these diseases is the major factor in reducing the death rate in the middle age groups discussed above. And it is clear that, with the exception of smallpox, specific medical treatment had little to do with this conquest. There were for instance no effective treatments available for tuberculosis before the 1940s. Isolation in sanatoria, which was increasingly practised in the interwar years, had no specific therapeutic effect, although it almost certainly helped to reduce the spread of the disease through contact, and may have helped individuals through improved diet. By the beginning of the interwar years the death rate from the various types of tuberculosis was one third of its 1860 level (1·09 per thousand instead of 3·3), but still accounted for 9% of all deaths in 1923. By the end of the period, in 1937, the death rate from this disease had fallen by a further 35%, to 0·7 per thousand though this still left it as a major cause of death, especially for those between 15 and 44. The other major infectious killers of the nineteenth century had by this time almost completely yielded to better conditions, although diphtheria was a partial exception and continued to claim some three thousand deaths a year throughout the period. As the infectious diseases retreated, they were starting to be replaced as major causes of death by the degenerative diseases of middle and old age — various forms of cancer and heart disease. At the beginning of the interwar years cancer and heart disease accounted for 23% of all deaths, but 37% by the end. By 1937 the death rate from heart disease was about the same as that from tuberculosis in 1860, and had doubled since 1923, although some of this increase may have reflected improved diagnosis.

The pattern of death rates for age groups other than those in the middle range was different. As conditions improved it seemed that the strongest and least vulnerable ages benefited first, while gains for the old and very young came later. The reduction in deaths from infectious diseases enabled a higher proportion of people to survive through middle age, but nothing in the new situation delayed the biological process of ageing, and even in the 1970s there seems little prospect of achieving this in the foreseeable future. Hence the death rate in the older age groups showed a far smaller fall. Whereas between the ages 5 and 45 death rates in 1920 were generally between a third and a half of their 1870 levels, for the 65-75 age group the rate was still three quarters of that level and for older groups over four fifths of it. A similar pattern of change continued through the interwar years themselves. Death rates for the middle age groups continued to fall, so that by 1937 they were down by roughly another 20%, but death rates in older groups again fell much less and for those over 75 they increased slightly. Since these older groups were now beginning to form a larger proportion of the population, this tended to stabilise the crude death rate for the whole population, which fell only slightly in this period.

The slow rate of change in death rates for the older age groups is simple enough to interpret, but at the other end of the age scale the infant mortality rate, that is the rate of death of children under one year of age, presents more problems. In the 1970s a few countries with high standards of living and efficient medical services have achieved infant mortality rates of between 10 and 15 per thousand, for instance Holland's rate in 1971 was 11·1 and Sweden's in 1968 13·0. In the early 1970s the British rate was about 18. The Swedish and Dutch rates quoted represent what must be close to the lowest possible level. By contrast, rates during the course of the nineteenth-century industrialisation were typically fifteen or more times higher. In Prussia in 1860, to take one example, the rate was 199 and in England and Wales in 1870 the rate was 160.[24] Thus over the 100 years since the 1870s the fall in infant mortality has been, if we consider the best figures achieved so far, the largest of all the improvements in mortality experience. However, unlike the fall in the rate for the middle and less vulnerable age groups, the fall in the infant mortality rate did not start, in either Britain or in the rest of Europe, until the turn of the century. The rate for England and Wales in 1900 was still 154. From then on the decline proceeded steadily, dropping to 80 in 1920, 60 in 1930, 30 in 1950 and 18·4 in 1970. As we have seen, the 1970 rate is not the lowest that can be achieved and is still falling, though very slowly. Thus whereas by the interwar years the death rates for the middle phases of life were already down to levels not very different from what we know today and which are unlikely to be much further reduced, infant mortality rates were at levels intermediate between the high rates of the nineteenth century and modern levels. The England and Wales rate of 60 in 1930, for instance, was about the same as that for Italy in 1950 or for the Philippines in 1970.

The reason for the different pattern in infant death rates as compared with middle life rates seems to be that for the young child, improvement in conditions and diet is not enough to protect him against the hazards of infection during the critically vulnerable early days of life. What is needed in addition is knowledge of the mechanisms of infection and this means that progress will depend not only on better general conditions but on specific medical knowledge and its application. This knowledge started to be available by about 1900 with the growing understanding of the nature of infective organisms and the development of midwifery and district nurse services which enabled at least a rudimentary application of what had been learnt.[25] The precise timing of the start of the fall in infant mortality rates however is a subject that deserves more study, since there is very little detailed information about the ways in which the available knowledge was brought to bear or whether other factors were at work.

The broad pattern of death rates in Britain in the interwar years is one of fairly rapid improvement, with middle life rates approaching modern levels. The subject cannot be left however without considering the variations which occurred between areas. The spread of rates between different areas of the country is an old phenomena, certainly pre-dating the industrial revolution. During the early stages of industrialisation, rates in the industrial towns were far higher than in predominantly middle-class or rural areas and mortality in the industrial slums reached very high levels. In the mid-nineteenth century the expectation of life for men in Manchester was, according to William Farr, 24·2 years, compared to 51 years for men in Surrey.[26] During the interwar years, despite the general fall in mortality, the spread between areas was probably hardly reduced, and some of the differences are large. When standardised so as to eliminate differences due to the age structure of the population, death rates in most of the urban areas which suffered high unemployment were between one and a quarter and one and a half times higher than the national average. Areas thus affected included South Wales, the Glasgow area, Lancashire, and the north-east of England. For instance the standardised rate for the whole of Glamorgan in 1938 was 1·24 times the national average for England and Wales, and, within Glamorgan, urban areas had higher rates still; Merthyr Tydfil was 1·52 times the average and had an infant mortality rate of 78 (England and Wales average 58). Aberdare's rate was 1·43 times, Caerphilly 1·36 times and Rhondda 1·44 times the average. Similar examples can be given from other depressed urban areas, such as Manchester (1·24), Burnley and Blackburn (1·31), Nelson (1·45) and Wigan (1·34), the last with an infant mortality rate of 99. From the north-east, Jarrow and South Shields were both about 1·3 times the average, Jarrow having an infant mortality rate of 72. These examples clearly show the uneven distribution of resources across the country and the way in which the areas of high unemployment and industrial depression suffered in the most vital human matters of life and death. At the other end of the scale, the standardised death rates for Buckinghamshire, Hertfordshire and Surrey were all about 20% less than the average, and Buckinghamshire's infant mortality rate of 32 was 45% below the average and less than one third of Wigan's. These are the extremes. Large blocs of the population had a mortality experience close to the average; for instance London, Birmingham and Bristol were all fairly close to the mean. The spread between extremes was however impressive and William Farr's comment made in 1885 — that such divergencies were 'unnatural and susceptible of remedy' — seems equally applicable to the situation of 1938.

Although the birth and death rates have been discussed separately, it is possible that there were interactions between them. In so far as married couples aimed at a certain completed family size, then they would need to have fewer children to achieve this as the death rate, and particularly the infant mortality rate, fell. And the infant mortality rate itself could well have been reduced by the reduction in the birth rate, which enabled parents to concentrate their care and resources on the smaller number of children. Family size is not easy to discuss, since it cannot be deduced from birth or death rates, and census figures for 'separate occupiers' or, after 1911, 'private families' are not exactly the same as the usual idea of the biological family. For what they are worth, the change in the average household size at various census dates is given in table 7·4. It can be seen that the fall in family size is a good deal less than the fall in the number of live births

202 Interwar Britain: a Social and Economic History

per married woman which was discussed earlier. The total outcome of the movement of the various rates discussed was to reduce the rate of population growth and we now turn to the views of contemporaries on the subject and to some of its presumed and actual effects.

Table 7.4 *Household Sizes in England and Wales as Recorded in the Census.*

Year	Persons per family (pre-1911 definitions)	Persons per private family on 1911 definition
1861	4·47	
1891	4·73	
1911	4·51	4·36
1921		4·14
1931		3·72
1951		3·19

Source General Register Office, *Census of England and Wales 1951, Housing Report*, table A, p. xxiii. The definition of the family in the second column differs mainly in counting lodgers not taking their meals with the family as a separate household. Both definitions include servants living in as part of the family. Family size was estimated on both bases in 1911.

III *Views on the Falling Rate of Population Growth*

The falling rate of population growth caused alarm in interwar Britain. This is not to say that the ordinary citizen was alarmed, if he thought about it at all, but writers and intellectuals were worried, and in some cases the fears assumed almost hysterical proportions. It was in this case perhaps a merit of the British political system that it tended to inhibit prompt action. In Germany, France and Italy various measures were taken to stimulate the birth rate, such as family allowances and tax rebates, special taxes on bachelors, loans on the occasion of marriage and the suppression of information about birth control. The merits of family allowances as an anti-poverty and re-distributive measure are beyond doubt, though these merits are quite distinct from the pro-natalist arguments. In the countries mentioned they were introduced for the wrong reasons and in association with other largely irrational measures which contributed nothing to the welfare of the populations concerned. In Britain, though there were books and talk, nothing was actually done, which in retrospect looks just as well. However, the literature of the falling population scare has some interest as an example of how intelligent people can deceive themselves about a situation of this sort. Demographic forecasting is not and never can be an exact science, in that what is required is a forecast of human actions. This is in principle impossible. Human beings may simply decide not to do whatever it is that someone has said they are going to do. This is not to say that one cannot make forecasts about what is likely to happen, and some such forecasts are more sensible than others. However, a feature of the interwar debate on population was that people searched for, and in some cases believed they had found, a statistical device for overcoming such uncertainties. The device was called a 'reproduction rate' and it offers a good example of statistically naive laymen allowing themselves to be blinded by pseudo-science. The 'reproduction rate' was devised by Dr Kuczynksi. It attempted to reduce to a single figure the extent to which a population was 'replacing itself' by aggregating the age-specific birth and death rates of various generations of women in a single year. The fatal flaw in all such calculations, however statistically refined, is that they cannot distinguish between a reduction in the number of births to each woman over her whole child-bearing life and a change in the spacing of births over that life. Thus if for some reason, such as an economic depression or a war, women use contraceptives or are separated from their husbands, and thus have fewer children, the reproduction rate for those years will fall. But the women may not have fewer children in total. When the depression passes or the husbands return, they may still have all the children they originally planned, and the number of children they have over their child-bearing life may be unaffected. Demographically nothing has happened, but in the meanwhile the reproduction rate will have fluctuated substantially, first downwards and then upwards, and those who follow it as an index for the future may have been flung into all sorts of unjustifiable anxieties.

The special attraction of reproduction rate calculations in British conditions was that they appeared to offer a way round the grave deficiencies of British demographic statistics. Modern demographic forecasting, which does not make spurious claims to deterministic predictions of the future, relies on cohort analysis. That is, it looks at the progressive performance of a cohort of women born in a particular year and asks — How many children are they going to have by the end of their child-bearing life? This is a question that cannot finally be answered until they have actually reached the end of their child-bearing life, by which time it is too late to be of any use for a prediction. Nevertheless, if one follows a cohort through the child-bearing period one can see how they are doing. If after say ten years of marriage, they have had fewer children per woman than previous cohorts had by that stage of their married lives, it may be reasonable to assume that they are going to have fewer in total, provided there is no obvious reason for postponed births. In effect, one compares the reproductive performance of the cohort in question with the performance of their predecessors at the same stage of their lives. From this one can make an estimate —

it can be no more − of what their final performance will be. This technique requires statistics of the number of children born to each married woman. That is, when a child's birth is registered, one needs to know whether it is the first, second or the nth child of its mother. Although the birth of all children in England and Wales had been registered since 1837, this birth parity information was not included in the registration data until 1938 when an Act of Parliament of that year made it a requirement. Moreover, no British census, with the single exception of that of 1911, had ever collected birth parity information in the form required. Thus British demographic statistics, which in this respect compared very unfavourably with some other countries, notably Sweden, were quite inadequate for cohort analysis. But a reproduction rate could be calculated from the birth and death rates of one year. In the 1930s the conclusions offered by these calculations were that the British population was 'failing to replace itself'; that is the reproduction rate had fallen below unity. The forecast for the future that followed from this was that the population would decline; in some versions of the calculations the decline was expected to be rapid.

The actual calculations involved in reproduction rates were fairly complex, involving the use of life tables. Probably few of the commentators who quoted the results understood the techniques involved and many were bowled over by the appearance of scientific precision. Even such a subsequently distinguished figure as the young R. M. Titmuss was uninhibited in his enthusiasm and this led him to join in the chorus of despondency about the future viability of the British race.[27] However, there were many more extreme prophets of impending disaster than Titmuss. The title of G. F. McCleary's book, *The Menace of British Depopulation*,[28] speaks for itself, and the contents fully live up to the title. More responsible commentators were hardly less gloomy. Eva Hubback's *The Population of Britain*, published in 1947, accepted that a large decline in British population was virtually certain. This prospect she found daunting in the extreme. Her admission (p. 140) that it is impossible to say what effects a smaller population would have on living standards, passes almost unnoticed in a welter of gloomy prophecies about the effects on British status and power in the world and the psychological ill-effects of belonging to a community which 'lacks the vitality and spirit to reproduce itself'. 'Does it matter if human life stops?', she asks, and in case this stretches the reader's credulity, she adds: 'This is by no means an imaginary danger'. After this a relapse into poetry (Browning) follows fairly swiftly. Sir Dennis Robertson, addressing the Royal Economic Society in 1945, said that every Englishman should make a note in the agenda section of his diary: 'Must raise net reproduction rate to at least one.[29] (one being the value at which the population was thought to be replacing itself exactly). And J. M. Keynes, speaking to the Eugenics Society in 1937, said that 'we know much more securely than we know almost any other social or economic factor relating to the future, that . . . we shall be faced in a very short time with a stationary or declining population'.[30]

It was in response to widely expressed and discussed fears of this sort that the Royal Commission on Population was established. It reported in 1949. This was one of the most thorough and distinguished of commissions, and it did an extensive demolition job on the alarmists, while at the same time producing valuable additions to British population statistics. It conducted the first fertility census (providing birth parity information) since the fertility census of 1911, and it also made a pioneering investigation into the contraceptive practices of a sample of married women. Its conclusions were firstly that it was impossible to say definitely that the British population was going to decline and that many of the interwar predictions based on reproduction rate calculations were highly misleading. 'Reproduction rates', the Commission noted acidly, 'are by no means reliable instruments for indicating the fundamental trends underlying the crude figures of births and deaths.'[31] Secondly the Commission thought that such evidence as there was did not support the view that a decline in the population was in any way likely, and that if there were to be a decline, it would not happen for a very long time; about eighty or one hundred years. And thirdly the Economics Committee of the Commission concluded that a slowly declining population would be no bad thing anyway, and that 'from a purely economic point of view we have good reason to welcome the prospect that the number of people in this island will soon cease to grow'.[32]

IV *Economic Consequences of the End of Rapid Population Growth*
A good many of the fears expressed in this period were either purely irrational or were based on a notion of national prestige and power which the arrival of atomic weapons was soon to render completely out of date. Despite this, the interwar years did see the end of an important historical era, the era of rapid population growth which had been associated with the early stages of industrialisation. Clearly such population growth could not continue for ever; by 1920 Britain was already one of the most densely populated countries in the world. A projection of nineteenth-century rates of population growth into the future would have produced an absurd population density in the fairly near future. It was entirely reasonable to suggest that the rate of

population growth was going to be lower in the future than in the past, and that it was perhaps going to be near zero. Keynes, in the paper already referred to, clearly saw that this presented both an opportunity and a danger. The opportunity was that for a given rate of increase in output, the per capita increase would be greater the lower the rate of population growth, an arithmetical truism that has been made all too clear to many poor countries in the 1960s. The danger was that this opportunity might be thrown away by increased unemployment. Unemployment was rightly a main topic for economic discussion in the interwar years. And by the end of the period Keynes and some other economists had analysed the problem as one of deficient demand. Demand could be conceptualised as having three components: the demand of consumers, the demand of the government for goods and services, and the demand for investment; the now familiar $C + G + I$ of the economics textbooks. If the total of C, G and I was less than the productive potential of the economy at any time, then unemployment would result. Keynes and some other economists, for instance Keynes's American disciple Alvin Hansen, reasoned that in the past a good deal of the investment demand had arisen from the need to provide fixed capital assets for an increasing population. Hansen thought that in the USA in the nineteenth century, about half of all the investment that took place had been attributable to population growth and the opening up of new territory,[33] In the minds of these economists there was a further reason to fear that in future investment might be too low to maintain full employment. This was their belief that economic progress was close to satiating all human wants. Taken together, the end of population growth and the satiation of material desires could lead either to a utopia of leisure and plenty or to the disaster of mounting unemployment and the social breakdown which might follow. This view of the future was in many ways optimistic, indeed almost utopian. The fact that it did not prove accurate in the short term does not make it irrelevant to the longer term economic outlook, even if it turns out to be the problems of the environment rather than the satiation of wants which ultimately limits the possibilities for the indefinite expansion of investment and output. The essence of this Keynes-Hansen view of the population situation was the recognition of the opportunity offered coupled with a very reasonable fear that the social wisdom necessary to grasp it would not be forthcoming. Keynes expressed support for 'the old Malthusian conclusion' that other things being equal, the faster the growth of population, the lower the increase in resources and output per head. Other things might not be equal; the new devil of unemployment might replace the old Malthusian devil, but it need not if we could understand the way the economy worked and acted on our knowledge. Keynes himself had already made large contributions to the knowledge and understanding that would be necessary.

The Economics Committee of the Royal Commission on Population considered the question in more detail, and came to the same basic conclusion. A successful policy on unemployment was the key, but they thought that 'even if our employment policy is only moderately successful we are led by our analysis to conclude that for Great Britain today the balance of economic advantage is strongly in favour of a stationary population'. In a far-sighted section, well ahead of its time, the Committee recognised that modern economic growth is space intensive. It creates demands for space, for all sorts of uses: 'parks, green belts, playing fields, gardens . . . in the more thickly peopled parts of Great Britain lack of space is a serious obstacle to the wider provision of such amenities'. 'We must expect', they continue, 'that the peace and beauty of the countryside will be increasingly threatened by the wider enjoyment of regular holidays, by the spread among town dwellers of the taste for regular outings, by improved transport facilities and by an increase in the numbers of those possessing motor cars and motor cycles.'[34] All these considerations added to their welcome for the possibility of a stationary population.

There were possible disadvantages. Prominent in the views of the alarmists on the subject was the 'ageing of the population'. Eva Hubback wrote that 'it is usually considered that elderly people have not the flexibility and adaptability of the young' and that 'from the point of view of the community it is indeed far more encouraging to spend money on children than to spend it on old people'; an illogical conclusion which confused the number of old people with the proportion of old people in the population. She was presumably not suggesting euthanasia. Factual information on the effects of the change in the age structure associated with the end of rapid population growth are harder to come by than assertions about 'lack of adaptability'. J. J. Spengler in a paper written in 1948[35] quotes a number of studies. Palmer and Brownell took a sample of 249 weavers, spinners and non-ferrous metal workers in the USA. The finding was that productivity was on a plateau from 25 to 55 years of age and that, compared with the level of that plateau, productivity was 5% lower between the ages of 55 and 64, 10% lower between the ages of 15 and 24 and 10-15% lower after age 65. Other evidence quoted by Spengler suggested that although interruptions of work increased with age, labour turnover decreased. Spengler concluded that 'output varies less with the age of a representative individual than from individual to individual of a stipulated age'.[36] On the wider issue of the general values held by a society Spengler reached the apparently reasonable conclusion that 'the system of values held by a people is determined by many factors of which age composition is merely one, and probably not even an important one'.[37] Fears about the debilitating effect of changes in the age structure then do not stand up very well to scrutiny, although on this topic even the Economics Committee of the Royal Commission hesitated. 'A society in which the proportion of young people is diminishing may well become dangerously unprogressive intellectually and artistically — a danger sufficient to provoke serious consideration.' To do the Committee justice however, they were referring there to the sort of changes of proportions which would follow from a substantial decline in population rather than a mere stabilisation.

There were other possible disadvantages; the economies of scale associated with large populations could probably be reaped through international trade; the maintenance of full employment could be dealt with through the management of demand. From the strategic point of view the decline in the proportion of the population available for military service was thought to be more serious, but the general conclusion was that the fears had been exaggerated and that the potential advantages of a stationary population were great.

V *Regional Distribution*

Two facts stand out in the experience of the interwar years with respect to regional distribution. The first is that despite very high unemployment in some parts of the country and much lower rates in others, the rate of internal migration was not particularly high by historical standards. The 'coefficient of redistribution' is a figure which compares the extent of internal migration as between different periods. For 1921 to 1931 the coefficient was 0·16. This compares with a figure of 0·45 for the forty years preceding 1921.[38] In other words, internal migration in the 1920s was proceeding at about one third of the rate of the previous forty years. In the 1930s it is not possible to calculate a coefficient in the same form, but internal migration was lower still.[39] Between 1931 and 1936 the rate of internal migration was such that it would have taken thirty-two years to level out the rates of unemployment across the country as a whole.[40] No simple or single explanation can be given for this observation. A possibility is that much of the previous internal migration had been from rural areas and agricultural employment into urban areas and industrial employment. The scope for this had been largely exhausted by the interwar years; agriculture, forestry and fishing accounted for only 9% of employment by 1921. Possibly people were less willing to respond to the push of unemployment than they were to the pull of the attractions of urban life, such as they were. Unemployment itself tended to reduce the financial resources available for migration. The costs of a move became more daunting if the move had to be undertaken after a prolonged spell of low income. Again unemployment was often seen as temporary; something that would disappear when 'better trade' returned. Internal migration did less in the interwar years than might have been expected to even out the incidence of unemployment.

The second fact which stands out in the interwar experience is the ending of the nineteenth-century pattern of movement which had seen the largest increases of population in the regions where textiles, coal mining and heavy engineering and shipbuilding predominated. This meant the northern region, the north-west, Humberside and Yorkshire, and South Wales. The south-east region had also been increasing its share of population regularly since the middle of the nineteenth century, but after 1921 its rate of increase exceeded the national average by a far larger margin. The south-east was joined in the interwar years by two other regions, the east midlands and the west midlands. In this period these three regions were the only ones which grew faster than the average and the only regions which gained population by migration. Many regions and areas lost population. Glamorgan and Monmouth for instance, which had seen very rapid rates of increase in the years before 1914 as the coal industry expanded, showed a decline of 9% between 1921 and 1937.[41] Wales, Scotland, the north, the north-west, and Yorkshire and Humberside all had a smaller proportion of the UK population in 1937 than they had had in 1921. Although Wales and Scotland had had a declining share of the UK population since the middle of the nineteenth century, the appearance of the other three regions in the proportionately declining group represents a major change from nineteenth-century experience. So too does the arrival of the east and west midlands in the proportionately increasing group. These changes reflect the shift in industrial structure away from the industries typical of the nineteenth-century development towards the far more heterogeneous type of development typical of later stages of industrialisation. This more heterogeneous development included a variety of forms of engineering, such as motor cars and electrical goods, a variety of consumer goods industries and a wide range of service industries. One can perhaps see these developments as a re-establishment of the traditional predominance of London and the surrounding area, which began long before the industrial revolution, but had been briefly interrupted by it, as prosperity and growth were temporarily centred on the textile, coal, iron and shipbuilding industries of the early stages of industrialisation.

Notes

1 *United Nations Demographic Year Book 1971*, p. 111.
2 United Nations, *Determinants and Consequences of Population Trends* (1953).
3 G. Hawthorn, *The Sociology of Fertility* (1970), p. 30.
4 Calculated from Cmd 7695 (1949), table 17, p. 26.
5 This is a necessarily cursory reference to a large philosophical topic. For one discussion see A. Ryan, *The Philosophy of the Social Sciences* (1970), chapter 5.
6 J. Hajnal, 'European Marriage Patterns in Perspective', in D. V. Glass and D. C. Eversley (eds.), *Population in History* (1965), p. 101.
7 Cmd 7695 (1949), Papers, vol. 1, *Report of an Inquiry into Family Limitation and its Influence on Human Fertility in the Past Fifty years* (by J. Lewis-Fanning).
8 Cmd 7695 (1949), *Papers*, vol. 1, p. 3.
9 Cmd 7695 (1949), *Papers*, vol. 1, tables, 2, 3, 5. The very small sample of women married before 1910 have here been discarded as a basis for comparison in favour of the larger 1910-19 cohort.
10 J. Latz, *The Rhythm of Sterility and Fertility in Women* (1932).
11 F. Campbell, 'Birth Control and the Christian Churches', *Population Studies*, vol. 14, no. 2 (November 1960), p. 131.
12 D. V. Glass, *Population Policies and Movements* (1940), p. 45.
13 Cmd 7695 (1949) *Report*, pp. 39-41.
14 E. A. Wrigley, *Population and History* (1969), chs 3 and 4.
15 M. Wynn, *Family Policy* (1970), p. 51. And compare the photographs in E. H. Phelps-Brown, *The Growth of British Industrial Relations* (1959), facing page 42. These show classes of primary school children at the same London school in 1894 and 1924. Two out of five in the front row in the earlier photograph are barefoot, and more will clearly be barefoot very shortly. At the later date all the children have what appear to be good shoes.
16 Cmd 7695 (1949) *Papers*, vol. 6, part 1, table 40, p. 110.
17 Cmd 7695 (1949) *Report*, table 21, p. 29.
18 J. A. Banks, *Prosperity and Parenthood* (1954), ch. 10.
19 Wrigley, *Population and History*, p. 124.
20 E. H. Phelps-Brown, *The Growth of British Industrial Relations* (1959), pp. 5-8.
21 Rates given throughout this section are per thousand. They are taken from various issues of the *Annual Abstract of Statistics and the Registrar General's Statistical Review of England and Wales*.
22 T. McKeown, and R. G. Record, 'Reasons for the Decline in Mortality in England and Wales during the Nineteenth Century', *Population Studies*, vol. 16 (1962).
23 R. Lambert, *Sir John Simon* (1963), p. 59 and appendix.
24 Wrigley, *Population and History*, p. 171, table 5.8.
25 Wrigley, *Population and History*, p. 170.
26 Quoted in Wrigley, *Population and History*, p. 173.
27 R. M. Titmuss, *Parents Revolt* (1942), p. 22.
28 G. F. McCleary, *The Menace of British Depopulation* (1937).
29 D. V. Glass, *Population Policies and Movements*, 2nd edn (1967), Introduction, p. vii.

30 J. M. Keynes, 'Some Economic Consequences of a Declining Population', *Eugenics Review* (April 1937), p. 13.

31 Cmd 7695 (1949), *Report*, p. 62.

32 Cmd 7695 (1949), *Papers*, vol. 3 p. 52.

33 A. H. Hansen, 'Economic Progress and Declining Population Growth', *American Economic Review* (March 1939), p. 10.

34 Cmd 7695 (1949), *Papers*, vol. 3, p. 50.

35 J. J. Spengler, 'The Economic Effects of Changes in Age Composition', *New York State Joint Legislative Committee on Problems of the Age in* (1948), reprinted in C. B. Nam, *Population and Society* (1968).

36 Nam, *Population and Society*, p. 594.

37 Nam, *Population and Society*, p. 603.

38 C. H. Lee, *Regional Economic Growth in the United Kingdom since the 1880s* (1970), table B. 3, p. 215.

39 Lee, *Regional Economic Growth*, p.132.

40 Lee, *Regional Economic Growth*, p.133.

41 Cmd 6153 (1940), *Royal Commission on the Distribution of the Industrial Population, Report*, p. 37.

Housing

I *The Nineteenth Century Heritage*

As population grew and industrialisation progressed in the nineteenth and early twentieth century, the building of houses probably constituted about one fifth of all the investment being carried on within the domestic economy. It is impossible to be sure of the figures before about 1870, but since then, they are as follows:

Table 8.1

Years	Investment in dwellings as percentages of total domestic investment
1870-9	21
1880-9	19
1890-9	19
1900-9	17
1920-9	26
1930-8	33

Source H. W. Richardson and D. H. Aldcroft, *Building in the British Economy between the Wars* (1968), table 27, p. 272.

The visible sign of this expenditure was the steady growth of cities, which covered ever larger areas with monotonous stretches of working-class houses. But this investment in dwellings is in many respects unlike investment in other items of capital equipment, both economically and socially.

Economically, a house does not fit easily into the economists' categories of capital and consumption goods. Like a consumption good, it is used by the final consumer, and indeed is one of the most essential and basic of consumer requirements, particularly in a climate like that of the British Isles. But on the other hand, a house is not in any obvious sense consumed. Rather it provides a flow of services over its lifetime, which is long, and its initial price is such as to make outright purchase impossible for a great majority of families, unless special facilities enable them to borrow against future income. In these respects a house resembles a capital good, and it is perhaps best thought of as the only capital good with which the consumer normally deals directly.

These rather hybrid characteristics may have something to do with the unsatisfactory way in which housing came to be treated from an economic point of view in Britain and in most industrial, urban societies. The owners of capital goods, after they have installed them, normally allow in their accounts for the fact that sooner or later the equipment they have just bought will wear out, or be outdated by new ideas and techniques. They provide for this by allowing in their accounts the depreciation of the value of the item in question as it wears out or becomes outdated. Thus the capital stock of the country is continually being renewed and updated, and the accounts of firms allow for this process. The principles of corporate taxation, which evolved with the growth of the tax system in the nineteenth century, recognised this fact and allowed firms to set such depreciation against their income in the calculation of taxable profit.

The housing stock on the other hand, though it represents a very important part of the total capital stock of any industrial country, was never treated in this way. When houses were built it was implicitly assumed that they would last for ever. All building was thought of as an addition to the stock and generally no person or institution made any provision for the eventual need to replace them. This crucial, unspoken assumption was built into the tax system simply by default.[1] It never occurred to anybody that a capitalist who makes his living by letting out houses should be allowed to set the depreciation of his capital assets against income for tax purposes. But if he made his income by letting out almost any other type of capital equipment, he would be allowed to do this. And in fact houses do wear out.

Houses of course last a long time. With thorough maintenance, which may be thought of as an alternative to allowing depreciation against the day when they finally fall down, some types of houses may last so long as almost to justify the assumption that they last for ever. But this is not true of the mile upon mile of working-class houses built during the nineteenth-century growth of the great British industrial cities. These houses were not especially well built, nor were they especially well maintained, but above all they were built to the standards of a relatively poor country in the middle stages of industrialisation. As the progress of industrialisation itself raised incomes, spread education more widely among the people, and raised the general levels of expectations, so it outdated these drab and depressing houses, just as a machine may be outdated by technological advance. But unlike the machine, no one had ever thought about or planned for the replacement of these houses; and the Inland Revenue would not allow an owner of a house to write off its value and set this against his income to help him replace it.

Thus, as each year throughout the nineteenth century and up to 1914, about one fifth of all investment at home was put into building more houses to accommodate the growing urban population, a problem was being laid up for the future. A large stock of capital was being accumulated, which was physically deteriorating, even if slowly, and which was being outdated by rising expectations. The problem was not a once for all matter of replacing houses built before a given date. It was rather the problem of incorporating replacement demand in the pattern of building, so that replacement demand and building for additional or newly moved members of the population could proceed side by side. Replacement demand would only become an important element in total demand as the first large blocks of urban housing started to become outdated, which we may suggest was somewhere around 1880 to 1900. But, as we have suggested, because of the hybrid economic nature of housing, there were available no social or financial institutions through which replacement demand could be made effective. A house, however dilapidated it was becoming, appeared in someone's account as an asset that had not been depreciated over time. No one therefore wanted to pull any houses down, except where there was some more profitable commercial use for the land.

The problem of getting replacement demand going in the field of housing, so that the housing stock was regularly renewed as well as enlarged, was made worse by many other aspects of the nineteenth-century building. Most working-class housing of the period was privately rented by small-scale capitalists. Although there is not much historical data on nineteenth-century landlords, most of them appear to have been the owners of only a few, and often only one or two, houses. They thus did not have the resources to undertake much in the way of replacement, and often not even much in the way of maintenance. But even if an individual landlord of a few houses had wanted to modernise his property, he would soon have found that its physical situation made this very difficult. Nineteenth-century towns were limited in the area they covered by the distance people could walk to work. This limitation was already being modified by about 1900 by the tramway and by the earliest motor buses, and in London by the underground railway, but by then a great deal of urban building had been carried out at very high densities, sometimes reaching up to 500 persons an acre. Many mid-Victorian tenements covered only 450-500 square feet per dwelling, about half of what was coming to be recommended by 1920. Thus rebuilding an individual house was rarely possible; redevelopment could only take place in larger areas, and this presented formidable problems of organisation and required resources beyond those of most small landlords. This was one aspect of the situation which was by 1914 swiftly turning housing into a problem of a nature bound sooner or later to draw in the only organisation which appeared to have the power to cut these tangled knots — that is the government.

II *The Quantity of Housing*

The number of separate households that are actually formed will depend on a number of factors; but mainly on the number of separate premises that are available to house them, the rate of growth of the population and its age structure and family size. If separate premises are not available for all the groups of people that would like to live separately, people will of necessity have to share dwellings. Whether they then get counted in the census as one or two households depends on the necessarily arbitrary techniques of the census enumeration. The definitions used by the census were changed in 1911 in respect of both 'houses' and 'families'. The new definitions adopted in that year were considerably closer to the ordinary ideas of the meaning of both words, but at the price of breaking the historical continuity of the statistics. The new definition of a private family still differed from the ordinary idea of a biological family in that it included lodgers taking their meals with the family or servants living in. The new definition of a 'house' was an attempt to identify the number of 'structurally separate dwellings' used for living accommodation. Previously a block of flats was counted as one 'house' but under the new and more realistic definition each flat would be counted as a dwelling.

The number of 'families' per 'house' between 1861 and 1951 is shown in Table 8.2. An attempt has been made to reconstruct the figures for the years before 1911 on the post-1911 basis, by applying to the earlier figures the ratios which are given in the 1911 census between the two sets of definitions. This must however be regarded as only a rough estimate. But the main trends in the figures are clear. From 1861 to 1901 there appears to have been an improvement in the housing situation quantitatively, though this trend was reversed between 1901 and 1911. The figure for 1921 shows a marked deterioration, which was due to the cessation of house building in the war. In 1921 there were 1·095 private families for each structurally separate dwelling available. Our rough estimates suggest that this was about the ratio prevailing in 1871. Even this may underestimate the extent of the setback due to the war. The shortage of housing will only be measured by the census if people actually share dwellings by setting up separate 'private families' in the same 'structurally separate dwelling'. If however they react to the shortage of housing by living together in one family, that is if they continue to take their meals together, they will not be counted as separate families. But their situation may conceal a strong unfulfilled desire for a separate place in which to live. The Housing Report of the 1931 census attempted to estimate the number of people still living together in this way because of the war. The method was to calculate the increase in the numbers of married women and the number of widows, widowers and divorcees under 65, plus 10% of the increase of the number of single persons between 20 and 45 years of age. This was then used as an indicator of 'normal' household formation between 1911 and 1921. On this basis the number of families recorded in the 1921 census appears to underestimate the number of people who would have been living as separate households but for the war by between 300,000 and 400,000. The figure of 1·095 private families per dwelling recorded in the 1921 census, bad as it was in historical perspective, may even so be an over-optimistic one.

Table 8.2 *Families per House, England and Wales, 1861-1951*

Year	Separate occupiers per building	Private families per dwelling
1861	1·145	(1·11)
1871	1·117	(1·09)
1881	1·080	(1·05)
1891	1·053	(1·02)
1901	1·049	(1·02)
1911	1·060	1·03
1921		1·095
1931		1·089
1939		0·971
1951		1·059

Source General Register Office, *Census of England and Wales 1951, Housing Report*, table A, p. xxiii. The year 1939 from Bowley, *Housing and the State*, appendix II. The figures in brackets are approximate estimates of private families per dwelling for the years before 1911.

It seems then that by 1921 there was a considerable quantitative shortage of housing, in that normal expectations of household formation had been frustrated by the cessation of building in the war. Much of the great dissatisfaction about housing after the war, the Registrar-General comments, 'is explained by the fact that between 300,000 and 400,000 groups of persons who but for the housing shortage would have set up as separate families, were obliged to live in the closest domestic contact with other persons from whom they desired to separate themselves'.[2] This situation, as the census report also points out, affected double the number of 'frustrated' potential families, since not only they, but the people they had to live with, were upset by the situation imposed on them. 'The radical hardship of this situation', the report continues, 'lay not so much in any condition of overcrowding as in the denial of that privacy and independence which are the distinguishing features of the Englishman's castle.'[3]

This estimate of a shortage of 300,000-400,000 houses is strictly a relative figure. It is relative to the situation prevailing before the war. It was possible to estimate a 'shortage' of almost any number of houses, depending on the standards adopted. Thus the Salisbury Committee[4] reported to the Ministry of Reconstruction in 1917 that 300,000 houses would be required if the war ended in 1917 – an estimate that agrees fairly closely with the Registrar General's calculations in his 1931 housing report. But by 1918 the Labour Party had included in its election manifesto a demand for the building of a million new homes, and the government itself in 1919 was talking in terms of a programme for 500,000 houses. All these estimates reflect the tendency to discuss the quantity of housing as if it were a static phenomena; the assumption is that somehow the number of houses 'needed' can be calculated; if the number of houses existing is then subtracted from this figure the result is the 'shortage'; what is then required is a building programme for this number, and the shortage will be removed. And then, one is tempted to add, we all lived happily ever after. These static estimates do indeed have an almost fairytale aspect to them.

The reality is that the balance between the supply and the demand for housing will be struck at a point which reflects the economic and social factors acting on both sides of the equation, and that this balance is a dynamic, constantly shifting point, with no final resting place. The principal factors acting on the side of supply are the availability of land suitably placed in relation to employment opportunities, the price of raw materials used in building, the rate of interest on capital, and the productivity of the building industry. On the demand side there are changes in the rate of formation of potential families, the level of incomes, the social conventions which determine the balance between the different ways that these incomes might be spent, and the institutions which enable the financing problem to be overcome, either through renting or borrowing capital for purchase. The outcome of the intricate balance between these and other factors determines the amount of houseroom that people occupy, its quality and the amount they pay for it. Before the war, there was an increasingly strong feeling however that the balance struck in respect of the quantity and quality of housing available was an unsatisfactory one. 'There was a growing dissatisfaction with working-class life in general and with housing in particular.'[5] Expectations and social norms about what was acceptable in the matter of housing were rising faster than the reality of the housing situation was improving, if it was improving at all. We have already seen two important reasons why this should be so, the institutional problems of updating the housing stock in line with current practice and the space limitations imposed by the journey to work in the large towns where the majority of the population lived. Now, superimposed on this pre-existing dissatisfaction, came the war. The effect of the war was first, as we have already seen, to stop the building of houses completely and thus ensure that there would be a fairly major backwards shift in the quantitative balance between houses and potential households, a shift back, we have suggested, to the standards of about 1870. But on the side of demand the war had a major effect on the level of expectations.

This change in the level of expectations cannot be measured precisely, but it was almost certainly a reality. Partly, it reflected an increasing public awareness of the nature of the Victorian urban legacy, itself created by the rising interest in social problems in general just before the war. But the main shift in the war came as a result of the government's own efforts to enlist the sympathy and support of the working classes in the war effort. This support was more necessary in the first world war than ever before, as the whole economy and working population became involved in the production of munitions, or in the deprivations made necessary if such production was to be possible. In the spring of 1917, with the war at a critical stage from a military and naval point of view, the war effort was threatened by a renewal of the social unrest that had been so prominent in the years before 1914. 'There was a general growing discontent among the British working class — unfocussed distrust manifesting itself in lack of confidence in government promises.'[6] To counter this distrust the government embarked, as governments are always prone to do in such circumstances, on a programme of promises for the future. If only you will work and fight now to save the state, the working classes were told, we will make life better for you later. Housing figured prominently, though unspecifically, among these promises. People were led to believe that after the war there would be significant improvement in the standard of housing, despite the fact that by the end of the war the average standard of housing was certain to be lower than at the beginning.

Not only was the level of expectations raised, but so, as we have seen in Chapter 1, was the average level of working-class incomes. Higher taxation and full employment, and later the extension of unemployment benefit of one sort or another and the squeeze on profits in the deflation of 1921, had led to a significant redistribution of income in favour of the working classes. This redistribution was not so great as to have any very large effect on the rent-paying capacity of many working-class families, but nevertheless, in conjunction with wartime and postwar election promises, it meant that more and better houses figured prominently in the expectations of large sections of the working classes after the war.

Despite these expectations, a number of factors conjoined to make it very unlikely that many houses would be built very quickly after the war. An obvious corollary of the fact, already discussed, that houses last a long time, is that the annual output of the building industry is small in relation to the total stock. The average increase in the number of houses each decade between 1861 and 1911 was 14%;[7] even making some allowance for demolitions, the annual average output cannot have reached 1·5% of the stock. With an industry geared to annual outputs of this order, it will clearly be extremely difficult to make any quick impact on the total supply of houses. There are difficulties in the rapid expansion of any industry; skilled men take time to train, materials may be in inelastic supply, firms will almost certainly have organisational difficulties, particularly in an industry like building consisting mainly of small producers. In the case of building after the war, the major difficulty of the supply of skilled labour was intensified by the attitude of the trade unions who were extremely reluctant to allow an increase in the number of apprentices, or to allow any form of dilution of labour. But in the years immediately after the war, in addition to these supply difficulties, there was the special consideration that building to let was extremely unlikely to be a profitable undertaking. This was because prices and interest rates were high, though their level was considered abnormal and the expectation was that they would fall. In these circumstances, building carried out at the high level of prices with money borrowed at high rates of interest was likely to turn out to be an unprofitable investment when prices and interest rates returned to their normal level. It was logical in such circumstances to postpone investment decisions in building. This tendency was exaggerated by the introduction, in 1915, of legal control over the level of rents. Although this control, introduced as an emergency measure to alleviate social unrest in the war, did not apply to newly built houses, it affected the general level of rents. Further, there was a continual fear that once the government had committed itself to such controls, they might be extended in ways that could not be foreseen and which might reduce the profitability of investment in housing.

For these reasons, the prospects for the renewal of speculative building of working-class houses to let after the war were poor. Indeed, as we can now see, the war signalled what was to be the beginning of the end of this particular variety of small-scale capitalism. The speculative builder and the small landlord had between them provided the great bulk of nineteenth- and early twentieth-century urban housing. Now the conditions under which they had flourished were changing. The spectacular movements of prices in and after the war had destroyed the confidence in the future course of prices and profits. The government's intervention in rent control and its increasing use of legislation in an attempt to raise standards were removing the confidence in the workings of the free enterprise market. And perhaps most important of all, there were an increasing number of opportunities for the small investor in other spheres; the war had greatly enlarged the volume of government debt, and the building societies were increasingly offering a safe and reasonably profitable haven for small savings, which was to channel these savings into a different form of housing tenure; that of the owner occupier.

III *The Intervention of the Government*
These were the circumstances then that brought the government into the business of providing houses. The quality of the nineteenth-century legacy was poor, and quantitatively the war had involved a setback, while at the same time raising expectations and to some extent the incomes which enable them to be realised. But the conditions immediately after the war were such that the nineteenth-century system for providing working-class houses — speculative building and letting by small landlords — was unlikely to function. Hence the government felt obliged to invervene.

There are many ways in which the government could, if it wished, interfere with the market situation in the supply and demand for housing. It had already, by 1920, made a most important decision by default in the tax treatment of housing to let as an investment. It was about to make another such decision by default in its tax treatment of money borrowed to finance housing for owner occupation. For in just the same way as no one had ever thought of allowing depreciation on the value of a house which was being let when it had been bought with the owner's savings, so no one ever thought of not allowing interest paid on borrowed capital as a charge against income. All interest was and always had been so allowed, and when it became common, as it did in the interwar years, to borrow money from building societies for house purchase, the practice was automatically extended to include these borrowings. These two 'decisions' taken together, although they were never thought of as policy and are rarely discussed as 'decisions' at all, have made a substantial contribution to determining the shape of British housing. Together, they have contributed to a major trend in the housing scene: the decline of privately rented housing and the rise of the (often mortgaged) owner occupier. The long-term changeover between these two sectors is shown in Table 8.3.

Table 8.3 *Housing Stock by Tenure: Great Britain* (percentages)

Year	Private rented	Local authority rented	Owner occupiers	Others
1914	80	1	10	9
1939	46	14	31	9
1950	44·6	18·0	29·5	7·9
1970	14·9	30·5	49·5	5·1

Source 1950 and 1970 from *Social Trends No. 1* (1970), table 90. 1939 and 1914 are only approximate estimates. 1939 is calculated by extrapolating from the 1950 situation. 1914 from M. F. W. Hemming, 'The Price of Accommodation', *National Institute Economic Review* (August 1964), p. 39, with an arbitrary allowance for 'other tenures'. Other tenures means tied cottages, company houses, etc.

But in the discussion of housing policy at the end of the war, there was, as far as we know, no discussion of the encouragement of owner occupation as a major policy aim. Rather, attention centred on the way the government could set about providing working-class houses itself. And though by the end of the interwar period about 18% of working-class families were owner occupiers, it was among the middle class that owner occupation spread fastest, whereas the housing problem was seen, rightly, as essentially a working-class problem. To provide houses for working-class people at rents which they could, or would, pay, two basic steps were taken. Firstly local authorities were charged with a responsibility for the provision of working-class housing; and, secondly, subsidies were provided out of taxation to enable both local authority and privately built houses to be let or sold at less than market price. There were many ways in which subsidies could have been paid, including subsidising the people who needed the houses or subsidising the houses themselves. As so often in history important decisions are taken by default, and this is such a case. There was in practice no consideration of tying the subsidy to the people rather than the houses, although on the face of it the mainly Conservative governments of this period might have found this more selective principle attractive. If those who could not afford to pay market rents could have been identified by a means test and then subsidised until they could, the extra demand resulting might have been expected to have brought forth an adequate extra supply from the market. Such a system would have had many difficulties, but so did the system actually adopted, and the former approach might well have made more impression on one fundamental stumbling block of the whole period: the problem of getting assistance to the poorest families who needed it most.

In the outcome, the main pattern of events can be summarised briefly. Firstly, the government embarked on an ambitious scheme under the 'Addison Act' of 1919. Houses under this scheme were to be let at the generally prevailing level of working-class rents. If this rent policy resulted in a loss to the housing authority then the central government would pay the whole difference, except for the proceeds of a penny rate. The housing authority was thus offered complete financial security whatever it did, or however inefficient it was in the management of its houses. As Marion Bowley comments, 'financially these rent rules were heroic',[8] and the whole Act was the product of war-induced hopes of a better world to follow. It was the brain-child of the Minister of Reconstruction, Christopher Addison, and was introduced during his short spell at the newly formed Ministry of Health. Addison represented the spirit of euphoria induced by the war. As the forces of financial orthodoxy and the realities of the peace reasserted themselves, Addison departed from the political scene, and so did his Housing Act.

There then followed a brief period, from 1922 to 1923, when the government attempted to turn back in its tracks and withdraw from the housing market, although rent control was continued. Then in 1923 to 1924 there was another reversal, more tentative and less ambitious than the plunge of 1919, but in fact more final in confirming the government as a permanent feature on the housing scene. The 1923 and 1924 Acts were passed by Conservative and minority Labour governments respectively, and were sponsored by the respective ministers of health, Neville Chamberlain and Joseph Wheatley. The Wheatley Act did not repeal the Chamberlain Act so that in the period up to 1934 when government policy took another twist in its tortuous path, the two Acts were the main financial influences on the course of subsidised housebuilding. Housing authorities and private builders could choose to build houses under either Act, or under both, or of course they could choose not to build at all. Housing authorities could also choose the extent to which they subsidised the houses they built out of the rates, except that, if they built under the Wheatley Act, they were required to provide a rate subsidy in certain conditions. The Chamberlain subsidy was continued until 1929 and Wheatley's until 1934.

Table 8.4 *Building during the Period of the Chamberlain and Wheatley Subsidies: England and Wales, 1923-34* (thousands of houses)

	Private enterprise	Local authority	Total
Chamberlain subsidy	362·7	75·3	438·0
Wheatley subsidy	15·8	504·5	520·3
Unsubsidised	1085·8	———	1085·8
	1464·3	579·8	2044·1

Source Calculated from M. Bowley, *Housing and the State* (1945), p. 271, table 2. The figure of 504·5 thousand includes 11,000 'Wheatley' houses actually built in 1935.

Table 8.4 will help in assessing the importance of the subsidies. The first point to emerge is that only about 47% of the houses built in this period were subsidised at all and only just over 28% were built by local authorities. The Chamberlain subsidy was aimed at and principally used by private enterprise builders, while the Labour Government's act was, as might be expected, almost entirely restricted to local authority building. The Wheatley subsidy was larger, but involved restrictions on the rent that could be charged and normally required a rate contribution. With the full rate contribution the subsidy reduced the rent of a typical three-bedroom local authority house by about 12½p a week, that is by about 20%. Clearly, though they were significant, the subsidies were not a decisive feature of the housing scene. The reduction in costs that they afforded was not spectacular; more houses were built without subsidy than with; and twice as many houses were built by private enterprise than by local authorities. Moreover, the almost universal judgement of commentators on the effect of the subsidies is that they were not large enough to enable the poorest families to rent (or of course buy) new houses. 'The market for local authority houses was largely confined to . . . the better off families, the small clerks, the artisans, the better off semi-skilled workers with small families and fairly safe jobs.'[9]

After 1934, building by local authorities for general needs, that is for families other than those actually displaced by slum clearance programmes, declined to small proportions, and government subsidies were concentrated on the slum clearance programme. By this date the problem of quantity, the housing shortage, was judged to have been solved and the remaining problem was seen more as one of quality, in the continued existence of slums and overcrowded households. The pattern of government intervention may therefore be summarised as follows:

1919-1921	The Addison programme. Ambitious attempt at large-scale building of working-class houses by local authorities. Terminated by economy campaign in 1921, though building under the Act continued through 1922.
1922-1923	A hiatus, during which the government withdrew from the housing market.
1923-1934	The period of the Chamberlain and Wheatley 'general needs' subsidies. A more cautious approach than Addison's, leaving the poorest families with little direct help.
1934-1939	The replacement of the general needs subsidies by slum clearance and overcrowding subsidies, aimed at the problem of the quality of urban housing on the assumption that the quantity of houses was now nearly adequate.

Of all these programmes, only the Addison phase was in any sense a radical attempt to tackle the housing problem; only the Addison Act gave the need for more houses a clear priority over the need for financial caution. And despite the difficulties of inflation and materials shortages, the Addison Act produced in 1922 one of the highest totals of local authority building in England and Wales in the interwar period. In that year 80,000 houses were built by local authorities, a figure exceeded only in 1928 and 1939. The Addison houses were however very expensive, and the liability of the Treasury was in effect open-ended. The high cost of building houses at the time was largely due to inflation of prices in general and to the inflation of the price of building materials in particular, which was increased by the attempt to raise the output of houses. Most attention at the time however was focussed on the form of the subsidy, which gave local authorities no incentive to control costs. Their liability was finite, the product of a penny rate, and if contracts were let at extravagant prices, only the Treasury lost. Further, the approximately 1,500 local housing authorities in Great Britain included many which were inexperienced in such matters and scarcely able to cope with the very complex operation of starting up as large-scale landlords. The upshot was that, as the boom gave way to slump with rising unemployment in late 1921 and 1922, demands for economy and allegations of extravagance mounted and eventually discredited the Act. In July 1921 it was announced that no further contracts were to be placed, and that effectively the Act would be phased out as the houses already planned were completed. A disappointed Christopher Addison was removed from the ministry and later from the government, and wrote a bitter indictment of the abandonment of his policy entitled *The Betrayal of the Slums*.[10]

No act or policy subsequently pursued in the interwar years with respect to housing approached the boldness, or if preferred the rashness, of the Addison Act. From 1923 on, the total financial liability of both central and local government was carefully limited to a relatively small proportion of the cost of house building. Thus throughout the whole period from 1919 to 1939, central government expenditure in England and Wales totalled £208 million, but of this no less than £131 million was spent on the 209,000 houses built under the Addison Act.[11] Apart from the Addison houses, which cost the central government an average of £625 each, annual average expenditure on subsidising housing ran at just under £5 million a year. Expenditure built up slowly over the period as more houses were built qualifying for a continuing annual subsidy. But in a typical year in the 1930s, 1935, gross expenditure on public and subsidised housing was £42 million in England and Wales. Of this total £25 million was paid by tenants in rents, £13·5 million was provided from central government out of taxation and £3·5 million was provided from local rates.[12] Thus in this year subsidies totalled £17 million. This figure can be put in perspective by giving the average annual total of consumers' expenditure for the years 1935-8, which was £4,246 million, of which £450 million was spent on housing. Total government expenditure (central and local) on all public social services in 1935 was £441 million so that expenditure on housing constituted only 4% of the total. In short, after the termination of the Addison Act, government subsidies for housing were on a limited scale which could not and did not have more than a fairly limited effect on the rate of house building.

The effects of the entry of the local authorities into the provision of houses to let was not however confined to the question of subsidy. Local authorities raised capital on favourable terms, and between 1920 and 1938 the total capital expenditure on housing by local authorities was £713 million.[13] Total capital expenditure on residential construction during these years was £2,423 million,[14] so that of all the capital raised for building houses in the interwar years, 29% was raised by local authorities. This contrasts with the very much smaller percentage of current expenditure on housing that was provided by subsidy out of taxation. The question then is: if local authorities had not raised this capital and used it to build houses, what effect would this have had on the total output of houses in the interwar period? It is unfortunately a question that has never been answered and very probably never could be, since it is almost impossible to answer 'counterfactual' questions of this sort with any degree of confidence. Without a great deal of further research all that can be suggested is that the activities of the public sector must have made some contribution to house building, although it is not reasonable to regard the whole output of the public sector, and even less the subsidised output of the private sector, as a net addition to housing output in this period. Some of this output, but not all of it, would have been built in any case.

IV *The Pattern of Building in the Interwar Years*
The activities of the state in providing subsidies and raising capital have been dealt with first, since the entry of the state in this way and on such a scale represents the most obvious historical break which occurred in this period. But perhaps the most significant feature of house building in the interwar years is not the fact that for the first time a substantial amount of it was carried out on behalf of public authorities and that some subsidies were provided, but that house building in this period proceeded at a historically very high level. Compared with both preceding and following periods, the interwar rate of house building was very high, and this statement can be supported whether the absolute figures alone are considered, or as is more appropriate, the figures taken are those in relation to population changes or to the existing stock of houses.

Table 8.1 has already shown how investment in the building of dwellings rose to a historically high proportion of total investment especially in the 1930s. Table 8.2 showed how the high level of building through the interwar period as a whole had succeeded, by 1939, in making good the effects of the war and had raised the ratio of houses to households to a level that was an all time high in the history of industrial Britain up to that time. Table 8.5 below shows another aspect of the high rate of building in this period.

Table 8.5 *Additions to the Housing Stock, 1861-1939*

Percentage addition during each decade to the stock at the beginning of that decade (England and Wales)

Decade ending	Percentage addition to stock
1861	14·3
1871	15·2
1881	15·4
1891	11·6
1901	15·2
1911	12·5
1921	3·7
1931	17·8
1939	25·0

Source General Register Office, *Census of England and Wales 1931, Housing Report*, p. x. 1939 figure calculated from M. Bowley, *Housing and the State* 1945, appendix 2, table 1. The 1939 figure is for the decennial rate achieved between 1931 and 1939.

The totals of housebuilding for the whole interwar period (1 January 1919 to 31 March 1939) are as follows:

Table 8.6 *Building in Great Britain, 1919-39*

	England and Wales	Scotland
Built by local authorities	1,112,505	212,866
Built by private enterprise with subsidy	430,327	43,067
Built by private enterprise without subsidy	2,449,216	61,444
	3,992,048	317,377
Total: Great Britain	4,309,425	

Source Cmd 6153 (1940), *Royal Commission on the Distribution of the Industrial Population*, p. 67.

This represents an annual average output of 212,800 houses for the twenty years. This annual average is a larger number than had ever been built in any earlier year in Britain. The addition to the stock of houses in England and Wales of 3·3% in 1936, when 347,000 houses were built, was a record which has never been exceeded. For the five years ending 31 March 1939 building in England and Wales passed the 300,000 mark each year, historically an outstanding performance. The level of 300,000 houses was not reached again until 1954, and the 1936 figure of 347,000 was not reached until 1965, when it still represented of course a smaller percentage addition to total housing stock.

The most surprising thing about this high level of building is that it occurred at just the time when rates of population growth were slowing down. Historically, high levels of building were associated with high rates of population growth; the largest percentage addition to the stock of housing recorded before 1931 was in the two decades 1821-31 (20·5%) and 1831-41 (19·8%) and this probably reflected, among other factors, the high rates of population increase in the early years of the nineteenth century. However, the relevant factor in determining demand for housing is not people in total but potential households. In a situation where population growth is falling from a high level towards stability, as in the interwar period, the decline in the rate of growth of population will precede the decline in the rate of growth of households. This assumes, as was the case at this time, that the mechanism of the decline is a reduction in the number of children born to each family with a simultaneous reduction in the death rate. The population in this situation is in effect reorganising itself into smaller groups, at the same time as its growth of total numbers declines towards zero. Eventually the rate of increase in the number of groups, or families, will stabilise like the increase in total numbers, but it takes longer. It is the number of people who would like to form groups living in separate dwellings that is the relevant factor in housing demand.

The number of potential families increased about as fast between 1911 and 1931 as at any time in the nineteenth century. Thus the fairly high rate of building in the 1920s served mainly to keep pace with this increase. After 1931 however, not only the rate of population growth but the rate of increase of potential families also slowed down, and the exceptionally high rates of building in the 1930s thus saw the housing stock, as it were, pulling up level with and indeed passing the number of families, leading to an easing of the housing situation quantitatively in a way which had no parallel since the start of the industrial revolution. In 1937 the Ministry of Health stated in evidence to the Ridley Committee that, although there was still considerable pressure on housing accommodation in the inner areas of London and some other large cities in England, 'there are parts of England where there is no longer any housing shortage'. Even in Scotland, where the housing position was in general much worse than in England, witnesses agreed that there was no difficulty in most places in obtaining empty houses, at rents from about £35 per annum upwards.[15] Indeed if the situation of the late 1930s could have been developed by continued high rates of building and increased rates of demolition, and if the then current rates of economic growth and population growth had been maintained, Britain could have moved into an entirely new era in the field of housing. Many factors have however intervened since then to ensure that this opportunity was not fully grasped.

What factors led to such high rates of building? A number of theories have been advanced in an attempt to account for the observed fluctuations in the level of residential construction.[16] Although there is no difficulty in listing factors which, as a matter of common sense, are likely to affect the level of building, it is much harder to assess the quantitative importance of any particular factor. There is indeed no reason today to modify the conclusion of the writer of a survey article on theories of this type. 'There is no prospect of obtaining a conclusive quantitative explanation of fluctuations in building.'[17] The best that can be done is to offer a list of factors which can reasonably be argued as having contributed to the high rate of building in the interwar period, and particularly in the 1930s, without attempting anything other than an impressionistic assessment of their relative importance. Such a list might be as follows:[18]

> On the side of demand
>> The rise in the level of real incomes.
>> The increase in the effective area for building made available by the development of motor transport and suburban (usually) electric railways.
>> The development of building societies and the publicity they instigated in favour of home ownership.
>> The changing structure of the working population.
> On the side of supply
>> Low prices for building materials, especially in the early 1930s.
>> In the 1930s only, low interest rates.

Such lists of factors are not of course really explanations, but rather rationalisations, offered after the event to make the event seem unsurprising. Such a listing of factors could never be used to predict in advance that the event in question was going to happen. With this rather severe qualification in mind, we may look at the list in a little more detail.

The increase in the effective area available for house building was a factor which comes most obviously to mind in connection with the interwar period. Until the innovations of the bicycle, motorcycle, motor bus and electric suburban railway, urban building had been confined within areas determined by the working man's journey to work on foot. Thus for almost the whole course of the nineteenth century the area available was limited by this physical constraint. The growing population of Great Britain concentrated itself at increasing densities around the centres of employment, so that crowding and lack of open space was perhaps the most obvious and depressing feature of the urban scene. By contrast after the second world war, although technically it became possible to disperse industry itself through the use of electric power and improved communications, and although improved transport made an even greater dispersal of residential accommodation practicable, dispersal of this sort came to be severely limited by planning regulations. These regulations were designed to preserve open countryside — countryside which had been preserved without difficulty in the nineteenth century simply due to the technical difficulties involved in 'colonising' it. Now that these technical difficulties were removed, they were deliberately replaced by legal obstacles. But, for a brief space of twenty years between the wars, neither difficulty prevailed, and the result was a fairly rapid expansion across the countryside near the great towns at fairly low densities of building. The Tudor Walters Report of 1919 had recommended that new housing should be at a density of not more than twelve houses per acre,[19] and this was the standard generally followed for most new housing throughout the period.

These circumstances did a great deal to determine the character of much interwar building. Houses were built along main roads, or in estates in green field sites on the fringes of the big urban areas. The census maps of 1951 for the six largest conurbations show in every case an outer ring of low density interwar housing, surrounding a much higher density nineteenth-century inner ring, which in turn surrounded the original commercial centre, where, in many cases, residential densities, once very high, were now declining as houses were replaced by commercial buildings. Thus in the interwar period, the west midlands conurbation centred on Birmingham was reaching out towards Solihull and Sutton Coldfield in the south-east and north-east respectively and to Tettenhall and Sedgley in the west. In the Merseyside conurbation, the interwar residential areas included for instance Hoylake, Wirral and Neston, whilst the west Yorkshire conurbation was spreading south-west to Holmfirth and Colne Valley. A good deal of growth took place too on the edges of smaller towns, so that despite the geographical spread of the conurbations, in only three of the six largest did population grow faster than the population of England and Wales as a whole between 1921 and 1931, and in only one (the west Midlands) between 1931 and 1951. This contrasts with the typical nineteenth century situation where all these conurbations were growing much faster than the whole population, as for instance between 1871 and 1881, where the population growth of all six was about fifty per cent above the England and Wales average.[20]

The merits or demerits of this dispersal of population across the countryside was one of the most important environmental issues then and now. People's preferences are very difficult to test in this matter, since they are rarely in a position to make a choice which is not constrained by many other factors. Thus although the interwar period suffered less in the way of physical and administrative constraints over dispersal than the periods before or since, it could hardly be claimed that it produced an ideal pattern of building. Densities were largely determined by official policy even though there was relatively little restriction on the use of such land as could be bought in the market; but more important still, layouts were mainly determined by the whims of speculative developers and council housing committees, both of whom were usually unimaginative and lacking much in the way of aesthetic understanding of the housing problem. And the buyer or tenant rarely had the knowledge or the financial resources to make his preferences articulate and effective. A house for most people is an urgent necessity which must be obtained soon and little picking and choosing is possible. Nevertheless, there can be little doubt that most of the new speculative and council estates, spreading their usually unlovely tentacles across the green fields in this period, were so much of an improvement on the cramped life of the nineteenth-century urban centres that they brought people into a different world. Space, light, ventilation were all so much improved, while the defects which often went with dispersal were in the main avoidable.

It would be extremely difficult to assess the extent to which the growth of building societies was a cause or an effect of the growth of owner occupation in the interwar period; some element of reciprocal interaction is probably involved. There is no doubt that the building societies were, especially in the thirties, instrumental in promoting interest in home ownership, through publicity, quite apart from the relatively low rates of interest they were able to offer. Building society assets increased more rapidly than any other form of small savings medium at this time.[21] After allowing for price changes, the value of their assets increased by six and a half times between 1923 and 1938, while between 1928 (the earliest date for which figures are available) and 1937 the number of borrowers rose from 554,000 to 1,392,000. [22] For comparison, in the same period, the assets of the Trustee Savings Banks and the Post Office Savings Bank only about doubled, while those of industrial insurance companies increased by a little less than three times, and the real value of bank deposits rose about one and a quarter times. It was in this period that the building societies consolidated their position as sound and respectable parts of the financial system, with professional management. The large inflow of funds meant that increasingly they became concerned actively to promote the demand for mortgages, and this led, in the 1930s, to successful attempts to reduce the initial deposit which was the main stumbling block for many would-be owner occupiers. The system used was for the builder to co-operate with the building society by covering part of the loan with a deposit, which enabled the building society to advance a total of 95% of the purchase price to the buyer, though effectively part of the advance came from the builder. Perhaps most important of all was the 'image' of owner occupation as conferring advantage and status as compared with the subservient position of the payer of rent. 'Get rid of your rent man', the advertisements said, and though they may have pushed this trend on its way, no doubt deeper social forces were involved as well.

The changing structure of the working population merits a brief reference. The steady increase in the number of clerical and administrative workers and the relative decline in the number of manual industrial workers continued in this period. These 'white-collar' workers were, the argument goes, more interested in higher standards of housing and in establishing themselves as 'respectable' in the eyes of the community.[23] It would probably be difficult to distinguish this effect, if it exists, from the general desire of all workers, whether manual or not, for better houses as their incomes rise. As Sir Harold Bellman wrote: 'The essential driving force behind the boom has been the almost revolutionary [change] in the conception of what are tolerable housing standards among a vast section of the population'. [24] For many people, the cramped and dreary streets of the nineteenth-century legacy were seen for what they were — a desperately unsatisfactory way for humans to live; the demand for something better was a natural enough outcome of this legacy as soon as circumstances and income levels enabled it to be expressed.

As far as supply is concerned, the central question is the cost of houses and of the land on which they are built, in relation to the wages of prospective buyers. The building of houses, unlike large sections of the rest of the output of industrial societies, has not proved easily susceptible to mechanisation. Hence the price of houses has remained roughly constant in terms of the average manual worker's wage between about 1920 and 1960. In contrast nearly all other products cost less in 1960 than in 1920 when their price is expressed in this form. It should at once be pointed out that the definition of a 'house' has not remained constant over this period, but the improvements in quality have probably been less dramatic than in many other products whose price has fallen in real terms. Thus, to take a crude comparison with the price of motor cars: in the interwar period it was possible to buy a car for say £150, or one year's average wages. In 1960, with average weekly earnings at £15 a week, the price of a car with a far higher performance than its interwar equivalent was very roughly eight months wages. During the same period the building costs of a house, whose quality had perhaps improved no more than that of the car, changed very little in terms of average annual wages.[25] At the same time the price of many houses (including the price of the land) has, in many areas of England, risen substantially over this period. In 1961, the average price of new dwellings mortgaged to private owners was £2,810 or 3·65 times the average annual earnings of adult males in manufacturing. The average annual wage of a manual worker in 1936 multiplied by 3·65 comes to £550. In 1936, a house could certainly have been bought for less than this; the average capital cost of local authority three-bedroom houses in that year for instance was £384[26] and the average value of new advances on mortgage was £458.[27] Thus the long-term pattern is for houses not to get cheaper in terms of average earnings, and in some areas at least, for them to get dearer. However, although this is true in the long-term comparison between the interwar and postwar periods, within the interwar period the price of houses fell. Thus the average capital cost of local authority houses remained above £400 before 1931 but fell below £400 between then and 1937, reaching a low point of £361, or 2·4 times the average wage, in 1934.[28] This fall in prices was certainly an important factor in the high level of interwar building. It was particularly important in the years of lowest prices between 1931 and 1937, which saw the highest rates of private enterprise building. Three reasons stand out for this fall in prices. First, there was a relative abundance of building land, for reasons already discussed. Second, rates of interest were low in the 1930s and capital was abundant. Third, the price of important raw materials used in building fell in this period, notably timber. *The Economist*'s index of building costs which stood at 109·6 in 1924

(1930 = 100) fell steadily to 90·7 in 1934, and though it rose thereafter, did not again reach the 1924 level.[29]

We may conclude that one of the reasons for the high level of building in this period was the movement of the price of houses, which was, contrary to the general trend considered over the longer term, falling in terms of average wages. Thus we see how a number of factors in both demand and supply came together to produce historically high levels of residential building. This high level of building did not result in anything approaching a housing utopia. But nevertheless, it must be rated as an outstandingly favourable aspect of these years. 'House and home', as Professor Donnison comments, 'stand at the centre of people's lives.'[30] If we could ever discover a way of measuring welfare, as opposed to merely measuring income, we might well find that improvements in housing contribute far more to people's welfare than improvements in most other parts of the output of the economy, unfashionable as such a highly unrigorous and subjective assertion may be.

v *The Quality of Housing*

The most important way in which the interwar housing stock was improved was by building new houses to much higher standards, so that as these postwar houses came to form an increasing proportion of the total stock, the average quality of the housing stock also was raised. In March 1939 there were approximately 11¼ million houses in England and Wales, of which 4 million, or 35·6%, had been built since the war. In Scotland, there were a further 1·4 million of which 317,000, or 22%, had been built since the war. Thus by 1939, roughly a third of the population of England and Wales was living in a postwar house. The distribution of houses built by rateable value is given below in Table 8.7. Very roughly, it may be assumed that the highest group in rateable value were middle-class houses and the lowest group were almost exclusively working-class. It can be seen from the table that the largest proportionate increase occurred in the middle group, probably occupied in the main by the better off sections of the working class and by clerical workers, school teachers, higher paid shop assistants and so on. Thus not only was the stock improved by the fact that all houses built after the war were to higher standards than their counterparts built before the war, but also the pattern of building was such that the composition of the stock was altered towards the upper end by the relatively large numbers of houses built in the middle and upper groups.

Although houses in the £14-£26 range only formed 20·9% of the 1919 stock of houses, interwar building increased the stock of such houses by 95% and they comprised, by 1939, 27·8% of the total stock. By contrast strictly working-class houses, which formed 67·6%

of the 1919 stock, were increased in the interwar period by only 29%, much less than the 47% by which the whole housing stock was increased in this period, and by 1939 they had fallen as a proportion of the total to 59·3%. This pattern of building could have reflected one of two things: on the one hand, it could have been an accurate reflection of a changing social structure, or, on the other, it could have represented a misdirection of the building effort, so that too many relatively expensive houses were built, leaving the working classes with a disproportionately small share in the general improvement which took place. Most observers would almost certainly favour the latter interpretation, and this is valid to the extent that people who started the period with the lowest incomes and the worst housing tended to get the least chance of a new or better house. But many working-class people who did not get a new house were able to move into an older but none the less better one made available by a better off family moving. This process of 'filtering-up' cannot be documented in any rigorous way, but it must have been extensive. Thus it is reasonable to see the output of new houses as having a widespread effect in improving the housing standards of the population as a whole, and not just of those usually better off people who were actually able to live in them. Nevertheless at the beginning of the period, a strong case could have been made for an attempt to reduce the very wide inequalities in the standards of housing enjoyed by different sections of the community. To do this it would have certainly been necessary to build a higher proportion of working-class houses of less than £14 rateable value than was actually done.

Table 8.7 *Composition and Changes in Housing Stock by Rateable Value (%), 1919-39* (England and Wales)

| | Rateable values | | | |
	Below £14	£14-£26	Above £26	Total
Stock in 1919	67·6	20·9	11·5	100
Increase in stock between 1919 and 1939	29	96	65	47
Stock in 1939	59·3	27·8	12·9	100

Source Calculated from M. Bowley, *Housing and the State*, appendix 2, tables 3b and 3c.

In principle, the improvement of the housing stock should be affected both by the building of new and better houses and by the demolition of out of date or unsatisfactory ones. As we have seen, the conditions in which industrialisation occurred in Britain did not favour any systematic demolition of such houses. Before 1930, demolition of unfit houses in Britain proceeded at a very low rate. There are no reliable figures of how many houses were in fact demolished.[31] D. C. Paige has estimated[32] that up to 1930, demolitions for all causes, not only due to the houses in question being unfit, averaged only 0·25% of the stock per year. Given an average growth of stock of about 1·3% per year, this implied an average life for a house of 140 years. Although by 1939 there were nearly 4 million modern houses in England and Wales, there were rather more than 4 million that had been built before 1880. In Scotland the proportion built before 1880 was higher, and the general situation markedly worse, due to the lower rate of interwar building. Just how many houses in England and Wales were 'unfit' at the end of the interwar period is difficult to say, not least because of the extreme difficulties of definition. As standards change, so does the level of what is accepted as tolerable. Different observers apply different standards, and it is all too easy for the historian to bring the standards of a later, richer period to an earlier age. In the 1930s, the government's slum clearance programme scheduled some 300,000 houses for early demolition, whereas one writer, in 1935, called for the immediate destruction of 4·6 million houses on account of their age.[33] As an estimate of the number of houses providing desperately unsatisfactory living standards for their occupants in the late 1930s, the latter is almost certainly much nearer the mark than the former. Only the most scattered statistics on the detailed condition of older houses in urban areas are available before the war. R. M. Titmuss has brought together a collection of them.[34] These make it clear that, even by the end of the interwar period, baths and bathrooms for instance were by no means a normal fitting in many of the older areas of urban housing. In Hull, 40% of the houses were without baths in 1943. In Bootle the proportion was the same in 1939, and in Stepney the figure was 90%; in York about 66%; in Glasgow, in 1944, 50%; and in Birmingham, in 1946, about 33%. The proportion for the whole of Great Britain can only be guessed at, but in view of the above figures, any guess lower than a third would certainly be optimistic.[35]

If the worst-housed third of the British population in 1939 had probably to make do without a bathroom or a satisfactory bath, a substantial proportion also had to do without the exclusive use of a water closet, or even an earth closet, and some still lived in nineteenth-century back-to-back houses. In Birmingham in 1946 12% of the city's dwellings had no separate lavatory accommodation, 2% had no internal water supply and 10% were back-to-back houses. In 1944 it was estimated that 50% of the working classes (and 14% of the middle classes) had no indoor sanitation. Such statistics as these can give no real impression of the drab and depressing circumstances in which the worst-housed third of the population lived. As in the discussion of the distribution of income, so in housing there existed a spectrum running, as far as the working classes were concerned, from the owner occupied postwar house on a well planned estate with bathroom and separate lavatory, to the crumbling back-to-back slum with communal closet in the yard. If the war had not intervened, the next project in the field of housing, after the easing of the quantitative situation achieved by high rates of building, was to raise demolition rates to a much higher level, so as to reduce the average age, and substantially raise the average conditions of the worst-housed sections of the population. This was the objective of the next major Housing Act after the Wheatley Act of 1924: the Greenwood Act of 1930. Once again a minority Labour Government produced an important step in what was certainly the right direction, though not a very large step. A new subsidy was introduced specifically for slum clearance and rehousing. It was intended that this subsidy should operate alongside the Wheatley subsidy for general needs building, but in practice the Wheatley subsidy and all general needs building by local authorities was to be a casualty of the depression, the change of government and the economy campaign that the depression brought with it. Thus it happened that after 1933, contrary to the intentions of its originator, the Greenwood Act became the centre of the government's housing policy, which after that date was entirely concentrated on slum clearance. This clearance programme was pursued with considerable energy. Up to 1939, 272,836 houses were either demolished or closed as unfit[36] and 265,000 dwelling units (houses or flats) were built to rehouse those displaced.[37] A further 23,600 houses were built under the subsequent Housing Acts of 1935 and 1936 which specified standards of crowding, making it an offence to cause housing to be occupied at above specified densities per room.

These slum clearance and crowding provisions mark a new phase in the government's intervention in the field of housing. Only the government, as we saw earlier, was likely to be able to break into the complex problem of updating the centres and inner rings of housing bequeathed to the twentieth by the nineteenth century. In practice, even the government found it in this period to be no easy task, and progress was inevitably slow. No annual rate of demolition much below one per cent of the stock per year (about 100,000 houses) was going to make any spectacular impact on the urban centres. Even a programme of 100,000 houses a year demolished would have taken between forty and fifty years to remove all the houses built before 1880. Given that new building was proceeding in these years at record rates, such rates of demolition were, to put it mildly, historically improbable. In practice, all that can be said was that a beginning was made. Some of the very worst slums were cleared; the rate of demolition was raised a little from its previous very low levels. But by 1939 there was still a very long way to go on the journey of urban renewal, a journey that was brought to an abrupt halt by the war.

If at the lower end of the long spectrum of housing standards in Britain of the 1930s there were many examples of families living in conditions deplorable by any standards, at the other end there were houses which for the first time began to look recognisably modern in layout and amenities. The most basic requirement of a house is space, and the floor area of new working-class houses had risen steadily over time from about 450 square feet in the 1840s to between 700 and 800 square feet in the interwar period.[38] The Tudor Walters Report of 1919[39] had reflected the general feeling that standards of housing needed to be sharply raised. Its recommendations laid the basis for the higher standards usually adopted in most interwar housing. 'We consider that every house where there is a water supply should be provided with a bath, or a space for one if there is no water' (p. 26). 'In all schemes a large proportion of houses with parlours should be included' (p. 25), though the 'parlour question' was debated at great length, as was the problem of where the family in a modern house should eat and cook. If eating and cooking were separated, then an extra fire was needed and this meant extra expense, but nevertheless 'a steady tendency is at work to eliminate the cooking from the living room' (p. 25). The scullery was graduating into the modern 'kitchen', whereas previously it would merely have been a combined washroom and store cupboard, with cooking, eating and living (and for many sleeping as well) all carried on in the main or 'living' room. With the addition of a 'bathroom' in many interwar houses the process of differentiation of rooms by function was carried further, and as family size declined and living standards rose, so many more families became able to eliminate sleeping from the living room. Thus for the better-off working-class families, these years saw the emergence of the modern pattern of a living/eating room, kitchen for cooking, bathroom for washing and bedrooms for sleeping. Many interwar houses added a 'parlour' for entertaining and special occasions; a tendency which has been reversed in post second world war building, which has often preferred to use all the available space for a single much larger 'living room'.

As the standards of layout improved so too did the equipment available for heating, cooking and the supply of hot water. By the end of the period about one third of all families with incomes below £300, and a quarter of those with incomes below £160, had a piped hot water supply.[40] In the majority of cases, this supply came from a back boiler. Electric hot water heaters, being expensive to run, were still largely a middle-class fitting, and only just under half a million were in use in 1939, and about 300,000 of these had been installed since 1935.[41] Thus even by 1939, probably three quarters of working-class families were still boiling water for washing in some form of copper over an open fire, or perhaps on a gas cooker. Gas cookers were by the end of the period remarkably widespread. Market penetration by 1939 had certainly reached two thirds of all households, and possibly more.[42] Many of these cookers were hired, and although of primitive design by modern standards, must have been a great improvement on struggling with open fires, especially in summer.

Nevertheless, the open coal fire, with all its associated dust and hard work, and a thermal efficiency of perhaps 15%,[43] remained the predominant means of heating in the great majority of British homes throughout the period. In the *Heating of Dwellings* inquiry, quoted by *Political and Economic Planning*, 74% of the sample families were able to afford the heating of one room only; 96% used coal for heating but, by 1939, about three fifths of the households sampled also had electric or gas fires which were used as supplementary heating, and occasionally to heat a bedroom in times of illness. The heating of bedrooms however by any means was definitely exceptional right up to the end of the period. Approximately two thirds of all homes were wired for electricity by the end of the period, an innovation that must have done a great deal to add convenience and comfort to life, though few homes could afford to use it other than very sparingly.

Thus there were three main ways in which the quality of housing was improving over this period. A very high rate of new building was providing the most fortunate families with houses with altogether higher standards of space and layout, and enabling other families further down the income distribution to move into better houses. Secondly a quite wide range of houses was being fitted with improved equipment for heating, lighting, cooking and water supply, although again there remained large sections of the working class unaffected or only very slightly affected by these developments. Thirdly, at the bottom end of the range, a small number of the very worst houses were demolished in the thirties and their occupants rehoused by local housing authorities.

New building and better equipment affected mainly the better off sections of the community; slum clearance benefited the worst off. And quantitatively of course, new building and better equipment were on a far larger scale than slum clearance. Thus there remained a large section, at least a third, of the working class who were deplorably badly housed and who benefited relatively little from the widespread improvements elsewhere.

VI *Some Social Aspects of Housing*

The new social phenomena of this period was the estate. Nineteenth-century towns had grown without any sort of plan. Houses had been added by speculative builders and were almost universally let to working-class people by private landlords for a weekly rent. Although the environment in which many urban dwellers lived was drab and the houses cramped and often insanitary, as the years passed the urban dwellers had of necessity reached some sort of equilibrium with their surroundings which enabled them to survive and even to be happy. There was the close contact with relatives and the sense of belonging within a neighbourhood where few were strangers. Further, there had grown up in these inner urban areas what Professor Titmuss describes as 'an array of supporting agencies . . . social, economic and institutional, such as clothing clubs, check traders, hospital almoners, dental repair shops and foot clinics';[44] not to mention the pubs and friendly shops where credit might be obtained and which were within easy walking distance of the home.

The builders of many of the earliest estates ignored the part this array of facilities had come to play in many people's lives and built only houses, often with little reference even to the journey to work, let alone more subtle social considerations. An extreme example was the Norris Green housing estate, which was commenced on the outskirts of Liverpool in 1926.[45] Norris Green was a large estate and grew extremely fast, reaching a population of 25,000 in three years. The houses were to modern standards, and were satisfactory, but almost every other aspect of life on this estate was totally neglected. There were no shops, no fish and chip stalls, no pubs, and to start with, even no paved streets. Not only were these facilities not planned in the design of the estate; some were positively prohibited by the council. Public houses were still prohibited in 1939 and this gave rise to a 'ring of public houses surrounding the estate . . . judging by the popularity of these establishments it is doubtful whether the estate has gained anything in sobriety as a result of the ban'.[46] The prohibition of shops led to a remarkable growth of illegal stores conducted in the tenants' houses; threats of eviction then led to protection rackets and the payments of 'hush money'. Norris Green was a rather extreme example of the neglect of the social environment in the planning of estates, but most council estates suffered in some degree from the rawness of an artificially created community with inadequate ancillary services. Transport particularly, both to work and to shop, was often a problem on these estates. The Barlow Report complained of the tendency to create extensive housing estates without regard to work place and quoted North Acton as a particularly bad example.[47] The Bristol survey investigated shopping facilities on new estates around the city and found that 'beyond question, money goes further for those within easy reach of a central shopping area',[48] but that many housewives felt unable to afford the fare to reach these cheaper shops. Compared to Norris Green however, the Bristol estates were relatively well supplied with shops, even if they were more expensive than those in the city centre.

A further problem typical of the estates was the mismatching of the size of houses with the sizes of applicants' families. The great majority of council housing built in the interwar period was three-bedroomed. At Norris Green for instance, 98·4% of all houses were of this type, but only about 43% of applicant families really needed a house of this specification. Another 47% could have managed with a smaller house; and the other 10% needed a larger one.[49] The only major variation introduced into the building of council houses was between those with and those without a parlour. Parlour houses usually had a higher rent and carried a higher social status; this usually meant that the financially more stable families, which were often the smaller families, occupied the parlour houses. At Bristol the average size of families with parlour houses was 4·1 persons, and with non-parlour houses 4·7.[50] This highlights the principal problem which council housing to a large extent failed to solve: the inability of the poorer and larger families to pay for housing that was socially acceptable by the standards of the time. A parlour was a poor substitute for the extra bedrooms needed by a large family, even if the large family could have afforded the extra rent involved. Social pressures sometimes prevented the parlour being used in the most rational way, as a bedroom, in these circumstances. When the Bristol housing authority made an attempt to get large families into parlour houses, and tried to persuade the tenants to use the parlour as a bedroom, the results were not encouraging. 'In one case, where the wife took the instructions of the housing department seriously and installed a bed in the front downstairs room, the remarks and curiosity of the neighbours quickly drove the bed upstairs again.'[51]

In an attempt of this sort, the housing authority was up against the basic problem of the mismatching of needs and incomes, a problem still unsolved in the field of housing and elsewhere. The large families were often the poorest but had the greatest housing needs; efforts to overcome this in the interwar period did not extend beyond the moderate degree of subsidy already described and the bare beginnings of means-tested rent rebates. By 1938 only 112 out of about 1,500 housing authorities had rent rebate schemes of any sort, and most of these only applied to families rehoused under slum clearance schemes.[52] Further, in their selection procedures, it was extremely difficult for housing authorities not to favour reliable, 'respectable' tenants who were likely to be good rent payers; not to do so was to invite trouble all round, both in the form of damage to the houses and arrears of rent, and also in the form of complaints from other tenants. Polarisation of estates into 'good' and 'bad' areas often quickly followed the introduction of 'rough' or slum clearance tenants.[53] None of this is to deny the sincere efforts of many housing departments or the very large improvements made in the housing conditions of very large numbers of people in this period. Generally the tenants, although they had their grumbles, many of them legitimate, approved of their houses, and in the Bristol survey the rate of movement out of council estates appeared to be quite low.[54] Many of those who did move did so because they were in a position to afford better houses rather than through positive dissatisfaction with their existing ones.

Probably the most important social trend which became apparent during this period was the decline of the private rented sector and the beginning of its replacement by a society polarised between owner occupiers and council tenants. Further it was already becoming clear that unless energetic steps were taken to prevent it, the poorest and often the neediest families would be excluded from both groups and left to struggle in the declining private rented sector which would make increasingly inadequate provision for them. At the end of the period, about half of all British families still lived in privately rented houses, but the proportion was declining fast and it was not at all clear that owner occupation or council tenancy in the forms then available were going to provide a fully satisfactory substitute for the poorer families.

Notes

1 A. A. Nevitt, *Housing, Taxation and Subsidies* (1966), p. 43.
2 General Register Office, *Census of England and Wales 1931, Housing Report*, p. xx.
3 *Census 1931, Housing Report*, p. xx.

4 Cd 9087 (1918).
5 M. Bowley, *Housing and the State* (1945), p. 4.
6 B. S. Gilbert, *British Social Policy 1914-39* (1970), p. 11.
7 Calculated from census reports.
8 Bowley, *Housing and the State*, p. 18.
9 Bowley, *Housing and the State*, p. 129.
10 Published by Herbert Jenkins, 1922.
11 Gilbert, *British Social Policy*, p. 148.
12 Cmd 5609 (1937), *The Public Social Services.*
13 C. H. Feinstein, *Domestic Capital Formation in the United Kingdom 1920-38* (1965), p. 216.
14 Feinstein, *Domestic Capital Formation*, p. 219. This represented 31% of total gross domestic investment in this period.
15 Cmd 5621 (1937), pp. 22-3.
16 For a survey of such theories see C. E. V. Leser, 'Building Activity and Housing Demand', *Yorkshire Bulletin of Economic and Social Research* (July 1951), p. 131.
17 Leser, 'Building Activity', p. 148.
18 For a rather similar list see A. P. Becker, 'Housing in England and Wales during the Business Depression of the 1930s', *Economic History Review*, vol. 3 (1950-1), p. 321.
19 Cd 9191 (1919), p. 13.
20 General Register Office, *Census of England and Wales 1951, Report on Greater London and Five Other Conurbations* (1956).
21 E. J. Cleary, *The Building Society Movement* (1965), p. 275.
22 Bowley, *Housing and the State*, appendix 2, table 7a.
23 Becker 'Housing in England and Wales', *Economic History Review* (1950-1).
24 British Association for the Advancement of Science, *Britain in Recovery* (1938), p. 432.
25 D. V. Donnison, *The Government of Housing* (1967), p. 64.
26 Bowley, *Housing and the State,* appendix 2, table 6.
27 Bowley, *Housing and the State,* appendix 2, table 7b.
28 Bowley, *Housing and the State,* appendix 2, table 6.
29 Bowley, *Housing and the State,* appendix 2, table 5.
30 Donnison, *The Government of Housing*, p. 9.
31 *Census of England and Wales 1951, Housing Report* (1956), p. xxiv.
32 In W. Beckerman and Associates, *The British Economy in 1975* (9165), p. 337.
33 A. Block, *Estimating Housing Needs* (1946), p. 37. The writer quoted is Craven Ellis MP, *The Rebuilding of Britain* (1935).
34 R. M. Titmuss, *Problems of Social Policy* (1950), p. 131, note.
35 Many houses used portable baths of one sort or another, which complicates any statistics. In 1947 a national survey showed that 13% of all households had no baths of any sort, while 29% had only portable baths.
36 *Census of England and Wales 1951*, Housing Report (1956), p. xxiv.
37 Bowley, *Housing and the State,* appendix 2, table 2.
38 D. C. Paige, in W. Beckerman and Associates, *The British Economy in 1975*, p. 374.
39 Cd 9191 (1919).
40 Political and Economic Planning, *Report on the Market for Household Appliances* (1945), p. 158.
41 Political and Economic Planning, *Market for Household Appliances*, p. 156.

42 Political and Economic Planning, *Market for Household Appliances*, p. 67.
43 Compared with about 75% for a modern central heating system.
44 R. M. Titmuss, *Problems of Social Policy* (1950), p. 177.
45 N. Williams, *Population Problems on New Estates* (1939).
46 Williams, *Population Problems*, p. 9.
47 Cmd 6153 (1940), *Royal Commission on the Distribution of the Industrial Population Report*, p. 175.
48 R. Jevons and J. Madge, *Housing Estates* (1946), p. 41.
49 Williams, *Population Problems*, p. 13.
50 Jevons and Madge, *Housing Estates*, p. 48.
51 Jevons and Madge, *Housing Estates*, p. 51.
52 R. Wilson, Fabian Society Research Series No. 28, *Rent Rebates*.
53 J. Tucker, *Honourable Estates* (1966).
54 Jevons and Madge, *Housing Estates*, p. 64.

Chapter 9

Social Policy

I *The Stages of Social Policy*
Social policy can be thought of as passing through three stages, although these may, and in practice do, overlap. First there is what may be called a 'destitution' phase, for example the English poor law. The English poor law consisted of a commitment by the state to prevent any of its citizens actually starving. To qualify for help under the non-medical side of the poor law an applicant had to show he was destitute, and destitution over most of the period for which the poor law operated meant something fairly close to starvation. Of course, as the average per capita income of the country grew, so the definition of destitution or poverty started to move away from a level that was close to physical hardship. By the interwar years applicants to the poor law were maintained at a level well above starvation. But nevertheless the principle of helping only those in urgent need remained. So too did the principles that such help as was provided should not encroach on the lowest levels offered by the wage system, and that the help offered should carry with it the penalty of stigma, an intrusive means test, and in the background the threat of entry into the workhouse.

Towards the end of the nineteenth century and early in the twentieth century important social and economic developments set the stage for the beginnings of the second stage of social policy. Rising real incomes opened up the possibility of providing more extensive support to those who, at any moment in time, found themselves in the bottom ranks of income distribution. The widening of the franchise and the rise of political parties and ideas which questioned the justice of the prevailing distribution, coupled with the desire of those in the elites of society for stability, led to pressure for an extension of social support beyond the minimum levels of the poor law. The type of social policy which emerged as a result of these pressures could reasonably be called a 'selective' social policy, but unfortunately the word 'selective' has been pre-empted by the postwar discussion about 'selectivity' and 'universalism' in social policy. The case for using 'selective' to describe the policies emerging after 1906 is that they were based on the selection of groups of the population as being in need of support on the basis of certain criteria, other than mere destitution. The three important criteria used at first were those of unemployment, sickness and old age. The groups in question were selected by the relevant criteria and then provided with support. Since 'selective' however has been pre-empted, we will describe this stage of policy as the 'contingency' phase — a period when specific contingencies such as unemployment, sickness, etc. were provided against.

The postwar discussion which has revolved around the ideas 'selective' and 'universal' is not, we would suggest, a very useful type of approach in an historical perspective. In so far as social policy aims to pick out certain groups of the population for support of some form (whether in cash or kind) it is bound to be selective. The heat in the post-1945 discussion was generated not by a disagreement about whether any criteria should be used, but rather by a disagreement about the use of one particular criterion; that of poverty. The use of the criterion of poverty of course harks back to the 'destitution' phase to some extent, even if the level of poverty used in the criterion is well above anything that would have been recognised as destitution in the days of the poor law. It is possible to imagine however a social policy that did not use any criterion, other than membership of the community. Such a policy would have a genuine claim to be called 'universal', whereas in the recent discussion 'universal' has come to mean merely a policy which does not involve the criterion of poverty. Serious suggestions for a universal policy have been put forward, but not implemented in any country to date. An example is a scheme for a social dividend which would divide up a large part, say half or more, of the national income simply on a per capita basis regardless of social situation or work record.[1] The extensively discussed proposals for a guaranteed income in the USA are a move in the direction of a genuinely universal social policy.[2] After the destitution and contingency phases of policy, the next logical category of policy would seem to be the universal policy in this sense. This of course is not to beg any questions about whether it or any other social policy is desirable.

Social policy in Britain can be thought of as going through an important transitional period between 1900 and 1940. Before 1900 there was little beyond the destitution policy of the poor law. In the 1940s, the Beveridge proposals and the legislation of the Labour Government of 1945-51 aimed to establish a 'contingency' policy.

During this transition, the poor law continued as a major instrument of social policy, operating on traditional 'destitution' principles, but it was supplemented by three major 'contingency' schemes; for unemployment, sickness and old age. Not surprisingly, these developments were a source of controversy. Social policy affects, or threatens to affect, fundamental aspects of society and its systems of values. The two major threatened values are the market system and the distribution of material reward, that is of income and wealth. A contingency system threatens to provide levels of living for those selected as needing support which is higher than that provided by the wage system for others who fail to get selected. This may have two effects, both seen as potentially disruptive of the social status quo. First, it may mean those in the selected groups deliberately opt not to work, by feigning unemployment or sickness; secondly, it tends to open up the question of the justice of the income distribution as a whole. If one is better off 'on the dole' than one is in work, one can conclude either that the dole is too generous or that wages are too low; that the dole ought to be reduced or that the general distribution of material reward in society ought to be altered in favour of those at the lower end. Similarly, a public medical service is likely to find that to belong to the lower end of the income distribution is to incur a higher risk of illness and that much disease is the product of working and living conditions. The doctors may conclude that the only proper prescription in such cases is a prescription for a higher income and better working conditions. Hence it is not surprising that social policy was regarded with suspicion and was, like the poor law had long been for much the same reason, a topic of controversy.

A feature of the controversy over social policy however was that the form the discussion took was such as to obscure what we are suggesting is the real subject. This is because it was approached from the establishment point of view, with a number of built-in assumptions which begged a large part of the argument — assumptions in particular relating to income distribution and the possibilities of altering it by taxation. With the arrival of the second world war it was immediately found that these assumptions no longer held. The emergency which then overtook the whole nation was deemed to justify very large increases in taxation. It could have been argued that the emergency which overtook the unemployed and the poor in interwar Britain was just as pressing for them as anything that threatened the nation as a whole in the war, but of course it was not so argued. Unemployment and poverty among the working class was not such an emergency and did not justify any radical changes in the organisation of society.

II *Unemployment Insurance and Assistance*

Unemployment was an outstanding feature of the interwar years and unemployment insurance and assistance held the centre of the stage in discussion about social policy in this period. If we try for a moment to divest ourselves of the assumptions about the social status quo current at the time, and ask: what ought to be done about the unemployed?, the answer is even then not at all straightforward. This is because it is impossible to discuss this question without very quickly being led on to the further question: what ought to be done about the distribution of material reward in society as a whole? If a man has a family which he is unable to support, presumably the community ought to help him. But how much help ought it to give him? Why should it provide any given standard of living rather than another? If unemployment is accepted as being not his 'fault', as simply a contingency beyond his control, is there any reason why he should have a very low level of support, below anything he could earn if he did happen to get a job? In short, is there any moral justification, or any justification at all, for the old poor law principle of less eligibility, the principle that the level of support should be determined by the wage system itself, and that no justification, moral or otherwise, is needed for the wage system? In the interwar years, and for that matter today, people cannot make up their mind about these questions. It seems to many improper that an unemployed family should suffer poverty and ill health because the community opts to provide a very low level of support. At the same time it seems very difficult to provide a higher level of support than a man can obtain in the market by selling his labour, because in that case the incentive to go on selling his labour will presumably be drastically reduced. On the other hand, the market system itself has many advantages, but to modify it in the direction of less unequal distribution of income through minimum wage laws or similar interventions seems difficult or impossible. These very difficult questions must of necessity lie in the background to any discussion of social policy. The contemporary discussion of social policy in the interwar years avoided them, even very often on the Labour side. It tended to concentrate on the mechanics of the schemes, to limit the area of discussion and prevent the larger and more disturbing questions coming to the foreground.

The main mechanism for limiting the area of discussion was the widely accepted premise that support for the unemployed ought to take the form of an insurance scheme, that is that people who were likely to be unemployed at some time or other in their lives should make regular contributions to a fund which would build up a claim to support. This was the system adopted in the original 1911 unemployment insurance scheme. The use of the insurance idea at the time was a logical development of the extensive arrangements developed privately in the nineteenth century by trade unions, friendly societies and industrial insurance companies. To the public scheme, the state gave its authority and a little, but not much, cash. The 1911 Unemployment Insurance Act covered only about 2¼ million workers in a labour force of about 19 million. It was the first such scheme to be implemented in any country, apart from some experiments on a much smaller scale. The 1911 scheme avoided any general problems of the type referred to above by its insurance aspect. The worker acquired certain rights on the strength of his contributions but these rights were precisely defined and limited by the accounting framework adopted. Only 15 weeks' benefit could be drawn in any year; and each week's benefit drawn required at least five previous contributions to the fund. Contributions were 'tri-partite'; that is to say they were made by the employee, the employer and the government at the rate of 1p, 1p and 0·7p a week respectively. It was calculated that by adhering to these rules the fund would be self-supporting over a number of years, even if there were deficits in particularly bad years. The rates of benefits were 35p for a man and 30p for a woman and there was no allowance for dependants. When the first benefits were paid in 1913, the 35p benefit was 22% of average weekly earnings, and about one third of Rowntree's income for 'Class B' families in 1899, since when the retail price index had risen by about 10%. Clearly this was a very limited scheme, providing only a supplement to savings, if there were any, and operating only for a limited time. No family could survive on unemployment insurance benefit and if that was all they had they would soon be driven to the poor law.

However, by 1921 this very limited scheme had been expanded out of recognition. By then it covered 12 million workers instead of 2¼ million, and the benefit rates now included allowances for dependants which raised the benefit to a family of man, wife and two children to about one third of the average wage. The legislative and political story of this extension has been told by B. B. Gilbert.[3] He concludes that the government did not proceed to unemployment insurance in deliberate and calculated steps but was driven to it by a series of concessions and expedients which arose out of the war.[4] The war had involved a larger upheaval for a greater proportion of the population than any previous one. Some 5 million men were to be demobilised from the armed forces and many more millions were affected drastically by the abrupt ending of munitions production. In these circumstances and particularly in view of the fears aroused by the spread of radical agitation and the example of the Russian revolution, the government felt obliged to provide an 'out of work donation' for both returning troops and civilian workers rendered unemployed in the transition to a peacetime economy. Once accepted, however, the obligation to provide for the unemployed proved difficult to discontinue. But the state of establishment opinion was by no means ready for an unqualified acceptance of universal state support for the unemployed, with all the questions that such a commitment would have raised. It was therefore necessary to attempt a compromise, and the obvious form for such a compromise was an extension of the prewar insurance scheme. This was put into effect with the 1920 Act, which for the most part followed the 1911 arrangements, on a larger scale. Contributions and benefits were scaled up to allow for the rise in prices, and the terms for benefit were slightly stiffened, 6 weeks' contributions being required for each payment of a week's benefit, and benefit in any year being limited as before, to 15 weeks. In addition the applicant had to be capable of work but unable to obtain suitable employment, and to prove this he was required to sign on daily at the labour exchange in working hours. Thus did the government and the establishment of the day try to return to the normalcy of prewar, with a clearly defined and limited scheme, based on insurance principles which again served to rule out of the discussion fundamental questions about the 'rights' of the unemployed to any particular standard of living or the obligations of the community, if any, to support them. In 1921 a further important extension was made with the innocently named Unemployed Workers Dependants (Temporary Provisions) Act, which provided additional benefits for an unemployed man's wife and children (25p for the wife, 5p for each child). This was in response to the rapidly rising level of unemployment once the postwar boom collapsed; as the title of the Act suggests, it was seen as a temporary provision to avoid large-scale resort to the poor law in what were seen as exceptional but passing circumstances. However, dependants' allowances were to be a permanent feature of unemployment insurance and assistance from then on.

With the 1920 and 1921 Acts, the basis of the interwar system of unemployment insurance was laid, as were most of its battle lines and attitudes. The scheme had been extended to a majority of manual workers. The important exclusions were agricultural workers, domestic servants and the self-employed, the first two on the grounds that both their wages and their expectation of unemployment were low, making them unsuitable subjects for insurance, since they could neither afford the contributions nor did they need the benefits. In the case of domestic servants there was the further reason that their middle-class employers did not want to pay their part of the tri-partite contribution.

The self-employed were assumed to be capable of looking after themselves, an assumption not at all justified in the case of many thousands of small shopkeepers whose standard of living often fell below that of many manual employees. The scheme had been put back firmly on a limited insurance basis, and the financial liability of the state was small and predictable. The benefits, though larger for families than before the war, were still too small to live on and were strictly limited in duration, but then, as before the war, there was the poor law.

It is possible that this programme might have worked out as the government hoped had the rate of unemployment remained of the same order as before the war, but this was not to be. By 1921 unemployment was at a level which was seen as highly exceptional by contemporaries but which was to be common during the interwar years. The expanded insurance scheme, with its limitations as to who might draw benefit and for how long, was soon excluding by these rules large numbers of the unemployed from any right to benefit. At the interwar rates of unemployment, society was faced with the alternatives of allowing large numbers of unemployed to undergo the tests of destitution required by the poor law or making some other provision. And the general development of ideas on social policy had reached by then a state at which this decision proved very difficult to make. The whole story of interwar unemployment support is the story of this dilemma, perpetually unresolved. Should the unemployed who were not covered by the insurance scheme, which at the high rates prevailing very quickly came to mean most of the unemployed, be made to face the poor law or some other test of destitution?; or should the principles of a 'contingency social policy' be extended to provide unconditional state support for them? To provide unconditional support seemed prohibitively expensive and implied a level of taxation, and hence of redistribution of income, which threatened powerful vested interests. On the other hand to throw the unemployed on the poor law also seemed to threaten the stability of society. It might provoke civil disturbance or worse. The details of unemployment insurance and assistance legislation in the period are involved and tedious; no year passed without some Act of Parliament on the subject and often there was more than one. Reorganisation followed reorganisation, and crisis followed crisis. Basically, all the arrangements followed similar lines. The establishment insisted that the norm was the insurance scheme; the only 'rights' were those gained through contributions and granted within the rules of the scheme. But the pressures from organised labour and the fears of disturbance were such that it was also never possible to deny payments to the unemployed who did not qualify under such rules. The compromise was always that although such payments would in fact in most cases be made, they were always exceptions and might be withdrawn. These extra payments were made to unemployed persons who would not have qualified for any payment under the insurance scheme. They were successively known as uncovenanted (1921), extended (1924) and transitional benefits (1927), and then as transitional payments (1931). They contrasted with 'standard benefit', this being the benefit which the worker received as of right because of his unemployment insurance contributions. An employee might never qualify for standard benefit, that is he might never have been employed long enough to acquire any rights in the insurance scheme; or he might have exhausted his benefit by drawing his 15 weeks in one year (extended to 26 weeks in 1921). In either case he was a candidate for 'uncovenanted' benefit. Here again, there were rules determining his eligibility, which were varied from time to time. The rules for uncovenanted and other 'extra' benefits were in general more complicated than for standard benefit, but in particular they tended to be more like the destitution test of the poor law. They involved checks upon the household status of the applicant. For instance from 1921 single men and women residing with their parents were excluded if their parents could be shown on a means test to have enough to support them. Similarly married women whose husbands were in employment were excluded.[5] Thus these extra benefits beyond the insurance scheme very quickly started to include an income criterion, and involve the applicant and his household in investigations reminiscent of the poor law. This reversion to a 'destitution' policy was symptomatic of the transitional state of thinking on social policy of the period, and of the hesitant and limited acceptance of the ideas of a 'contingency' policy.

For those who failed to qualify under the rules either of standard benefit or of the extra benefits that were regularly allowed after 1921, there was the poor law itself. Support of the unemployed between 1921 and 1934 thus had three aspects: the standard insurance scheme; the succession of uncovenanted, extended and transitional benefits that were allowed year after year to those who did not qualify; and thirdly the poor law. An applicant might go through each stage, or, particularly before 1924 when the extra benefits were made continuous in time, he might find himself alternating between each system in a way that must have left many of the unemployed without any comprehension as to who was paying them and why and just how ashamed they ought to be about it. To quote the detailed changes in the arrangements would take the rest of the chapter, but to get their flavour some examples will serve. In 1922, under a Conservative Government inclined to take a hard line on the question, provision was made for two 'special periods' during which uncovenanted benefit could be drawn. The first followed a previous special period of 22 weeks, and was of 15 weeks' duration but with a gap of 5 weeks between each 5 weeks of benefits. The second special period was of 22 weeks' duration, but later in 1922 the duration of the first period was also increased to 22 weeks. In 1923 there was a further special period of 44 weeks' duration, and the gaps were shortened to 2 weeks after 22 weeks' benefit. In 1924 under a Labour Government inclined, within the limits of its minority in the House of Commons, to take a soft line on the question, the 'gaps' were abolished (and were never reinstated) and 41 weeks of uncovenanted benefit was allowed in the first benefit year. This Labour Government edged a little way towards making the 'second stage' payments – then renamed 'extended benefits' – a matter of right rather than discretion, but in 1925 a Conservative Government inclined to take a hard line on the subject reversed this trend and restored the 'ministerial discretion'. This meant restoring the investigations into family circumstances and income. In 1926 extended benefit was still being paid, was still at the Minister's discretion, and legislation extended the period in which it could be paid to 31 December 1927. It was still thought of as a temporary expedient and there was still no sign of it being possible to discontinue it. If the reader finds this recital of details confusing, and they are meant to be examples of the sort of thing that went on rather than a comprehensive description, he can perhaps imagine how the unemployed found it at the time.

The payment of extra benefits over the standard benefit raised the question as to how they should be financed. The unemployment insurance fund could not pay for them; its income was nothing like adequate. The answer to this question reflects much of the contemporary attitude to the problem; the extra benefits were financed by running up a deficit in the insurance fund and covering this by borrowing; that is by the issue of government securities, and hence by an addition to the national debt. This was regarded by almost everyone, including very often Labour spokesmen, as an almost immoral process, and the figure for the debt of the unemployment insurance fund was used as a barometer of national solvency. If the debt was increasing, this meant that the weather was unsettled; if the debt got too large a storm was on the way. Eventually when the storm did break in 1931, it washed away Ramsay Macdonald's Labour Government and sent the labour movement scrambling for cover. The figures however need to be put in proportion. The national debt at this time was about £7½ thousand million. By 1929 the accumulated deficit of the unemployment insurance fund was £36 million, or 0·5% of the national debt. With the onset of the depression in 1929, unemployment, and with it the deficit on the fund, rose rapidly. By the end of 1930 the deficit was £60 million. In 1931, as Percy Cohen puts it, 'the unemployed tide swept on; its advance irresistible; its consequences devastating to the state's finances'.[6] In the spring of 1931 about 2½ million people were unemployed, which implied an annual expenditure on standard and transitional benefits of £120 million. Against this, income, including the government's share of the tri-partite contribution (which in 1929 had been raised to one half of the combined contributions of employer and employee), would be only £44 million. At this level of unemployment the government was committed to finding about £80 million a year over and above its contributions under the insurance scheme proper. £80 million was 2·0% of the gross national product for 1931 and 7½% of the total public authorities' current expenditure in that year. It was about three quarters of defence expenditure in that year, and only about the same as the increase in defence expenditure between the years 1936 and 1937. It can be argued therefore that it was not a very serious sum of money to have to pay. When an emergency in foreign policy made rearmament necessary much larger sums of money were found without difficulty. The increase in defence expenditure between 1937 and 1938, when defence spending was seriously building up in response to the threat from Nazi Germany, was more than the total needed to support the unemployed in 1931. But support of the unemployed at this rate was not socially acceptable. The differences in attitude to the two sources of expenditure need to be sought in social attitudes rather than in any objective differences. Britain could, if she had wished, have as easily raised the money for the unemployed as she did in fact raise the money to fight the Germans.

There is a further reason for pressing this comparison. Rearmament was a 'real' cost; it actually made demands on the productive capacity of the economy. It was, in short, expenditure on goods and services. Support of the unemployed was transfer expenditure which made no direct demands on the productive capacity of the economy. The resource cost of unemployment insurance and assistance was probably roughly nil. It may in fact have been a 'negative cost', by which is meant that it might have increased the output of the economy above what it would have been in the absence of such payments. This possibility arises because, where there is spare capacity in the economy, as of course there was with so many unemployed, transferring money from a section of the community who save a certain proportion of their income — say the middle classes, or the employed, or lenders to the government to a section of the community who save less, such as the unemployed, will raise the level of demand. As long as the economy has the capacity to meet the extra demand, which in 1931 it had, then output may be raised. Support of the unemployed has then 'paid for itself'. Of course such arguments were not accepted at the time, although they were sometimes heard. But generally the costs of unemployment support were thought of as costs, and the deficit in the fund as a disaster; and all discussion focussed on how to stop it increasing any more, and then preferably on how to 'pay it off'.

The government which happened to be in power to face this cruel dilemma was a minority Labour Government. They as much as anybody else implicitly accepted the styles of economic reasoning which saw the deficit of the fund as an approach to national insolvency; indeed their Chancellor, Philip Snowden, was in such respects a financial 'hawk' of the most rigid type. But for a Labour Government the conflicts of thought and feeling proved tragically irreconcilable. The deficit of the fund must be controlled; the final imperative for this arose from abroad. The balance of payments situation was registering a currency outflow which needed to be financed. The reserves were inadequate, so that short-term official borrowing was necessary, though on a scale that thirty years later would have been regarded as routine. But in 1931 the world's bankers were in pessimistic mood and demanded in effect that the government should change its policies as a condition of a loan. The principal change demanded was a reduction in the rate of government spending and the budget deficit.[7] Hence it was made to seem that the need for cuts in unemployment support were externally imposed and not of the government's own making, but this was misleading. The government itself, and the establishment in general, had repeatedly paraded the deficit in the unemployment insurance fund as a matter of regret; as a fault that ought to be corrected. The 'May Committee' appointed to investigate the national finances earlier in 1931 had reported, in July, that large cuts needed to be made. Further, as subsequent events showed, there was the perfectly possible option of suspending the convertibility of the currency. So the government itself cannot escape the responsibility for the prominence given to the expenditure on support of the unemployed. But although powerful forces converged in cutting the level of such support, equally powerful forces from the side of organised labour and from the ideological bases of the labour movement suggested the opposite; that the level of support must be maintained. The conflicting forces divided the government and the labour movement; Ramsay MacDonald, unable to obtain agreement in his cabinet, resigned, but then added to the trauma of the occasion by in effect crossing the party lines to form a nominally national but basically Conservative government, of which he remained as Prime Minister until succeeded by Baldwin in 1935.

The political dramas that were enacted around these themes greatly exceeded in their range and scope any actual changes that were made or proposed in the system of unemployment insurance. The cuts in benefit that had split MacDonald's cabinet down the middle so fatally, were swiftly enacted by the new government, but with the fall in prices they did not in fact reduce the real value of benefits below the level of 1929. Some administrative changes were made. The extra or second stage benefits, renamed yet again as transitional payments, were now to be made conditional on an overt and formalised means test, this time administered by the Public Assistance Committees of the local authorities. The Public Assistance Committees were the product of a reorganisation of local government in 1929, which had in name abolished the poor law. This might be thought of as a major turning point in social policy, the end of the 'destitution' phase perhaps, but in fact it was much more a change of name than of substance. The Public Assistance Committees of the local authorities were the poor law under another name, and continued much the same policies as before. To make them responsible for the means test associated with transitional payments therefore brought unemployment assistance a step nearer to the poor law once again. This was perhaps the worst phase of the interwar years for the unemployed, at least in the public mind. The household means test, the reductions in the money value of benefits, the sense of national gloom generated by the 'fall of the pound' and the rise of fascist governments abroad, and above all the very high levels of unemployment, particularly in the depressed areas, combined to make the years 1930-4 the worst of the whole period. The crisis did not however bring any fundamental reappraisal of the role of social support for the unemployed. Instead there was administrative reorganisation, which took account of some of the realities of the situation which had developed, without attempting to alter them. The extra payments, beyond standard benefit, which had persisted from 1921 and whose cost had played such a large part in the political traumas of 1931, were finally recognised as permanent. They were to be subject to a means test. And they were to be no longer a charge on the unemployment insurance fund, but a direct charge on the Treasury, that is they were to be financed out of general taxation rather than by government borrowing. This much was brought about in 1931. In 1934, these changes were consolidated by the creation of a new body, the Unemployment Assistance Board, which was to take over responsibility for the support of all the unemployed other than those entitled to standard benefit. In 1935 the UAB took over all those in receipt of transitional payments, whose rates of benefit had been determined by the Public Assistance Committees. It applied to them uniform rates of benefit determined by a standardised means test. In 1937, in a further administrative rationalisation, the UAB took over the third group of unemployed, those who failed to qualify either for standard or transitional payments and who had fallen back on poor relief.

In retrospect, the rationalisation of unemployment support under two sections, the insurance scheme and the UAB, is an important landmark in the administrative history of the welfare state. The UAB progressively extended its range of operation in the second war and eventually was destined to be the body which finally superseded the poor law. Renamed the National Assistance Board, it became in 1946 a part of the Beveridge system of social security. Just as in 1935 and 1937 it had assumed the role of providing 'second line' support for the unemployed behind the insurance scheme, so in 1946 it took over as provider of second line support behind all the 'contingency' social security schemes which were greatly extended in scope under the Beveridge plan. The idea was that this extension of the 'contingency' systems would be sufficiently effective to reduce the role of the National Assistance Board to that of a 'sweeper' behind a defence that was in any case virtually foolproof. Such expectations were unfortunately very far from being realised, and the 'sweeper' was soon very active, but that is a story that belongs to a later period. In the interwar years, the arrival of the Unemployment Assistance Board as provider for the 'out-of-benefit' unemployed was heralded by a major row. The UAB standardised the rates which had previously varied from one authority to another. It did so with little thought for the fact that some of its standardisations were large reductions, and in some cases even complete cancellations of benefit. The result was a remarkable upsurge of feeling, sufficiently strong to stop the government in its tracks. A 'standstill' order, the Unemployment Assistance (Temporary Provisions) Act, 1935, was hastily rushed through Parliament to give applicants the original Public Assistance Committee rates where the new UAB assessments were lower.[8] The Board was a typical specimen of the British administrative and social attitudes to such problems at the time. It was designed to be outside politics, though it is hard to think of a more fundamentally political problem than the extent of social commitment to disadvantaged groups such as the unemployed. The minister responsible for most aspects of the Board's work was the Minister of Labour, and he answered questions in Parliament about its work with the formula 'I am informed by the Board that . . .'. The Board was an *ad hoc* body consisting of a full time chairman and deputy chairman with three part-time members. It opened 327 offices in 1935 to carry out its work of assessing the benefits to be paid to the unemployed, and recruited a staff of about 6,000. Some 5,000 of these were the investigating clerks, whose job it was to visit the homes of the unemployed and obtain the information on which the assessment of their benefits would later be made at the office. These investigating clerks, who were the public's only point of contact with the board, were untrained junior clerical workers, some of them taken over from public assistance work and others recruited from junior staff in the Ministry of Labour. Their only instruction in their delicate task was usually a day out with another investigating clerk. After that they were on their own, and they were expected to get through twenty-five visits a day.[9] It was not thought necessary that the board should have either a press or public relations department, or that anything much in the way of explanation or information should be offered to applicants about the way the assessments were reached. The visitors indeed were not authorised to provide such information; they did not make the assessments but merely collected the information on a form. In short, the traditions of the poor law cast a long shadow over the administration of the UAB and continued to cast it over the National Assistance Board when that was formed in 1946.[10]

With the change in government, the administrative reorganisation and eventually, in 1933, the beginnings of economic recovery, the excitement over the cost of unemployment support died down, though the cost did not undergo any dramatic reduction. The reductions in benefit rates of 1931 presumably reduced the cost somewhat below what it would have been without them, although for reasons already given, even this cannot be certain. If the cuts had not been made, unemployment might have been a little lower than it was, and that might have offset the higher rates. By 1935 the gross cost of supporting the unemployed, not including expenditure on 'poor relief', was £99 million, of which £44 million was raised in contributions. Net expenditure was £55 million or about 5·2% of public authorities' total current expenditure in that year or 1·2% of the gross national product. Defence expenditure in that year was 3% of GNP and interest on the national debt 6%.[11] A feature of the discussion of the cost of unemployment support throughout this period is the way in which the savings were regarded as net savings. This ignored the fact that if support was withdrawn from an unemployed man he would be very likely to apply to the Guardians, or after 1929, the Public Assistance Committee, for poor relief. The cost of this however fell mainly on the local rates and not on either the national debt or the national budget, so it was ignored in most discussions of the subject.

Table 9.1 *Unemployment Benefits, 1919-36*

	Money rates			'Real' rates[a]	
		Dependants		Single	Man and
	Adult			man	wife
Year	Male	Adult	Child	(1931	= 100)
		(in modern pence)			
1919	55	–	–	49	34
1920	75	–	–	59	40
1921 (March)	100	–	–	87	59
1921[b] (June)	75	25	5	80	72
1924	90	25	10	101	87
1927	85	35	10	100	96
1930	85	45	10	105	109
1931	76·25	40	10	100	100
1934	85	45	10	118	123
1936	85	45	15	115	119

[a]'Real' Rates; by this is meant money rates divided by the retail price index and multiplied by a factor which sets the relationship for 1931 equal to 100.

[b]The adult male rate was reduced to 75p in June, but dependants' allowances were introduced in November. Prices were falling rapidly in 1921 and the index for 1922 has been used in calculating the real rates which resulted from the June and November changes in money rates.

The weekly rate of benefit paid to an unemployed man throughout the period varied, apart from the very short periods in 1919 and 1921, between 90p and 75p, the average manual workers wage for most of the period being in the region of £3, rising to about £3·37 with the rise in real earnings and prices by 1938. The 1931 cut was from a rate of 85p, established in 1927, to 76·25p, a cut of 10·3%. Between 1927 and 1931 the retail price index for food fell by 18·5% and the general retail price index by 11·5%. In 1934 the cuts were restored, and in 1936 the allowance for children was raised from 10p to 15p. This produced the most generous level of allowances of the period, since the retail price index had not returned to its 1927 level by the start of the war and the index of food prices hardly rose at all, being only 7½% higher in 1938 than in 1932. Table 9.1 gives the level of allowances throughout the period and the value of the allowances compared with changes in retail prices. Nevertheless although the allowances may have improved as the period progressed, and improved particularly rapidly over the period of the depression when prices were falling, they were never sufficient for anything other than a very low standard of living, and never sufficient to get even a small family over the poverty line as defined in many of the numerous interwar social surveys.

III *Health and Insurance Pensions*

Unemployment insurance and assistance has been treated at some length because it was the centre of interest for much of the period, and because it illustrates very clearly the conflicts and problems of the transition through which social policy was passing in the period. The two other major contingencies defined in the legislation of 1909-11 were ill health and old age. Both these schemes continued throughout the interwar years without drastic modification and without ever becoming the centre of controversy. This is not to say they were without defects or critics. The system of health services and health insurance in existence in Britain in this period was extraordinarily complex, but can be thought of as falling into two main sections as far as the working-class population was concerned. First, there was an insurance scheme with a coverage similar in principle to, but somewhat wider than, that of unemployment insurance. This was designed to provide cash benefits during interruptions of earnings through sickness. And secondly, there was 'medical benefit', which provided free access to a general practitioner for those covered by the insurance scheme. These arrangements came into being in 1911 and remained substantially unchanged until after the second world war, when they were transformed by the introduction of the National Health Service. In addition to maintenance of income and access to a general practitioner, a person who was ill might of course need to enter hospital or be treated by a specialist. But although the first two aspects of illness were covered to a certain extent by the health insurance scheme of 1911, there was almost no official provision for hospital or specialist treatment until the arrival of the National Health Service. The Beveridge Report thought that this omission was the worst defect in the whole network of Britain's interwar social services.

'Provision for most of the many varieties of need through interruption of earnings and other causes . . . has already been made in Britain on a scale not surpassed and hardly rivalled in any other country in the world. In one respect only . . . namely limitation of medical service, both in the range of treatment which is provided as of right and in respect of the classes of person for whom it is provided, does Britain's achievement fall seriously short of what has been accomplished elsewhere.'[12]

The report referred here to treatment beyond that which could be provided by a general practitioner. The coverage of the health insurance scheme itself was good by international standards, including in the 1930s at least as large a proportion of the population as any other European country, and of course far more than in the USA, where there was not, and still is not, any national scheme of this sort.[13] But although an insured person could get benefit of about 75p a week and see a general practitioner without charge, his prospects for further treatment were extremely problematical if he could not afford to pay, and depended very much on the energy of his general practitioner in finding a hospital bed and on the area where he lived.

The health insurance scheme was introduced in 1911 in a welter of controversy,[14] as a result of which the scheme came to be administered in a complex way through 'approved societies'. An 'approved society' was a non-profit making organisation set up specifically to collect the contributions and pay the benefits due under the act. Approved societies were in practice set up by friendly societies, trade unions, industrial insurance companies, and employers. Technically, the approved societies associated with such bodies were separate entities financially; even where the sponsoring body was a commercial company in business for profit, the associated approved society had to be non-profit making. The basic reason, in brief, for this arrangement, was the opposition of the existing friendly societies and industrial insurance companies to any scheme which excluded them, since sickness benefit, and particularly funeral benefit, had been, and continued to be, the centre of their activities. The industrial insurance companies wanted to be admitted to health insurance, even though they were debarred from making a profit on it, since they felt, and probably rightly that the access of their agents to the insured persons' homes to collect contributions and pay benefits under the Act would greatly assist the sale of further insurances, such as burial insurance, on which they did make a profit.[15] The outcome was that interwar British health insurance was administered through thousands of financially and administratively separate agencies. In 1924 there were 1,192 such societies, but many of these had separate branches, the number of such branches being 7,226.[16] The number of societies and branches declined slowly in the interwar years, but by 1938 there were still in total 6,600.[17] Since each society and branch was financially independent, the benefits paid could vary widely. Under the Act, an approved society was bound to pay the minimum benefits, but could pay more. Whether it did pay additional benefits over the minimum depended on the sickness experience of its members. If this was better than average, additional benefits might be substantial. In 1938 there was a wide range for such additional benefits, which might be as high as 75p a week or as low as 5p, but which averaged 16·25p.[18] Beyond additional cash benefits during illness, an approved society might offer a further range of additional benefits, such as hospital treatment, dental or ophthalmic treatment. The panel below gives the actual benefits given by one approved society, that associated with the Hearts of Oak Friendly Society in 1936.

Table 9.2 *Benefits Given by the Hearts of Oak Friendly Society* (1936)

Item	Minimum rate	Hearts of Oak rate
Absence from work due to sickness		
men	75p/week	90p/week
women	60p/week	65p/week
married women	50p/week	55p/week
Disablement: men	37½p/week	45p/week
Maternity grant to the head of the household:		
if male	£2	£2:30
if female	£2	£2·10
Dental treatment	Nil	Half the actual cost
Ophthalmic treatment	Nil	£3-£15 or full cost, whichever is the less
Medical and surgical appliances	Nil	The first £1, plus half of any further cost, maximum payment £2·50

In addition the society would pay the full cost of maintenance in convalescent homes and might at its discretion pay the whole or part cost of nursing, but for men only. It also might, again at its discretion, make further payments in cases of 'want or distress'. This particular society would not contribute towards the cost of hospital treatment. Membership of the society in 1936 was approximately 530,000.

This society provided a range of benefits fairly typical of the major societies. But in 1938 37% of all insured men and about three quarters of all insured women were not entitled to any additional benefits.[19] Thus a first and major criticism of the working of the scheme was this diversity of benefits, which were entirely unrelated either to contributions, which were equal for all contributors, or to need.

The second criticism commonly heard was that general practitioners treated their 'panel patients' (as the insured non-fee paying patients were called) as second-class patients, and did not take them as seriously as they did the middle-class fee-payers. The majority report of the Royal Commission on National Health Insurance reporting in 1926 came to a complacent conclusion on this: 'we can say confidently ... that medical benefit has proved a most successful and most valued factor in the advancement of the health of the nation'.[20] Herman Levy, writing in 1944, doubted this conclusion, using evidence from the Royal Commission's own minutes of evidence. One witness, not quoted in the Report, said that 'patients particularly complain about lack of examination'. Patients, this witness thought, often had nothing wrong with them, but, he continued, it was no good saying, as it appears some doctors did, 'you are all right; get out'. Levy comments that the middle-class patient 'paying good fees, would not hear the curt "you are all right; get out".[21] The report by *Political and Economic Planning* in 1937 thought that in many practices 'middle-class patients go to the doctor's front door and working-class patients to the surgery door; one class of patient comes by appointment, the other . . . may have to wait'.[22] But more serious than any deficiencies that may have existed in some doctor's attitudes to panel patients was the failure of the scheme to admit insured contributors' dependants to the panel at all. The minority report of the 1926 Royal Commission suggested the extension of medical benefits to dependants[23] and estimated the cost at the modest sum of £9·5 millions a year. But this recommendation was never adopted in the interwar years. Throughout the period, the wives and children of working-class subscribers had to pay to see a doctor, or if they could not, go to the out-patients department of a hospital. Large numbers of them took out subscriptions to 'contributory schemes' whereby, for subscriptions of between about 1p and 1·5p a week, they obtained rights to free treatment of various types, mostly in voluntary hospitals, either as in- or out-patients. In 1937 there were 5¼ million subscribers to such schemes, and one report estimated that, since many subscriptions were for whole households, about 10 million persons were covered.[24]

If many people had difficulty in getting to a doctor, when they did, the gravest deficiency of the interwar medical services would only then become apparent. This was the lack of provision for specialist or hospital treatment, to which attention was drawn in the Beveridge Report. The British hospital system in these years was a hotch-potch of differently administered and financed institutions that hardly deserves the name of a system. The main elements were the voluntary hospitals, the municipal hospitals and the poor law hospitals. Voluntary hospitals were charities, often with a long history, relying for their income on donations, legacies and patients' fees, which they charged to those whom they judged could afford it. They included a great variety of institutions, from the London teaching hospitals with international reputations, to small non-specialist institutions in the provinces. Outside London, about half their income came from patients' contributions of one form or another, about half of this being from the contributory schemes described above. In London the proportion of income derived from fees was about a third. The rest came from investment income, charitable gifts or legacies.[25] Thus throughout the interwar years a very important part of the medical services of the country was financed on much the same basis as the lifeboat service is today – by appeals to the public.

Parallel with the voluntary hospitals were two other groups of hospitals, the municipal and the poor law hospitals. Both were publicly financed from the local rates. Municipal hospitals were run by the public health departments of the local authorities and poor law hospitals by the Public Assistance Committees. The latter group of hospitals had grown up from the differentiation of poor law workhouses into those for the sick and those for the able-bodied poor, many of the former being expanded into hospitals for the poor. Their quality varied greatly, some being little more than hostels for infirm people, with minimal facilities and nursing attendance. In 1935 these three groups of hospitals provided 220,000 hospital beds (voluntary 83,000, municipal 57,000, poor law 80,000). Including another 69,000 beds in special purpose infectious disease and tuberculosis hospitals run by local authorities, the total of hospital beds in Britain was equal to about one bed for each 160 inhabitants (compared with, for instance, 110 per bed in the United Kingdom in 1969, and 90 and 1,620 in West Germany and India respectively in the same year).[26] Entry to any part of this extraordinary mixture of institutions, whose quality varied over the whole range from good to very bad indeed, was either by payment or by charity, except for that minority of the population who were insured with approved societies whose additional benefits included hospital treatment. The variety of hospitals, the variety of benefits paid by different approved societies, the exclusion of dependants from the insurance scheme, and the varieties of benefit offered by the numerous contributory schemes, together made the health care situation in interwar Britain one of great complexity, but not in general a satisfactory one. There were many other aspects of public health provision not covered here, such as the school medical service, district nursing and midwifery services, and the mental hospitals. A summary judgement of all these services taken together is obviously extremely difficult. What is certain is that when the government eventually grasped the nettle of reviewing the whole situation under the stress of war in the early 1940s, there was no other sphere, except perhaps education, where such sweeping and all-embracing change seemed necessary. The insurance services could be expanded and rationalised into a single system, but the proposals for a 'National Health Service' made in 1944 involved a complete sweeping away of the accumulated historical debris of the transitional period and the establishment of the first truly complete 'contingency' service; a service which aimed to, and to a considerable extent did, offer a free service in kind to anyone on the basis of only one criterion: that he was ill.

Less needs to be said about pensions. They were less controversial and pursued a relatively uncomplicated course in the interwar years. The pension scheme of 1908 was different from the other two major insurance schemes in that it was non-contributory. The corollary of state finance was a means test. Subject to means, 25p a week was to be paid to all persons reaching the age of 70. To this non-contributory scheme was added in 1925 a contributory shceme which provided pensions of 50p a week without means test for insured persons reaching the age of 65 and for the widows and orphans of insured men, of any age. Pensions payable under the earlier Act of 1908 were also raised to 50p a week after the war, so that throughout the interwar years anyone over 70, and after 1926, most people over 65, and most widows and orphans, received pensions of 50p a week, or about one sixth of the average manual worker's weekly wage. The 25p payable under the 1908 Act had also been about one sixth of the average wage, and in 1970, the rate for the old age pension at £5 a week was still almost the same proportion of average manual earnings.[27] Pensions at this level were not intended to avert poverty if they were the only source of income — in that case a person would be likely to become dependent on the poor law — but they were a substantial contribution to savings or to the household income where old people lived with relatives.

IV *The Social Services as a System*
The overwhelming impression given by any detailing of the social services of interwar Britain is of the complexity and the illogicality of the arrangements. In the attempt to break away from the 'destitution' concept, the ideal of provision for particular contingencies, and the building up of rights to such provision by contributions, had seemed a logical development. Society was not ready or willing for anything

approaching a comprehensive scheme which would redistribute income radically or detach the right to income from the market place. It was implicitly accepted that social security must not affect the income distribution dramatically nor must it interfere with the incentives to work in the market for labour. On the other hand it was increasingly felt that individuals could not be expected to cope with all the contingencies of life unaided, and that the state had a role to play in the provision of contingency schemes against unemployment, sickness, old age, as well as other eventualities, which have not been discussed in detail here, such as childbirth, death, injury or disablement, blindness, or mental deficiency. But throughout the period there remained in the background the ultimate contingency of destitution, covered by the poor law.

From the start of the modern welfare state in the period of Liberal government after 1906, until the Beveridge legislation of the recent postwar period, a series of interrelated but autonomous schemes were devised, modified and added to, but little attempt was made to consider the problem of social policy as a whole, or to face any of the larger and more philosophical problems which have been referred to here. The impression is of a battle between conflicting ideas. From the side of the establishment, represented by middle-class opinion, the Treasury and the Conservative Party, were ideas tending to perpetuate a 'destitution' policy: to introduce income or poverty as criteria into contingency schemes; to ensure that the level of benefits were not such as to reduce incentives, and that any benefits claimed by right were earned through actuarily sound contributory schemes and that further payments carried with them something of the stigma of the poor law as a deterrent. On the other hand there were other pressures, not in this period very well organised or articulated, acting in the opposite direction: to do away with means tests; to reduce the role of the poor law; and to provide maintenance to the unemployed and the sick and old and other disadvantaged groups as a matter of right, in a way that carried no shame and provided a standard of living that was reasonably in line with other members of society. The outcome of these various forces was a situation which can be viewed in different ways. Compared with the nineteenth century, the range of schemes in existence represented a great change. On the other hand, the establishment could be seen as being reasonably successful in restricting the development of radical ideas. The virtues of social insurance remained the conventional wisdom of the period. Payments made beyond those earned by contributions on the whole continued to carry means tests and stigma. Levels of support remained in all cases at a level which did not seriously interfere with the wage system. Large omissions in the coverage of schemes, notably the health insurance scheme's omission of dependants, survived throughout the period without ever being allowed to lead to a Beveridge-type reappraisal of the system as a whole. There can be no doubt that a large contribution was made to the standard of living in the interwar period by this mixture of schemes. Equally of course, it is not hard to imagine, without going to utopian extremes, considerably more generous and wide-ranging provisions.

The gross cost of social services in the interwar period, including transfer payments, and including expenditure on education, the poor laws and housing subsidies, but not capital expenditure, ranged between 8% and 11% of the gross national product. It reached a peak in the depression, due to rising expenditure on unemployment, but fell only slightly subsequently, owing to more generous benefits, particularly for the unemployed, and the extension of some of the insurance schemes to a larger proportion of the population. In round figures and in most years, about 60% of this expenditure was a charge on central government finance, another quarter was raised in contributions and the rest came from local government rates.[28] In 1935, when total expenditure from central government funds in England and Wales was £203·7 millions, the largest items were unemployment assistance, non-contributory pensions, war pensions, and education, each taking approximately £40 millions. The government's contribution to unemployment insurance was £20 millions, housing subsidies took £13·5 millions, and national health insurance £6·7 millions. For the rates, from which total expenditure in England and Wales in 1935 on social services was £104·6 millions, the largest items were poor relief and education. Education, though not treated here as a social service as such, was thus by far the largest single item of social expenditure in its combined demands, net of contributions, on central and local finance.[29] In the pattern of government expenditure as a whole in this period, debt interest, social service expenditure and defence were the major elements throughout the period. Debt interest, arising from the expensive borrowing of the first world war, took about a third of public authorities expenditure in the 1920s, but was reduced to about a quarter after 1933 by the fall in interest rates and the conversion operations on higher coupon government securities. Social services expenditure averaged 36% of the total in the 1920s, rising to a peak of 45% in the depression, and later falling back as a proportion of government expenditure, though not absolutely, as defence expenditure rose under the threat of war. Public authorities current expenditure as a whole was about a quarter of gross national product for most of the period, about double the rate prevailing before the war.[30] The proportion of government expenditure going to social services before the war had been of the same order of magnitude as after it (32·8% in 1910). If one looks for a pattern of change in the levels of public authorities expenditure, certainly the most obvious pattern visible is the way in which the level is raised in each of the wars.[31] In between the wars, there is the reduction of debt interest, the piecemeal extension of social policies, the rise of defence expenditure in preparation for the next war, and the unplanned expansion of expenditure on the unemployed during the depression, but there are no dramatic changes or strong trends. The conventions about what is possible in the way of taxation and social policy appear to have been abruptly shifted by the wars; in between the wars they remained comparatively stable. An economy measure like the possibility of paying much lower interest rates on the national debt was accepted as a desirable change; the foreign challenge made demands on the defence forces which were accepted, although reluctantly. Any major expansion of the social services however was implicitly treated as undesirable if it made large calls on public finance. Some extensions were made, and as we have seen, social policy expenditure did rise modestly as a proportion of GNP. Radical reappraisal was postponed however until the arrival of the next war.

Notes

1 A. B. Atkinson, *Poverty in Britain and the Reform of Social Security* (1969), ch. 9.
2 See for instance R. Theobald (ed.)., *The Guaranteed Income; Next Step in Socio-Economic Evolution?* (1966).
3 B. B. Gilbert, *British Social Policy 1914-39* (1970), ch. 2.
4 Gilbert, *British Social Policy* p. 56.
5 R. C. Davison, *The Unemployed* (1929), p. 115.
6 P. Cohen, *The British System of Social Insurance* (1932), p. 137.
7 R. Skidelsky, *Politicians and the Slump* (1967), p. 360.
8 J. S. Clarke, 'The Assistance Board', in W. A. Robson (ed.), *Social Security* (1943), p. 132.
9 Clarke, 'The Assistance Board', p. 138.
10 R. M. Titmuss, 'New Guardians of the Poor in Britain' in S. Jenkins (ed.), *Social Security in International Perspective* (1969), p. 157.
11 Figures from Cmd 5609 (1937), *The Public Social Services and The British Economy, Key Statistics 1900-1970* (1972).
12 Cmd 6404 (1942), *Social Insurance and Allied Services* (Beveridge Report), p. 5.
13 H. Levy, *National Health Insurance* (1944), p. 44.
14 See generally B. B. Gilbert, *The Evolution of National Insurance in Great Britain* (1966)
15 Levy, *National Health Insurance*, p. 217.
16 Levy, *National Health Insurance*, p. 26.
17 Cmd 6404 p. 24.

18 Cmd 6404, p. 27.
19 Cmd 6404, p. 27.
20 Cmd 2596 (1926), *Royal Commission on National Health Insurance, Report,* p. 38.
21 Levy, *National Health Insurance,* p. 109.
22 Political and Economic Planning, *Report on the British Health Services* (1937), p. 143.
23 Cmd 2596 (1926), p. 314.
24 Political and Economic Planning, *Report on the British Health Services,* p. 234.
25 Political and Economic Planning, *Report on the British Health Services,* p. 233.
26 Political and Economic Planning, *Report on the British Health Services,* p. 257; *Social Trends No. 4* (1973), p. 200.
27 Political and Economic Planning, *Report on the British Social Services* (1937), pp. 24, 26; *Social Trends No. 2* (1971), p. 87.
28 Actual figures for 1935 from Cmd 5609 (1937): gross expenditure £502 millions; contributions £148 millions (29·4%); central government £286 millions (57·0%); local rates £68 millions (13·5%). Figures for Great Britain.
29 Cmd 5609 (1937), pp. 8-9.
30 A. T. Peacock and J. Wiseman, *The Growth of Public Expenditure in the United Kingdom* (1961), p. 86.
31 Peacock and Wiseman, *The Growth of Public Expenditure,* p. 91.

Index

276 Interwar Britain: a Social and Economic History